Teaching and Learning in the New Latino Diaspora

Teaching and Learning in the New Latino Diaspora

Creating Culturally Responsive Practice

Edited by
Edmund T. Hamann, Socorro G. Herrera,
Enrique G. Murillo, Jr., and Stanton Wortham

Foreword by Sofia A. Villenas

TEACHERS COLLEGE PRESS
TEACHERS COLLEGE | COLUMBIA UNIVERSITY
NEW YORK AND LONDON

Published by Teachers College Press,® 1234 Amsterdam Avenue, New York, NY 10027

Copyright © 2024 by Teachers College, Columbia University

Front cover art and design by adam bohannon.

All rights reserved. No part of this publication may be reproduced or transmitted in any form or by any means, electronic or mechanical, including photocopy, or any information storage and retrieval system, without permission from the publisher. For reprint permission and other subsidiary rights requests, please contact Teachers College Press, Rights Dept.: tcpressrights@tc.columbia.edu

Library of Congress Cataloging-in-Publication Data is available at loc.gov

ISBN 978-0-8077-6730-6 (paper)
ISBN 978-0-8077-6731-3 (hardcover)
ISBN 978-0-8077-8120-3 (ebook)

Printed on acid-free paper
Manufactured in the United States of America

Contents

Foreword *Sofia A. Villenas*   vii

1. **From Challenges to Improvements: Creating Culturally Responsive Practice in the New Latino Diaspora**   1
   Edmund T. Hamann, Socorro G. Herrera, Enrique G. Murillo, Jr., and Stanton Wortham

2. **Imagineering More Inclusive Teacher Education: Systemic Approaches to Challenging the Predominance of Whiteness in Education**   8
   Amanda R. Morales, Lydiah Kiramba, Ricardo Martinez, and Edmund T. Hamann

3. ***Impacto sin Quemarse*: Building Understanding of the Latinx Immigrant/Migrant Experience Through Literature**   20
   Scott Beck, Alma Stevenson, and Yasar Bodur

4. **Reengineering Professional Development for Educational Leaders in the New Latinx Diaspora of the U.S. Midwest**   38
   Lisa M. Dorner and Emily R. Crawford

5. **Reframing Emergent Multilinguals as "First-Class Citizens" in the New Latinx Diaspora of New Jersey**   56
   Meredith McConnochie

6. **Imagining and Reengineering Inclusive Schooling for All Students in the New Latino Diaspora**   71
   Tricia Gray

7. **Lessons From the New Latinx Diaspora in Idaho: Negotiating Access to School Success and Well-Being**   87
   Eulalia Gallegos Buitron and Vanessa Anthony-Stevens

8. Intersectional Potentialities in Non-Urban K–12 Education: Envisioning the Future for New Latinx Diaspora Nebraska   103
   Jessica Sierk

9. Leveraging Existing Educator Expertise: Serving Latinx Students in the Rural Southeast   118
   Julie Yammine and Rebecca Lowenhaupt

10. *Luchando Contra La Corriente* (Fighting Against the Current): Historicizing Our Latinx Identities   132
    Socorro G. Herrera, Lisa Lynn Porter, and Katherine Barko-Alva

11. Transforming K–12 School District Structures to Center Latinx Newcomers   146
    Megan Hopkins and Hayley Weddle

12. Studying Up to Reimagine and Reframe the Dual Language Bilingual Education Agenda in the New Latino Diaspora   156
    Jessica Mitchell-McCollough

13. The Bureaucratic Paradox: Newcomer Unaccompanied Children, Educational Access, and Strategies for Increasing Flourishing Through an Ecosystem of Care   169
    Sophia Rodriguez, Lisa Lopez-Escobar, and Katya Murillo-Valencia

14. The Praxis of More Welcoming, More Just, More Successful Schooling in the New Latino Diaspora   191
    Edmund T. Hamann, Socorro G. Herrera, Stanton Wortham, and Enrique G. Murillo

Index   195

About the Editors and Contributors   204

Foreword

When Enrique Murillo, Jr. and I first started thinking about the idea of education in the New Latino Diaspora (NLD), we were doctoral students at the University of North Carolina at Chapel Hill. In the 1990s, North Carolina was experiencing a dramatic increase in the Latin American diaspora population with families arriving from El Salvador, Honduras, Guatemala, Colombia, and Mexico among other Latin American countries. Having moved from California, we had grown accustomed to drawing on our experiences as bilingual/bicultural children of working-class immigrant parents from Mexico (Enrique) and Ecuador (Sofia) and leveraging histories of Chicanx/Latinx activism in our work as adult educators and teachers in Los Angeles schools. In North Carolina, I felt as Murillo did, that our "categories of the world [did not] necessarily exist here and that they [could not] be easily imported" (Murillo, 1997, p. 265). Conceptualizing education in the "New Latino Diaspora" thus emerged from our own sense-making as educators, researchers, and community members who now found ourselves in other borderlands.

In articulating the NLD from our lived experiences, we wanted to draw attention to the configurations of power, place, and history that presented specific challenges and opportunities for the education of this newer and growing Latinx population in North Carolina. Because I experienced and viewed education as intimately connected to political struggle vis-à-vis the growing number of Latinx bilingual teachers in Los Angeles at the time, I wondered how students and their families in North Carolina might thrive absent attention to shared histories of solidarity (see Herrera, Porter, and Barko-Alva, this volume). I sorely missed that second-generation of bilingual/bicultural Latinx teachers and the non-Latinx Spanish-speaking educators who, as in Los Angeles, might be doing the work of bridging, translating, and advocating for children's cultures and language(s) and the rights of immigrant parents. I also confronted familiar forms of nativist and anti-immigrant xenophobia, and the education system's deficit perspectives. Simultaneously, I witnessed the good will and forms of mutual aid on the part of many people, including teachers from diverse backgrounds. Today much has changed and yet much remains the same. This volume beautifully and effectively approaches the NLD as a verb, as a generative term that points to the active, continuing shifts and changes in a population, and the equally shifting (but also enduring) challenges and responses to education.

The chapters in this volume teach us that education in the NLD concerns place and the immigration-related laws and discourses that shape the lives of im/migrant families and their children. It concerns the relationships, resources, school policies and practices, and forms of organizing needed for the struggle to create educational systems in which children and young adults of the Latinx diaspora can thrive. The authors precisely interrogate those closures and openings animated by the context-specific configurations of power in diverse NLD locations, including in Nebraska, Idaho, Georgia, Maryland, the Midwest, and the rural Southeast among other places. Most importantly, they set out to imagine, or imagineer, ways to create change in educational systems across the NLD. Featuring the diverse voices of parents/caregivers, teachers, students, teacher educators, administrators, and community members, the authors pose critical questions such as, how can schools be transformed by the experiences of emergent bilingual youths (Chapter 6), how can we create stronger webs of relationships to surround and nurture Latinx youth (Chapter 9), how do we make sure to center an intersectional approach in all our efforts (Chapter 8), and how do we counter the deficit and technocratic frames that have long framed schooling for Latinx youth across the United States (Chapter 10). These questions are not new, but the rich, context-sensitive research in this volume charts a powerful course for transforming education in the NLD and beyond.

REFERENCES

Murillo, E. G., Jr. (1997). Pedagogy of a Latin American festival. *The Urban Review*, 29(4), 263–281.

CHAPTER 1

From Challenges to Improvements
Creating Culturally Responsive Practice in the New Latino Diaspora

Edmund T. Hamann, Socorro G. Herrera, Enrique G. Murillo, Jr., and Stanton Wortham

Latinos form the second-largest population group in the United States, and yet they are too often still insufficiently supported in educational environments. Recent and older quantitative data point to higher dropout rates, lower college-going, and other indicators of educational challenge, with these challenges being acute in locations where the hosting of significant Latino enrollments is relatively "new" (i.e., mainly since the 1965 Immigration and Nationality Act and the 1986 Immigration and Reform Act; see Hamann & Harklau, 2022). In turn, there is a substantial and growing body of qualitative inquiry that highlights *how*, *why*, and *where* educational processes too easily fall short, disadvantaging Latino students and other Latino educational stakeholders, although clearly there is more here to note. So, it follows that documenting and analyzing the how, why, and where of schooling being inadequate should be a research priority.

Yet merely documenting what is "going wrong" or what is inadequate does not in and of itself actually ameliorate anything. Indeed, there is even space for the criticism that reiterating the point that Latino education is too often inadequate becomes a self-fulfilling prophecy and might even leave intact or rationalize deficit thinking that Latino education struggle is somehow inevitable—that students cannot succeed and/or that educators cannot adequately help. If it is important to document problems in order to understand them, we argue that it is becoming increasingly important to offer solutions, to point to what could be and then even to trace steps regarding how to get there. That is what we—both editors and contributing authors—propose to do here. As has long been noted (e.g., Flores, 2021; Romo & Falbo, 1996), education *of*, *by*, *with*, and *for* Latinos can be successful, but it often isn't. We endeavor here to share perspectives and strategies for how it more often could be.

In what is our third jointly edited volume on "Education in the New Latino Diaspora" (see *Education in the New Latino Diaspora* [Wortham, Murillo, & Hamann, 2002] and *Revisiting Education in the New Latino Diaspora* [Hamann, Wortham, & Murillo, 2015]), the task here is no longer the introduction of a field. In 2002 we proposed that dynamics encountered by Latino students and families in school districts and regions that had not historically hosted significant Latino populations might be different from those encountered in places where significant extant Latino populations often predated the incorporation of their geographic territories into the United States (i.e., Arizona, California, Colorado, Florida, New Mexico, and Texas) or where Latino populations had long formed significant portions of growing urban populations (as in Illinois, New Jersey, and New York). In 2002, we wondered if patterns of racism and discrimination that plagued education of Latino populations in sites where they have long lived might be avoided in environments not burdened by such histories. In posing that question, we were not oblivious to problematic framings—indeed Villenas's (2002) invocation in that volume of "benevolent racism" to explain the patronizing premise of immigrant targeting parent education programs and Murillo's (2002) outrage that Latino labor (and exploitation) were "welcome," but that whole human beings (with families, needs, aspiration, and complexities) were not, were both brilliantly critical. But still we had a hope back then that we were describing dynamics that were often new and improvisational and not automatically burdened as institutionalized and inflexible vehicles of structural inequality, and we noted this as rapidly growing Latino enrollments highlighted how important the new sites and settings for our inquiry were.

That initial work—the very insistence that Latino educational experiences also matter in Georgia, Indiana, Maine, North Carolina, and like locations, which included the naming of a geography of a New Latino Diaspora (NLD)—is no longer the primary case to be made. We are no longer just empirically documenting something that is new and was previously invisible. While we are not persuaded by Monreal and Tirado's (2022) argument that "new" was never an appropriate adjective, in this third decade of the 21st century, the word "new" may no longer be all that apt, except for a comparative claim that dynamics that are two and three generations old are "newer" than those that reach back five or six or more.

Our second joint NLD volume, in 2015, addressed geographic omissions from the first volume, adding examples from Connecticut, Iowa, Pennsylvania, Tennessee, Washington, and Wisconsin, for instance. It broadened the domains of formal education being scrutinized, adding examples of early childhood education, higher education, and even educator professional development through university and state department of education-organized travel study. It overtly broached topics like interracial adoption and being undocumented that were not central foci of the first volume. It also began to reject novelty and improvisation as fair excuses for weaker educational outcomes. Being caught off guard when Latino enrollment surges from nothing to half of enrollment in 10 years because of changes by local employers (e.g., Hamann, 2003), may be an okay excuse for feeling overwhelmed, but only temporarily. When, a decade or more in, practices are still improvisational, that is no longer a symptom of surprise so much as neglect. Still, the 2015 volume (which did not anticipate the Trump presidency and its related cultivation and renewal of white nationalism and xenophobia) was, like the first volume, primarily an empirical and descriptive body of work. Its main task too was to document "here's what's going on."

As we contemplated a third volume, we considered just updating and extending the first two. After all, there are still many locales of the NLD where educational topics have not been closely investigated (and this one adds some of those, like South Carolina and Idaho). Moreover, our second volume was even cautiously optimistic that Deferred Action for Childhood Arrivals (DACA) might be made permanent and that comprehensive immigration reform was in the offing, not anticipating the sharp xenophobic and racist backlash that was imminent. So, an update attending to the fraught and often anti-Latino/anti-newcomer zeitgeist could have been defended. But we also felt a kind of impatience that made repeating our prior strategy feel a bit indulgent.

Academia in general and social science in particular have roles to document and to analyze, and we get that, but perhaps reflecting the fact that the operating sphere of most of the editors and authors of this volume is in schools of education, where tasks are more applied than "just to engage in research," we wanted this volume to do more. Our task is not just to reveal a previously underconsidered dynamic or to document more interethnic interaction. Rather, if we depict dynamics that, per our review, are wanting and problematic, then the task is not only to describe the problem, but also to outline how it should and could be better. In other words, the task is to "imagineer" (Rutheiser, 1996)—that is, imagine what is possible and desirable and then to "plan backward" from there to depict and promote effective, inclusive, and responsive educational praxis.

The next 12 chapters that follow this one each start with the empirical documentation of what the authors describe as an educational problem, one that involves Latino populations in a circumstance where their/our presence is relatively new. But the task does not stop at depiction, at hoping that someone else will find our analysis, will find it cogent, and will "do something about it." Instead, all the authors here follow their explanations of the problem or challenge with a description of what could or should be. They outline how the identified problem can be resolved or at least mitigated. By intent, we are "putting our money where our mouth is" and, as such, hoping to push against accusations sometimes directed at academic research wherein academicians make careers out of highlighting the challenges of BIPOC (Black, Indigenous, and people of color) students, but do little to attend to those same challenges.

The 12 core chapters vary in a number of ways; not least, as readers will soon notice, is terminology. In the contemporary United States, the debate about the favored terminology to name those with roots, recent and/or historic, in Latin America is ongoing. While "Latino" versus "Hispanic" is one dimension of the debate, so too is the question of gender that comes with having a masculine noun—Latino—stand in as a collective label. Naming both Latino and Latina (i.e., adding the feminine form) attends to possible patriarchic implications of using just Latino, but it then struggles with seeming to reference gender in only binary terms. Latinx (which doesn't imply any gender) has become more popular recently, particularly in academic circles, but is criticized for reasons as varied as being difficult to pronounce to not being liked or used by many whom it supposedly names. A still newer term, "Latine," attends to the first of these, but not the second. Our stance in this volume has been to allow authors to use any of these terms, per their preference, noting the debate is unsettled (and, perhaps, "unsettleable"). In this chapter and the conclusion, we use "Latino" at the suggestion of coeditor Enrique G. Murillo, who, in addition to being the founding editor of the *Journal of Latino Education* (JLE) and founder of Latino Education and Advocacy Days (LEAD), says simply, "All of them have limitations and Latino is short, to the point, and broadly comprehensible." "Latino" is an imperfect choice, but so too are all the other options.

Excepting the concluding chapter, the remainder of this book is divided into two parts. The two chapters after this one exemplify the structure that is repeated more loosely in the chapters that follow. They start with a description of an extant problem related to Latino education in the NLD and then describe what could/should be done about it. Chapter 2, by Morales, Kiramba, Martinez, and Hamann, is first about the problems in Nebraska of too few teachers and too few Latino teachers (given student enrollment demographics), a problem that is not unique to Nebraska. The chapter then outlines a multifaceted solution that ranges from working with and recruiting high school students to go into teacher education, to better supporting students of color during preservice teacher preparation, to even incubating their successful induction as teachers, often back in districts where they were previously students.

Chapter 3 is Beck, Stevenson, and Bodur's recounting of the missteps that led to several Georgia Southern University students literally burning Cuban American author Jennine Capó Crucet's (2015) *Make Your Home Among Strangers*, which had been required reading for all first-year undergraduates. In this case the problem is both particular—a specific incident—but also much bigger: the means and strategies by which higher education can be made welcoming, inclusive, and empathetic. Similarly, the authors' proposed solution is both specific—advice to fellow Georgia Southern educators—and also much bigger, with attention to the implementation parameters that can keep a broad curriculum initiative intended to help cultivate a climate of inclusion from backfiring horribly.

Both chapters illuminate the concept of starting with an empirically grounded problem and then developing/illuminating a solution that would be both immediately practical and relevant to other settings. Capturing a range of additional geographies and problems, Chapters 4 through 13 consider a variety of educational tiers to describe what possible practices could and should be. Those 10 chapters are then followed by the concluding Chapter 14 wherein all four coeditors briefly consider our various takes on each of these four domains from our various professional perches with attendant responsibilities.

ADDITIONAL CONSIDERATIONS

One thing, of course, that this volume does share with its two predecessors is the assertion that education in the NLD is a substantial concern. That case can be made a number of ways, but one is quantitative. According to the World Population Review (n.d.), which draws from the 2020 U.S. Census and subsequent estimates, in 2024 the U.S. Hispanic population (echoing Census terminology) was 59,361,020, and of that, a not insignificant 25.2% of Latino individuals (14,966,923) lived in the NLD (i.e., the 41 states, plus Washington, DC, that are not Arizona, California, Colorado, Florida, Illinois, New Jersey, New Mexico, New York, and Texas). At that time, all nine "traditional" states had bigger Latino populations than any state of the NLD, and one, New Mexico, with 1,029,233 Latino residents, or 49%, was poised to become the United States' first Latino-majority state. That said, Georgia, with a Latino population of 1,013,057; North Carolina, with 991,051; Pennsylvania, with 971,813; and Washington, with 971,522, were all poised to soon overtake New Mexico in actual numbers of Latino residents. Some NLD states were about to host more Latino residents than some of the states where Latinos have been a long-standing constituency.

According to the U.S. Census Bureau's (n.d.) American Community Survey estimates from 2022, twenty-six NLD states had at least a 10% Hispanic population under age 18 (topped by Nevada at 41.9%), and several that fell short of that threshold nonetheless had under-18 Hispanic populations that topped 100,000 individuals, including Michigan (189,000), Ohio (177,700), Minnesota (116,000), and Missouri (100,700), while Alabama was close with 96,500 (U.S. Census Bureau, n.d). Connecticut, Delaware, Hawaii, Idaho, Kansas, Maryland, Massachusetts, Nebraska, Nevada, North Carolina, Oklahoma, Oregon, Rhode Island, Utah, and Washington were all NLD states where at least one of every six children and youth were Hispanic. Children and youth, of course, comprises most of the K–12 school-age population, although many states allow students who are up to 21 to continue with high school if they have not yet finished (which is more common with immigrant children who are more likely to have interrupted schooling). Acknowledging that this volume looks also at higher education, the coming-of-age population dominates who enters postsecondary education. So these tallies of Latino minors become rough approximations of prospective school enrollment.

A second set of numbers also matters: high school completion rates for Latino students in the NLD. Summarizing from Hamann and Harklau (2022), 55% of the 41 states (plus Washington, DC) in the NLD had Hispanic graduation rates in 2016–2017 below the national average of 80%,[1] including 12 that were below 74%. In turn, Hispanic high school graduation rates trailed total state averages by more than three percentage points in 74% of the NLD and by more than 10 percentage points in Connecticut, Louisiana, Maryland, Massachusetts, Minnesota, New Hampshire, North Dakota, Ohio, Pennsylvania, and South Dakota. Even as the Latino student population in the NLD is increasingly U.S.-born rather than immigrant (another point made by Hamann and Harklau [2022]), Latino school outcomes still often dramatically and problematically trail those of their non-Latino peers.

Numbers are not the only rationale for why this volume matters, however. Central to our motivation is to push back against the neo-nativism that has grown so much more common since the 2016 election. Much of the NLD is in "red-state" America, parts of the country that, at least at the ballot box, have proven willing to embrace xenophobic and racist stances. We need depictions of what thoughtful Latino parent–teacher partnerships might look like, what authentically welcoming 4-year college campuses would do to include first-generation Latino students, how high school literature classes could be different if their canon included Benjamin Alire Sáenz, Helena Viramontes, Jennine Capó Crucet, or any of the myriad other Latino authors. And the list goes on.

As a final introductory note, although neither is from the NLD, we take as two inspirations Guadalupe Valdés's (2003) *Expanding Definitions of Giftedness* (which argued for children's displays of bilingual interpreting adroitness counting as additional means to identify "giftedness") and Marjorie Faulstich Orellana's (2016) *Immigrant Children in Transcultural Spaces* (which unabashedly named *love* as a condition present in the after-school "B-Club"). While the chapters here start with an empirically documented challenge, sufficient to outline for readers the problem to be solved, the goal is to share visions of what ought to be and designs for how to get there. There's a lot of scholarship (ours included) that documents things going wrong; the task now is to depict what better educational praxis *for/with/by* Latino stakeholders might look like. What adroitness and resourcefulness needs to be allowed to flourish? What educational praxis would be more successful if it was pursued lovingly? The following chapters offer tangible answers.

NOTE

1. "Hispanic" is used here to echo the terminology of the National Center for Education Statistics (NCES), which is the source of the data.

REFERENCES

Capó Crucet, J. (2015). *Make your home among strangers*. St. Martin's.
Flores, A. (2021). *The succeeders: How immigrant youth are transforming what it means to belong in America*. University of California Press.

Hamann, E. T. (2003). *The educational welcome of Latinos in the New South*. Praeger.
Hamann, E. T., & Harklau, L. (2022). Changing faces and persistent patterns for education in the new Latinx diaspora. In E. G. Murillo, Jr. (Ed.), *Handbook of Latinos and education: Theory, research, and practice* (2nd ed., pp. 81–92). Routledge.
Hamann, E. T., Wortham, S., & Murillo, E. G., Jr. (Eds.). (2015). *Revisiting education in the new Latino diaspora*. Information Age Publishing.
Monreal, T., & Tirado, J. (2022). Don't call it the new (Latinx) South, *Estábamos aquí por años*. In Y. Medina & M. Machado-Casas (Eds.), *Encyclopedia of critical understandings of Latinx and global education* (pp. 97–121). Brill.
Murillo, E. G., Jr. (2002). How does it feel to be a problem? Disciplining the transnational subject in the American south. In S. Wortham, E. G. Murillo, Jr., & E. T. Hamann (Eds.), *Education in the new Latino diaspora: Policy and the politics of identity* (pp. 215–240). Ablex Publishing.
Orellana, M. F. (2016). *Immigrant children in transcultural spaces: Language, literacy, and love*. Routledge.
Romo, H., & Falbo, T. (1996). *Latino high school graduation: Defying the odds*. University of Texas Press.
Rutheiser, C. (1996). *Imagineering Atlanta*. Verso.
U.S. Census Bureau. (n.d.). *American Community Survey 2022: Annual state resident population estimates for 6 race groups by age, sex, and Hispanic origin*. Retrieved August 1, 2024, from https://www.census.gov/data/datasets/time-series/demo/popest/2020s-state-detail.html
Valdés, G. (2003). *Expanding definitions of giftedness*. Lawrence Erlbaum Associates.
Villenas, S. (2002). Reinventing *educación* in new Latino communities: Pedagogies of change and continuity in North Carolina. In S. Wortham, E. G. Murillo, Jr., & E. T. Hamann (Eds.), *Education in the new Latino diaspora: Policy and the politics of identity* (pp. 17–36.) Ablex Press.
World Population Review (n.d.). *Hispanic population by state 2024*. Retrieved August 1, 2024, from https://worldpopulationreview.com/state-rankings/hispanic-population-by-state
Wortham, S., Murillo, E. G., Jr., & Hamann, E. T. (Eds.). (2002). *Education in the new Latino diaspora: Policy and the politics of identity*. Ablex Press.

CHAPTER 2

Imagineering More Inclusive Teacher Education
Systemic Approaches to Challenging the Predominance of Whiteness in Education

Amanda R. Morales, Lydiah Kiramba, Ricardo Martinez, and Edmund T. Hamann

Using the idea of *imagineering* (Rutheiser, 1996) briefly traced in the opening chapter, we have imagined what a teacher education program would look like that attracted, prepared, and then supported the successful induction of Latinx and other BIPOC teachers into high-Latinx/BIPOC districts. And we have begun engineering a program along these lines that starts before college and finishes several years into a new teacher's career (while it does not go on forever, it is hard to say definitively when it ends). Given the gravity of growing racial tensions, both nationally and on the Great Plains amidst the Trump-inflected, neo-nativist, anti-immigrant social context, and the prospectively corrosive effect of these tensions on minoritized populations, those charged with preparing our increasingly diverse youth have great responsibilities (López & Pérez, 2018). In current educational contexts, the impacts of this country's *educational debt* (Ladson-Billings, 2006) incurred on minoritized communities are being experienced in both chronic/long-standing and new/short-term ways. Unfortunately, despite the rapid changes we see in the demographic makeup of the PK–12 student populations in our schools and the increased complexity that comes with enrollment heterogeneity, the teaching force remains predominantly white, monolingual, and female (Sleeter, 2017). Indeed, research indicates that the educator workforce is becoming less diverse relative to the overall population (Hansen & Quintero, 2019).

Educational debts, demographic mismatches (Easton-Brooks, 2019), and lack of shared cultural funds of knowledge (Gonzalez et al., 1995) are challenges in Nebraska, where we work; here, the proportion of BIPOC students—35% in 2020–2021—was 7 times higher than the proportion of BIPOC teachers: 5%. Further, the growth in BIPOC teachers has proportionally lagged the growth in

BIPOC students, meaning mismatch gaps are still widening. Looking specifically at Latinx student enrollments versus Latinx teacher positions, the 64,509 Latinx students in Nebraska public schools in 2020–2021 constituted just less than one fifth of total enrollment (19.9%), but the 644 Latinx teachers constituted just 2.7% of Nebraska's nearly 24,000 teachers. While the number of Latinx teachers grew by 60 from 2019–2020 to 2020–2021, the new total, according to the Nebraska Education Profile (n.d.), still lagged the 2017–2018 tally of 682.

Nebraska's Latinx public school enrollment is not distributed evenly across the state, nor are Latinx teachers. In 2020–2021 there were seven majority Latinx school districts in Nebraska—Schuyler (86%), Lexington (75%), Madison (71%), South Sioux City (64%), Crete (61%), Wakefield (60%), and Grand Island (53%)—while most of the state's metropolitan districts had more than 1,000 Latinx students: Omaha (19,351, or 37%), Lincoln (6,196, or 15%), Millard (2,259, or 10%), Bellevue (1,490, or 16%), and Papillion La Vista (1,380, or 12%). Four of the state's larger towns also enrolled more than 1,000 Latinx students—Fremont (1,836 out of 4,868) was 38% Latinx; Columbus (1,755 out of 4,159) was 42% Latinx; Scottsbluff (1,547 out of 3,452) was 49% Latinx; and Norfolk (1,210 out of 4,444) was 27% Latinx. Rural Minatare was 47% Latinx by enrollment, but that tally described just 79 students of the 168 total enrollment.

Latinx teachers have uneven distribution as well. Lexington had the highest proportion in 2020–2021 at just under 9%, with Schuyler second at 8%, and Madison third at 7% (although that 7% meant just three teachers). Omaha Public Schools had the highest number of Latinx teachers and the fifth highest in proportion (6.2%), with Scottsbluff just ahead at fourth, or 6.4%. No district other than Omaha has 100 Latinx teachers, although Lincoln Public Schools (95 full-time equivalent [FTE] out of 3,134 FTE, or 3.0%) was close.

Although we might wonder what effects the pandemic has had on both school enrollments and teacher retention, as is starting to be explored in the literature (e.g., Goldhaber & Theobald, 2023)—effects that would have been manifest in the examined 2020–2021 dataset, which was the latest available as of this writing—the 2020–2021 numbers were not a dramatic departure from previous recent patterns. Notably, a few districts (like previously noted Madison, plus Schuyler and Omaha) significantly grew their number of Latinx teachers between 2019–2020 and 2020–2021, which in one sense is a very good thing, but hints that much of the Latinx teaching force, such as it is, is likely new and more vulnerable than more veteran teachers to leaving the profession. In sum, dramatic shortfalls in BIPOC teachers in general and Latinx teachers in particular characterize contemporary schooling in Nebraska, while a few promising modest exceptions are likely fragile.

All of the chapters in this book start with a problem and then propose strategies to mitigate that problem. In this case, the problem is that the majority of BIPOC children in Nebraska complete their K–12 schooling having never seen or been taught by a BIPOC educator. Simply put, Nebraska is failing to recruit, prepare, and successfully induct teachers of color and thus has made little headway into diversifying its teaching force. Before we turn to our strategies to mitigate that problem (where we describe a pilot Youth Participatory Action Research [YPAR] project that proposes to attend to Nebraska's teachers of color shortage), it is worth clarifying what the research literature tells us regarding how and why our current overwhelmingly White teaching force is disadvantageous for BIPOC students.

THE IMPORTANCE OF DIVERSIFYING THE TEACHING FORCE

We make no claim here that White teachers cannot teach minoritized students well (which has been noted in small- and large-scale studies). Perhaps most vividly, two of the seven teachers Ladson-Billings (1994) ethnographically chronicles as particularly effective with African American students in her classic book *The Dreamkeepers* were White and they were excellent. However, we also do not claim that White teachers are equipped automatically to work as well with BIPOC students as they are with White students.

Researching from a very different methodology and scale, Meier and Stewart (1991) surveyed thousands of school districts, finding that Latinx students tended to fare better in districts with more Latinx teachers. They suggested a partially structural explanation: In districts with more Latinx teachers, more upward mobility for Latinx populations had been demonstrated. The idea of growing up to become a professional was intact. For Latinx students, exposure on a regular basis to Latinx professionals as integral members within their community can be powerful, broadening students' notions of *possible selves* (Ginorio & Huston, 2001) within and outside the field of education, making a range of future identities more tangible.

Ladson-Billings and a number of other ethnographers (e.g., Erickson, 1987; Suárez-Orozco & Súarez-Orozco, 1995) raise a key point—student wellbeing and academic success depends on their finding classroom spaces (and the educators who create them) to be safe, trustworthy, and engaging. Not surprisingly, because trust and comfort are subjective, creating these conditions requires culturally situated knowledge, critical care pedagogies that prioritize culturally sustaining practices, and an attention to subjectivity—to what individuals find familiar, responsive, and affirming. Moreover, because classrooms are not hermeneutically sealed from the dynamics of the larger society, teachers need to create safety and trustworthiness in the face of structural racism, economic inequality, and other challenges (Berry, 2010; hooks, 1994; Morales, 2018; Nieto & Bode, 2018). However, teachers do not bring equal backgrounds and life experience to this task.

Despite the profound positive impacts that BIPOC teachers can have for BIPOC students in today's classrooms, diverse ethnic and linguistic representation in teacher education and then school classrooms remains a chronic struggle (Easton-Brooks, 2019). Not only do BIPOC teachers tend to take longer, more indirect pathways into the profession (Carver-Thomas, 2018), they are leaving at faster rates than white teachers (Albert Shanker Institute, 2016). The teaching profession has "grown slowly less attractive to people of color, as evidenced by the larger diversity gaps across generations" (Hansen & Quintero, 2019, para. 17).

As aptly described by Keffrelyn Brown (2014), the relationship between the predominance of whiteness within the educator workforce and common ineffectiveness of teacher preparation and development programs to recruit, graduate, and retain teachers of color is clear. She called out the "dominant, (dis)embodied and normalized culture of Whiteness, White privilege and White hegemony" as a pervasive force still shaping teacher education and identified this force as one of our "most formidable challenge[s] to the goal of preparing teachers (of color) to teach in a manner that is relevant, critical and humanizing while also socially and individually transformative" (p. 326).

While the paragraphs above just scratch the surface in terms of depicting why and how teachers of color can be important for the academic success of students of color (a topic others have studied at much greater length—see Carver-Thomas, 2018; Dilworth, 2018; Easton-Brooks, 2019; Ingersoll & May, 2016), those topics are not the focus here, but rather the backdrop. Instead, this chapter claims that diversifying who goes into teaching (and stays in teaching) needs to change in the New Latinx Diaspora (NLD).

So, if we are to take up this challenge and reimagine teacher education as a more inclusive, affirming, and transformative space for a wider range of learners, what is to be done? More specifically, what might teacher education pathways in Nebraska and Kansas look like that effectively recruit, develop, retain, and sustain Latinx teachers, thus changing who goes into and who stays in the profession? What characteristics would agents of change within this teacher education pathway need to demonstrate? What knowledges would they need to possess? What mechanisms would need to be in place for agents to transform the systems that have historically pushed out, marginalized, and underserved Latinx pre- and in-service teachers within the profession?

Describing a successful, but grant-dependent program called BESITOS that was a vehicle for more than a hundred Latinx high school students to become teachers in Kansas, Herrera and Holmes (2015) identified the "3 Rs" of *recruitment*, *rhetoric*, and *retention* as keys to getting high school students into teacher education pathways (recruitment) and then keeping them there (rhetoric as means and retention as end) to become prepared and certified teachers. These 3 Rs function as guiding stars as this chapter describes the problem of diversifying who goes into teaching in the third decade of the 21st century in Nebraska and then describes a design and pilot project intended to grow the number of teachers of color, particularly of Latinx teachers, as that is the state's biggest population of color.

TOWARD A SOLUTION

One obvious obstacle to diversifying the teaching pool in Nebraska is the catch-22 that the current lack of diversity in Nebraska's teaching force correlates with relative disadvantage for Nebraska's BIPOC students. You will not become a teacher if you do not succeed well enough in high school to head to college. However, even for BIPOC students who succeed in school sufficiently to "make it" to tertiary education, the idea of becoming a teacher is less appealing if school has not been a particularly satisfying or welcoming place to be. To make teaching a more appealing career possibility for Latinx and other BIPOC students, there needs to be direct attention to how the next generation of teachers is recruited. More pessimistically, if current recruitment strategies do not change, who goes into teaching is not likely to change either.

If, per our argument, the big problem to be solved is to diversify who becomes a teacher in the NLD, a more tangible smaller problem is to change or expand who is attracted to teaching. We believe that sustainably diversifying who goes into teaching requires attention before college, responsive programming at college, and then supported induction beyond college (Morales, 2018). This conceives of the pathway into teaching as an 8- or 19-year plan (including the first years after one is licensed and practicing) as opposed to just 2 or 4 years. Retention of preservice teachers of color in teacher education programs and successful induction of new teachers of color into long-term teaching careers can both be struggles, but attending to these struggles does not matter much if prospective teachers of color have not been successfully recruited in the first place. These are not either/or challenges; it all matters. But recruitment matters first.

There are some overt teacher recruitment strategies beginning to be deployed in Nebraska high schools, particularly the proliferation of Educators Rising initiatives (https://educatorsrising.org/). Nebraska's former commissioner of education Doug Christensen serves on Educators Rising's board of directors, and the Nebraska Department of Education as a liaison to schools that want to start chapters. Educators Rising's mission promises to "[work] with aspiring educators who reflect the demographics of their communities and who are passionate about serving those communities through public education." However, the programming, with its emphasis on conferences and competitions, is not particularly geared toward engaging and winning the confidence of BIPOC students (nor is it geared to discouraging it). The Educators Rising Standards (https://educatorsrising.org/standards/), which include seven standards and seven "cross-cutting themes," promise to help future teachers develop "the ability to successfully teach students who come from a culture or cultures other than one's own" (cross-cutting theme 1) and to help future teachers "work vigilantly to provide all students with fair and equitable access to resources and learning opportunities" (cross-cutting theme 2). These are both laudable, but they imagine teachers and students coming from different backgrounds from one another and the emphasis on "all" leaves out how winning the confidence of children and youth from one group may differ from ways one most efficaciously wins the confidence of members from another group.

To clarify, we view Educators Rising as a complement to the YPAR initiative we organized and describe next. Educators Rising was not the "competition" because it attracted students (including some academically successful BIPOC students) who were not the same population who became interested in our pilot. Educators Rising can be an attractive program for students with the time and orientation to engage in extracurricular activities, but that does not describe all BIPOC students who could become interested in teaching and effective at it. Educators Rising may be part of the solution to growing and diversifying who goes into teaching, but we think our approach, which was piloted in 2021–2022, attends to that challenge more directly.

A LONG-TERM GROW-YOUR-OWN EFFORT TO DIVERSIFY UNL'S TEACHER EDUCATION PROGRAM

As the aphorism goes, "Stupidity is doing the same thing over again, but expecting different results." Recruiting new teachers and a broader diversity of future teachers to the University of Nebraska-Lincoln's (UNL) teacher education program is unlikely to be successful using just existing recruitment strategies; different or additional strategies need to be deployed. This final section of the chapter recounts both the piloting of some of those strategies and model development that can better be described as what "we should do" or "would like to do" rather than what we have done so far.

For the imagineering of what could be, the four authors of this chapter (partially prompted by a 2021 call from the Spencer Foundation for "Racial Equity Special Research Grant" proposals) imagined a 4-year applied research initiative that would partner us with high school students in four of Nebraska's seven majority Latinx school districts—Crete, Schuyler, South Sioux City, and Wakefield. Our proposal, which was highly scored but ultimately not funded, imagined creating *clubes igualdades* (equality clubs), a Spanish language wordplay on Nebraska's state motto, "Equality before the law." Club participants would engage in YPAR projects that came from their own questions, particularly questions about school, community, and the possibilities and rationales for becoming a teacher.

While YPAR specifically was relatively new to three of the four of us, it had been a point of specialization of coauthor Ricardo Martinez in his doctoral studies at Iowa State University, which he completed just after the COVID-19 pandemic started in spring 2020. As Ricardo mentored the rest of us in the application of YPAR, we learned its immense value and power to foster engagement and agency among youth. We gained insights from key scholars in the field, starting with the seminal work of Fals-Borda (1987) and including work from Ayala et al. (2018), Brown and Rodriguez (2009), Cammarota (2017), Cammarota and Fine (2008),

Ginwright et al. (2006), and Whyte (1991). As this literature base articulates, the goal of YPAR is empowerment as it "teaches young people that conditions of injustice are produced, not natural" and are therefore "challengeable and thus changeable" (Cammarota & Fine, 2008, p. 2). Further, it centers the capacities of youth as "intellectual beings capable of engaging in the practice of critical investigation of community issues and the production of viable, usable knowledge" (Caraballo et al., 2017, p. 315). YPAR allows for youth "engagement" efforts and teacher "recruitment efforts" to look different; to shift power, to decenter the goals of educational institutions (K–12 and postsecondary), and to take on a critical hope orientation as the youth and their adult co-facilitators critique and reimagine new, different, and more affirming educational systems for BIPOC students.

As a clear, tangible benefit of such authentic engagement, YPAR participation has been associated with higher likelihood of academic engagement in school and increased likelihood of youth going to college and succeeding at college (Strobel et al., 2006). In short, utilizing YPAR in our Midwestern context concurrently could serve as a vehicle for a lot of positive things: as a platform for youth voice; as a mechanism to collect youths' reasoned accounts about what does and does not inspire them about school and schooling and teachers and teaching; as a tool that positions educators to listen; and as a beacon to guide our efforts in transforming teaching and teacher education programs to be more attractive and affirming.

Lest the thread of our grow-your-own (GYO) effort gets lost because we focused too long or too early on our visions of what could be, we should return to our account of the unsuccessful Spencer Foundation proposal and how we moved forward in spite of its rejection. To be sure, crafting such a proposal and doing the legwork associated with establishing the partner relationships needed to implement it meant that we made significant progress toward setting an underlying foundation. We met with youth, teachers, and administrators within the four Nebraska communities noted earlier. And as we described our vision to the school superintendents, we gained their interest and support, which allowed us together to take the first steps in thinking about the prospective role of YPAR in both recruiting prospective teachers of color to preservice teacher education programs and also in having those prospective teachers engage in thinking agentively about what the schools and communities they called home needed in order to be better, more welcoming, more successful spaces.

In May 2021, a month after Spencer Foundation had shared its disappointing news, we decided to share our unsuccessful Spencer proposal with Nebraska's then-Commissioner of Education, Matthew Blomstedt. Our question to the commissioner: "Any advice/suggestions about what else we might do with this idea?" His response pleasantly surprised us. He pointed out that he had both support from the Nebraska Board of Education and the discretion to support initiatives that cost less than $50,000 without seeking further approval. He asked if we could refine our idea and turn it into a 1-year pilot project. We could. And in fall

2021 we began cocreating YPAR groups at South Sioux City High School and Wakefield High School. Shortly thereafter, because of its proximity to UNL's campus (less than a mile away) and its shared status with the other two high schools having a majority BIPOC student enrollment, we added Lincoln High to the project. This meant we could try our ideas concurrently at (a) a small, bicultural high school—Wakefield—where each grade enrolled just 30–40 students and students were either White or Latinx (of both Mexican and Guatemalan heritages); (b) a medium-sized (1,200 students) working-class metropolitan suburb high school, South Sioux City, where the majority of students were Latinx but there was a rapidly growing African immigrant population as well as White, Asian, and American Indian populations in smaller numbers, and (c) one of the largest and oldest high schools in the state, Lincoln High, where 2,300-plus students spoke more than 20 different languages and a new AVID initiative had been started targeting promising prospective first-generation college students.[1]

The pilot year engaged more than 50 students across the three schools, including 35 who were consistent participants and presented their YPAR projects at a one-day summit at UNL in May 2022. Before the summit, we visited each school in person at least eight times and additionally connected with students by Zoom when COVID spikes or winter weather argued against in-person visits. Students created and honed questions like "Why aren't there any teachers who look like me?," "What do I wish my teachers and peers knew about Guatemala?," "Is the dress code unfairly enforced against female students? And Black students?," and "What should be the relationships between teachers and students?" These questions were the seeds that developed into nine different joint Microsoft PowerPoint presentations conducted solely by the youth. They presented to an audience filled with their peers across the three YPAR programs, to assembled UNL faculty and Nebraska Department of Education administrators, and to a special undergraduate student group called Future Teachers of Color (FTOC). Authentic connections with YPAR peers and with near peers (the FTOC college students) developed rapidly, particularly after FTOC members engaged the youth in lively table conversations over lunch at a campus dining hall and later guided them on a personalized tour of the campus.

As of this writing, we do not yet know if this first YPAR foray with the three schools will measurably diversify and augment who comes to our UNL teacher education program, but we did note the enthusiasm and engagement of the high school students, the FTOC college students, and the faculty and administrators at the summit. We noted the seriousness of purpose with which the youth conducted their YPAR inquiries. We noted their quick connection to current preservice teachers. And we noted their connections to us as co-facilitators and teacher educators. Thus, if a challenge of large universities is their large scale and the sense of anonymity or loneliness, particularly for first-generation and students of color (Pascarella et al., 2004), then it is clear that connections to faculty and more advanced students can be a vehicle for countering that sense of anonymity.

LOOKING FORWARD

Ultimately, the pilot project catalyzed broader thinking about much of our work within teacher education at UNL. In addition to offering new considerations for how we engage and partner with majority BIPOC school districts in the state, it also pointed to concrete ways we can change our teacher education programs to make them more student centered and attractive to prospective BIPOC students (recruiting), more responsive and affirming if/when they come (retention), and more inclusive and welcoming (rhetoric) as they move through to graduation.

As such, at the beginning of the 2022 summer session we crafted two large, intertwined grant proposals, one to the federal U.S. Department of Education's Supporting Effective Educator Development (SEED) program and one to the Nebraska Department of Education for a special Educator Pipeline grant. Working through the development of these proposals, we were able to build greatly on our lessons learned during the pilot as we together continued to reimagine how to authentically engage and draw high school students from high Latinx-concentration high schools to a transformed version of our college teacher education program, and then on into successful induction into the profession. In other words, our intent was to continue to develop robust and meaningful preparation *architecture* that begins not in college, but in high school, and that extends not just to graduation and certification, but through successful induction.

Within these expanded opportunities, the main high school YPAR programs will continue and grow. However, it will also mean that more of our teacher education faculty can get involved, having meaningful and frequent opportunities to engage in the YPAR programming, thus positioning UNL as a familiar and regular presence in these partner high schools. And as UNL (or any higher education institution) becomes more familiar to BIPOC youth, it becomes a more tangible destination for them beyond high school. In addition, this increased engagement will assuredly develop a more nuanced lens among teacher education faculty to view and better understand the particular environments that we are directing some of our students to. The transformed preservice program will include more meaningful and well-connected practicums and student teaching placements in these schools and apprenticeships for members of the FTOC group to be mentors to high school YPAR participants. It will also include scholarships for students interested in becoming teachers from these schools in order to create and maintain connections between the schools and our program.

Finally, instead of ending our involvement with preservice teachers when they graduate and are licensed, we will continue to support their successful induction into long-term careers. This additional induction support will be provided in two ways: (a) through tuition remission for new teachers to begin coursework toward a master of arts degree that doubles as a professional space to brainstorm about new teacher challenges, and (b) through a direct connection with one of our colleagues who is an award-winning educator with rich experience mentoring new teachers. In this role she will not displace any existing mentor relationship that these districts already operate, but rather will provide more of the critical value-added support for new BIPOC teachers not feeling sufficiently supported by existing induction programs.

A second way to support diversification efforts long-term in our state involves a commitment to listening to the needs of our partners and understanding our role as teacher educators. For example, from the beginning of our work with high school students we must place a priority on nurturing, not severing, their connectedness to family, place, and community, understanding that our job is not to "recruit them away" from their communities but to prepare and equip them with tools to return home as transformative educational agents equipped with the knowledge and skills to reimagine more effective schooling for the children and families in those communities. As such, their impact would also mean more academic success for the Latinx and other BIPOC students, as a virtuous circle that links diversifying who goes into teaching with longer-term academic success generated by these "sending" districts. Sustainably growing the number and proportion of students of color who go on to become talented, successful, and satisfied teachers of color is a comprehensive and multifaceted process. We think we are starting to get better at describing and building what it entails.

NOTE

1. There is an extensive and long-standing literature on AVID (e.g., Bernhardt, 2013; Mehan et al., 1996). Almost always referred to by acronym, AVID stands for Advancement Via Individual Determination.

REFERENCES

Albert Shanker Institute. (2016). *The state of teacher diversity in American education.* http://www.shankerinstitute.org/resource/teacherdiversity

Ayala, J., Cammarota, J., Berta-Avila M., Rivera, M., Rodriguez, L. &, Torree, M. (2018). *PAR EntreMundos: A pedagogy of the Américas.* Peter Lang Press.

Bernhardt, P. E. (2013). The Advancement Via Individual Determination (AVID) program: Providing cultural capital and college access to low-income students. *School Community Journal, 23*(1), 203–222.

Berry, T. (2010). Engaged pedagogy and critical race feminism. *Educational Foundations, 24*(3–4), 19–26.

Brown, K. D. (2014). Teaching in color: A critical race theory in education analysis of the literature on preservice teachers of color and teacher education in the US. *Race Ethnicity and Education, 17*(3), 326–345.

Brown, T. M., & Rodriguez, L. F. (2009). *Youth in participatory action research.* Jossey-Bass/Wiley.

Cammarota, J. (2017). Youth participatory action research: A pedagogy of transformational resistance for critical youth studies. *Journal for Critical Education Policy Studies, 15*(2), 188–213.

Cammarota, J., & Fine, M. (Eds.). (2008). *Revolutionizing education: Youth participatory action research in motion.* Routledge.

Caraballo, L., Lozenski, B. D., Lyiscott, J. J., & Morrell, E. (2017). YPAR and critical epistemologies: Rethinking education research. *Review of Research in Education, 41*, 311–336.

Carver-Thomas, D. (2018). *Diversifying the teaching profession: How to recruit and retain teachers of color.* Learning Policy Institute. https://learningpolicyinstitute.org/product/diversifying-teaching-profession

Dilworth, M. E. (Ed.). (2018). *Millennial teachers of color.* Harvard Education Press.

Easton-Brooks, D. (2019). *Ethnic matching: Academic success of students of color.* Rowman & Littlefield.

Erickson, F. (1987). Transformation and school success: The politics and culture of educational achievement. *Anthropology & Education Quarterly, 18*(4), 335–356.

Fals-Borda, O. (1987). The application of participatory action-research in Latin America. *International Sociology, 2*(4), 329–347.

Ginorio, A., & Huston, M. (2001). *¡Sí se puede! Yes we can! Latinas in education report.* American Association of University Women Educational Foundation.

Ginwright, S., Noguera, P., & Cammarota, J., eds. (2006). *Beyond resistance! Youth activism and community change: New democratic possibilities for practice and policy for America's youth.* Routledge.

Goldhaber, D., & Theobald, R. (2023). Teacher attrition and mobility in the pandemic. *Educational Evaluation and Policy Analysis, 45*(4), 682–687. https://doi.org/10.3102/01623737221139285

Gonzalez, N., Moll, L. C., Tenery, M. F., Rivera, A., Rendon, P., Gonzales, R., & Amanti, C. (1995). Funds of knowledge for teaching in Latino households. *Urban Education, 29*(4), 443–470.

Hansen, M., & Quintero, D. (2019). *The diversity gap for public school teachers is actually growing across generations.* Brookings Institute, Brown Center Chalkboard.

Herrera, S. G., & Holmes, M. (2015). The 3 R's: Rhetoric, recruitment, and retention. In E. T. Hamann, S. Wortham, & E. G. Murillo, Jr. (Eds.), *Revisiting education in the new Latino diaspora* (pp. 225–243). Information Age Publishing.

hooks, b. (1994). *Teaching to transgress.* Routledge.

Ingersoll, R., & May, H. (2016). *Minority teacher recruitment, employment, and retention: 1987 to 2013* (Research brief). Learning Policy Institute.

Ladson-Billings, G. (1994). *The dreamkeepers: Successful teachers of African American children.* Jossey-Bass.

Ladson-Billings, G. (2006). From the achievement gap to the education debt: Understanding achievement in U.S. schools. *Educational Researcher 35*(7), 3–12.

López, P. D., & Pérez, W. (2018). Latinx education policy and resistance in the Trump era. *Association of Mexican American Educators Journal, 12*(3), 7–12.

Mehan, H., Villanueva, I., Hubbard, L., & Lintz, A. (1996). *Constructing school success: The consequences of untracking low achieving students.* Cambridge University Press.

Meier, K., & Stewart, J. (1991). *The politics of Hispanic education: Un paso pa'lante y dos pa'tras.* State University of New York Press.

Morales, A. (2018). Within and beyond a grow-your-own-teacher program: Documenting the contextualized preparation and professional development experiences of critically conscious Latina teachers. *Teaching Education, 29*(4), 357–369.

Nebraska Education Profile. (n.d.). Nebraska Department of Education. https://nep.education.ne.gov

Nieto, S., & Bode, P. (2018). *Affirming diversity: The sociopolitical context of multicultural education* (7th ed.). Pearson.

Pascarella, E. T., Pierson, C. T., Wolniak, G. C., & Terenzini, P. T. (2004). First-generation college students. *The Journal of Higher Education, 75*(3), 249–284.

Rutheiser, C. (1996). *Imagineering Atlanta: The politics of place in the city of dreams.* Verso.

Sleeter, C. (2017). Critical race theory and the whiteness of teacher education. *Urban Education, 52*(2), 155–169.

Strobel, K., Osberg, J., & McLaughlin, M. (2006). Participation in social change: Shifting adolescents' developmental pathways. In S. Ginwright, P. Noguera, & J. Cammarota (Eds.), *Beyond resistance! Youth activism and community change: New democratic possibilities for practice and policy for America's youth.* (pp. 197–214). Routledge.

Suárez-Orozco, C., & Suárez-Orozco, M. (1995). *Transformations: Immigration, family life, and achievement motivation among Latino adolescents.* Stanford University Press.

Whyte, W. F. (Ed.). (1991). *Participatory action research.* Sage.

CHAPTER 3

Impacto sin Quemarse
Building Understanding of the Latinx Immigrant/Migrant Experience Through Literature

Scott Beck, Alma Stevenson, and Yasar Bodur

During an October 2019 First-Year Experience (FYE) speech that Georgia Southern University freshmen were mandated to attend, the award-winning author of their required "Common Read" novel, *Make Your Home Among Strangers* (2015), Miami-origin Cubana Jennine Capó Crucet spoke of America's history of systemic sexism, institutional racism, and White privilege:

> When I speak at other predominantly White campuses, I remind the students of color and the women about this fact: This place never imagined you here . . . It was designed to keep you out. Undoing that inheritance is going to take radical action. I push students toward protest, toward using their understandable and justified rage to be heard. To literally and metaphorically burn things down. (Capó Crucet, 2019, minute 35)

The session ended with a heated question-and-answer session, wherein a student repeated an earlier incident on another campus described during the speech, challenging Capó Crucet's credentials. The audience loudly voiced both approval and anger at the question and the Q&A was soon halted. Soon after, a group of White students responded by burning a copy of *Make Your Home*—a fictionalized version of the author's own experiences as a college freshman at Cornell University. A video of the flames quickly went viral (elainaaan, 2019). "It was a chilling display: A terror often associated with Nazi Germany, unfolding on an American college campus . . . The actions, at least to the public, made Georgia Southern synonymous with intolerance. Even in a year saturated with explosive political division, these images were a horrifying low point" (Ellis, 2020, para. 7).

The university's administration, overseen by the University System of Georgia, stated that the burning of books was First Amendment–protected speech (Jamison, 2019). During the subsequent media firestorm, the hot potatoes of blame (for choosing Capó Crucet's book and inviting her to campus, for ill-preparing the students, and for the book-burning itself) bounced between the intentional ignorance of the students and the provocative stance of the author (Horton, 2019)—disregarding the underlying conflict between rhetoric about "inclusive excellence" (Georgia Southern University [GSU], 2019a) and the reality of budget cuts (Cannady, 2019).

This chapter, written by three Georgia Southern professors, each with the professional safety of tenure, will contextualize this event and summarize the rushed, underresourced, top-down curriculum process that set things in motion. We will then present data from an earlier, thoughtfully and responsively planned, and much more successful Georgia Southern FYE curricula and praxis that also focused on novels about the Latinx immigrant/migrant experience. Consistent with the larger volume's emphasis on "imagineering," where our status as researchers is to intertwine with our status as designers and implementers, this chapter ultimately attempts to describe ways that the FYE and complementary activities can help make Georgia Southern, and potentially other universities, places where students of color are more welcome, visible, and heard. However, for this to occur, we emphasize that efforts to address and reverse xenophobia must be carefully considered and implemented to avoid significant counterproductive backlash.

LONG-TERM CONTEXT

Georgia Southern University is located in southeastern Georgia, a region known for the cultivation of Vidalia onions and one of the definitive locales of the New Latino Diaspora (Lynn, 2015). The university was founded in the early 1900s as a small, White, state-funded college in a farm market town, Statesboro, that then included a segregated White–Black population of less than 2,500 (U.S. Census Bureau, 1913). The Sunbelt South economic and population boom of the second half of the 1900s prompted rapid growth of both Statesboro and Georgia Southern into a much larger and comprehensive university (GSU, 2020a). As of 2019, the Statesboro campus, where this research took place, had expanded to over 18,000 students, mostly undergraduate, spread across over 150 majors, 80 minors, and 100 advanced degrees (GSU, 2019b). Statesboro and surrounding Bulloch County, in turn, had grown to nearly 80,000 residents (U.S. Census Bureau, 2020).

Since the comparatively quiet integration of the Statesboro campus in 1965 (Brooks, 2006, p. 40), its African American student percentage has plateaued in the low to mid-20s (GSU, 2019b). This is a problematic number, lagging behind the state's approximately one-third Black populace (U.S. Census Bureau, 2020), but not as unacceptable as that of the state system's flagships—Georgia Tech and the University of Georgia—with African American enrollment percentages in the single digits (Board of Regents, 2020).

Since the 1980s, southeastern Georgia's Latinx population has expanded from negligible (U.S. Census Bureau, 1983) to accounting for up to one-third of some school systems' enrollment (Georgia Department of Education, 2024). This growth started when improved opportunities for low-wage workers combined with the expansion of Vidalia onion and poultry production left farmers and chicken processors desperate for easily exploited laborers (Weber, 2015). Like many other agricultural employers in the South (Guerrero, 2017), they turned to predominantly Mexican-heritage migrants from Texas and beyond the border. Over time, other employers hired this hardworking workforce to make batteries, build modular homes, and load trucks (Beck & Allexsaht-Snider, 2002; Lynn, 2015).

Through improved outreach and retention efforts, the Statesboro campus's Latinx student population has grown to 6% (GSU, 2019b), closer to that of the state's official proportion of 10% (likely significantly undercounted [U.S. Census Bureau, 2020; Visser, 2014]). As Georgia's Latinx population has bloomed, racial/ethnic disruptions and social tensions here have paralleled other places in the South (Beck & Stevenson, 2016; Hamann, 2003; Marrow, 2011; Stuesse, 2016). These challenges have further raised the necessity and stakes for diversity initiatives at Deep South institutions like ours.

Georgia Southern has long struggled to create a culture of equity and inclusion (F. Johnson, 2019; Walker-DeVose et al., 2019). University administrators have tried to address these failings in multiple ways during the past dozen years. Particularly relevant for our work is the fact that in 2011, all entering students were required to complete a one-credit-hour course regarding diversity. The course, FYE 1410 Global Citizens, had the following charge: "In this seminar, students explain factors that contribute to their cultural perspective, apply multiple cultural perspectives to global issues, and then apply this knowledge through engagement with local communities or problems" (GSU, 2011, p. 556). Sections of this course were overwhelmingly taught by faculty who addressed multiculturalism through a thematic case study of interest to them, including coauthor Beck. Themes included Music and Popular Culture, Technology and Innovation, Health and Nursing, Soccer, and Film Studies (GSU, 2015). Students could choose a section based on their interests. It was within this structure that the research presented later in this chapter was conducted.

Scholarship has repeatedly shown the difficulties of mandatory diversity and tolerance training (Dobbin & Kalev, 2018). Unsurprisingly, especially in the Trump era, these one-credit-hour classes did not prevent multiple nationally and even internationally publicized viral social and traditional media controversies that stained our institution's claim to openness to diverse ideas and populations. For example, in November 2015, a Georgia Southern student criticized Muslims and threatened Black Lives Matter protestors on Facebook and soon after was fired from her job at a local chain restaurant (Howell, 2015). In September 2016, a Georgia Southern student-athlete threw a bottle at a cheerleader from a nearby historically Black college and university (HBCU), Savannah State, during a football game—all while other fans called her racial slurs (Habersham, 2016). In 2016 and 2017, a Georgia Southern professor's journalism and research about Trump acolytes yielded death threats, including that he'd "be killed in a new Civil War" (Rhone, 2017; Sexton, 2016). In

July 2018, an incoming White freshman assigned to live with a Black student accidentally sent a text message to her new roommate describing the roommate's Instagram identity as "pretty normal, not too [N-word]-ish" (Logan, 2018). A year later, in July 2019 the university's Black star quarterback was falsely accused of and arrested for cocaine possession; however, the "drug" in question was bird poop that had dried on the hood of his car (Cary & Motsinger, 2019).

IMMEDIATE CAUSES

Meanwhile, the USG Board of Regents forced the consolidation of Savannah's smaller Armstrong State University into Georgia Southern University to save money (Cannady, 2017). Armstrong's enrollment had declined 7.8% since Assessment Year (AY) 2010–2011, whereas GSU had grown by 6.1% (GSU, 2020b). Armstrong originated as a junior college in the first half of the 20th century and, as of 2017, served a slightly more diverse population with many commuter, nontraditional, and military students. The resultant process was rushed, painful, and controversial due, in part, to state-level constraints and micromanagement. The uncertainty caused by consolidation, in turn, caused a downturn in overall enrollment and a consequent further budget cut (Hackle, 2019). The cross-campus curriculum consolidation negotiations combined with the budget cuts hit the FYE program particularly hard.

The problems that resulted from these cutbacks were predictable, according to Stacy et al.'s (2015) discussion of educational policy in the New Latino Diaspora: "[s]tructural responses must have enough support, economic and otherwise, throughout the implementation process" (p. 345). Nonetheless, the racist embarrassments of previous years drove administrators to plunge ahead with campuswide diversity training on the cheap (Ellis, 2020). FYE's previous two-credit-hour introduction to college and one-credit-hour diversity course were consolidated into a single two-credit-hour course wherein the problems of procrastination and systemic racism were to be taught side by side. Additionally, as documented by *The Chronicle of Higher Education*, FYE funding was slashed from "about $1 million . . . to about $33,000 [and] instructors would no longer be paid to teach" (Ellis, 2020, para. 30).

To many faculty, this revealed that the university's supposed commitment to diversity through "Inclusive Excellence" was just lip service. Many experienced and relatively diverse FYE faculty abandoned the program, dropping faculty from 80% to 24% of instructors between spring and fall 2019. They were mostly replaced by already-overworked, generally White mainstream student advisers and support staff—that is, many novice instructors much better situated to teach the "study skills" side of these now oddly hybrid classes, but with little to no experience teaching about diversity and multiculturalism. Meanwhile, class sizes spiked due to the shortage of instructors. Students were involuntarily assigned to FYE sections, diminishing their enthusiasm, and the long-time FYE director was reassigned to a teaching position outside FYE and not replaced (Ellis, 2020). Nonetheless, the administration hurried forward with the official intention of using the program to open conversation about the most fraught issues of the Trump era. Thus, "a lack of preparation, budget cuts, and insufficient foresight unwittingly spread the kindling for the spark that would come" (Ellis, 2020, para. 8).

Less than 2 weeks before the fall 2019 semester during which Capó Crucet would speak, the largely inexperienced instructors were presented with a master syllabus and teaching materials. They had little time to prepare and even less training regarding how to address controversial issues. According to retrospective coverage in *The Chronicle of Higher Education* that quoted instructors, training included:

> a detailed overview of the learning-management system. [But no] required programming on how to teach diversity . . . [Instructors] were "freaking out" . . . "Everybody had the feeling that this is something serious, this is something we don't need to botch . . . If we are addressing this issue, we need to do it in the right way." (Ellis, 2020, para. 38)

Further escalating the risks was the gap in expectations and understandings between Capó Crucet, the FYE planners, and much of her October audience. Most students had not read her novel because the syllabus did not provide substantial consequences for not doing so. Capó Crucet's controversial speech not only assumed that the students had read her book, but that they had *previously* discussed its challenging ideas in their FYE section. Instead, though, the FYE syllabus was structured to use her speech as a starting point for these difficult conversations. The master syllabus scheduled a session on identity and worldviews and two sessions on privilege *after* her speech. Moreover, the university-provided FYE materials for those later sessions were useful but were better suited to graduate courses than a freshman seminar (M. Johnson, personal communication, 2019). Thus, the weight of introducing and explaining these ideas was placed upon her book and her speech. Afterward, one faculty member said, "You don't make big words about diversity and inclusion and then throw a book at students, call a speaker, and hope it will all go down well" (Ellis, 2020, para. 49).

SAME COURSE, SIMILAR GOALS, DIFFERENT PLANNING AND IMPLEMENTATION

Things did not have to be this way. The undermining of FYE's capacity to address diversity and equity and the resultant speech and book-burning incidents were not inevitable. The previous FYE model, with experienced faculty addressing multiculturalism with smaller groups of freshmen in the context of a topic of interest to both, had functioned without major incident for several years. Moreover, some of the sections had documented positive effects on student attitudes. One such success was the instructional plan and process to be described here. As we will show, mixed-methods analysis (Creswell & Plano Clark, 2011) of our quantitative and qualitative data demonstrates that curricula based on literature about young people—similar to *Make Your Home*—can be thoughtfully "imagineered" to effectively and positively address issues of identity and immigration in the New Latino Diaspora.

Between 2012 and 2018, coauthor Beck taught 25 sections of preconsolidation FYE 1410 Global Citizens. He built his sections around the theme Controversial Young Adult Literature. Across those 7 years, a total of more than 700 undergraduates, mostly freshmen, read fiction about and discussed some of the central controversies that have become flashpoints for immigration and migration, gender and sexual diversity, and Islam. From spring 2012 to fall 2015, the course included young adult (YA) novels focused on Mexican-heritage immigrants and migrant farmworkers in the United States—the people Trump most defamed in his announcement of candidacy for the presidency. Although the 2019 FYE program used *Make Your Home* as a fictional Common Read, there had been no mandated reading shared across the pre-2019 sections of FYE. Thus, Beck's use of fiction was atypical.

THEORY, PEDAGOGY, AND DATA COLLECTION

As further elaborated on in Beck et al. (2018), this teaching and research project is based on Rosenblatt's reader-response theory (1938/1995), which asserts that each reader applies their unique background to a text and thereby negotiates their individual understanding of its meaning. Within this theoretical frame, books for young people are often used to begin and inform conversations about challenging issues (Taxel, 2007; Todres & Higinbotham, 2015). As Sumara et al. (2006) argue, "literature can broaden [readers'] understanding of social and cultural diversity" (p. 55). Since most people in their early 20s are still thinking with adolescent brains (Sowell et al., 2003), it is not surprising that this approach has been effective in college. However, as the events of October 2019 show, books for young people are not a panacea, and using such books in uninformed or culturally unresponsive ways can do damage (Meacham & Meacham, 2016).

During coauthor Beck's 2012–2018 FYE combined teaching and research project, his first class meeting started to build a community of learners and a safe space for them to express their questions, doubts, and stereotypes freely. This trust-building process began with the instructor using self-deprecatory humor to describe his identities and share his, possibly unexpected, roots in "redneck culture": alcoholism, racism, and depression. This model set a high ceiling for open honesty by students without forcing them to say more than they felt comfortable sharing. The students got to know each other in pairs or triads before introducing their peers to the whole class. Finally, the course syllabus, schedule, and Institutional Review Board (IRB)-approved consent process for the research were introduced, while the potential value of controversial and censored literature was discussed. During the next week, the students reviewed the syllabus, gave (or denied) their consent for the use of their data, and completed an online Likert-scale pre-survey of their demographic background and dispositions toward and knowledge about immigrants/migrants. These disposition prompts were

> intentionally provocative and reflected opinions found at both ends of the political and rhetorical spectrum, for example: "People in the USA without documentation should be protected by our laws" versus "Our country needs to deport all the illegal aliens right away." The repugnant term "illegal alien" was included in some prompts to accurately reflect the terms of the debate. . . . The prompts were screened . . . for content validity and accuracy in reflecting real-world opinions. (Beck & Bodur, 2015, para. 9)

Students could answer "unknown" or "rather not say" to any questions. Because of the IRB assurance that students who opted out of the study would not face any repercussions for doing so, the researchers did not see the pre- and post-test data until after the completion of the semester.

The class then spent the next few weeks, in literature circles of three to six students, reading and discussing YA novels and first-person memoirs about immigration and migrancy (see the Appendix). To monitor that the students were actually reading, an individualized role sheet was graded each week (Daniels, 2002). Each literature circle meeting was structured by the sharing of emotional responses, role sheet research findings, and mutual question-and-answer time. The instructor toured the literature circles to listen in on each conversation, assess how the group was responding to their book, and keep them focused and on task.

Unresolved questions from the literature circles often included "Why can't we just replace farmworkers with robots?" and "Why don't they just get legal papers?" The instructor used the whole class's preexisting knowledge and experiences to begin to scaffold answers. Rural students with agricultural backgrounds and immigrant/Latinx students often had much to contribute. The instructor brought in Internet sources (such as a video of a mechanical tomato harvester), multimedia presentations (such as Romano's 2010 documentary *The Harvest*), children's picture storybooks about the topic (Beck & Stevenson, 2015), and a summary of U.S. immigration history and policy to build more complete understandings. Finally, after 3 to 5 weeks of reading and discussing their YA novel, the groups worked to create and present an illustrated story map summarizing and reviewing their book for their classmates.

Each student then completed an online post-survey that reassessed their attitudes with the same disposition prompts and sought their opinion regarding the book(s) they read. After receiving a comparison of their pre- and post-survey responses, each student drafted, revised, and submitted a short, summative reflective essay about their book, the experience of discussing it, other class activities, and any changes in their survey responses. The survey data and the essays were stored for future analysis with student identities protected by pseudonyms—mostly chosen by the students. For comparability to the Capó Crucet cohort, this chapter will only examine data regarding the Latinx immigrant/migrant experience from freshmen in FYE classes.

THE PARTICIPANT FRESHMEN

The total number of students who originally enrolled in Beck's 2012–2015 FYE sections was approximately 400. However, given the high withdrawal and failure rates in freshmen courses, our dataset size is smaller. After removing all incomplete data and data without consent, and then scrubbing unreliable participants such as "straightliners" who unthinkingly clicked on the same Likert number for most or all prompts (Kim et al., 2019), the data under examination here include N=259 survey results and essays. After the data were cleaned, they were rechecked for accuracy against the original survey software data files.

The participants were nearly equally female/male and almost 80% under age 20, with another 17% aged 20–25. Of the students who reported their family's approximate annual income, 14% stated below $30,000, 23% stated above $100,000, with the remainder in the middle. Politically, they self-identified as 28% Democrat/Liberal, 17% Independent, and 55% Republican/Conservative/etc. This is substantially more conservative than contemporary poll numbers regarding Georgia's voters (Davis & Stirgus, 2012). Racially and ethnically, our participants largely mirrored the university's enrollment: 62% White, 24% African American, 6% Latinx, 6% Native American, and 5% Asian/Other.

QUANTITATIVE DATA FROM PRE- AND POST-SURVEYS

As explained in Beck and Bodur (2015), our quantitative data analysis began with Lakoff's (2007) parenting-metaphor explanation of U.S. politics based on nurturing liberals (generally supportive of immigrants and migrants) versus stern conservatives (generally nativist and opposed to immigration). We developed four composite averages (rescaled from 1 low to 10 high) to summarize the bulk of the survey data described in Table 3.1. Each average included prompts

Table 3.1. Composite Average Summary of Data

	Pre-Test		Post-Test		Progressive Net Change Toward Pro-Immigrant
	Nurturing Liberal	Stern Conservative	Nurturing Liberal	Stern Conservative	
Mean	$Pre\text{-}\mu_{pro} =$ 6.88 / 10	$Pre\text{-}\mu_{anti} =$ 5.52 / 10	$Post\text{-}\mu_{pro} =$ 7.45 / 10	$Post\text{-}\mu_{anti} =$ 4.97 / 10	$\Delta_{net} =$ 0.56 / 10
Range	4.2 to 9.5	1.8 to 8.6	3.8 to 9.1	1.4 to 9.1	−1.2 to 2.6

Across the entire sample, a paired-samples *t*-test showed that the difference from pre- to post-test for both μ_{pro} Nurturing Liberal ($t(258) < -10.6$; $p < 0.01$) and μ_{anti} Stern Conservative ($t(258) = 10.8$; $p < 0.01$) was statistically significant.

that our previous analysis showed as clustering together and thereby providing explanatory value. So, for example, the prompts "Immigration is one of the things that made this country great" and "Farmers should provide comfortable & safe housing for farmworkers" were part of the Nurturing Liberal average (μ_{pro}); meanwhile, "All people in the USA should be required to speak English in public" and "Illegal aliens cost us more than they contribute to our economy" were counted in the Stern Conservative average (μ_{anti}).

The histogram in Figure 3.1 helps visualize how the net change by individuals was distributed across the 259 participants, with the four rightmost bars representing progressive change, per U.S. norms. Remarkably, 99 students' net survey results Δ_{net} shifted in a progressive direction by more than a standard deviation ($\sigma = 0.68$). Meanwhile, only 10 participants substantially backlashed by more than a standard deviation ($\Delta_{net} < \mu - \sigma$) toward an increased anti-immigrant stance.

Figure 3.1. Histogram of Net Change Distribution

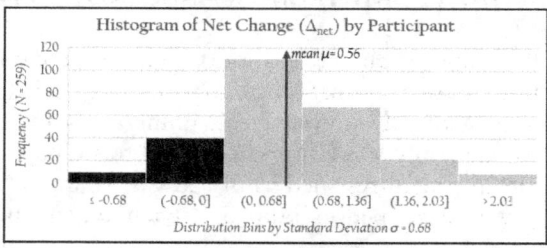

QUALITATIVE DATA FROM STUDENT ESSAYS

Stacy et al. (2015) call for greater prominence for student voices in the planning, implementation, and assessment of educational efforts because "how students interact with an initiative is the ultimate measure as to how well it served them" (p. 346). Thus, to better understand the feelings and thoughts of our student participants that underlie the results of our quantitative data, we turn to their summative reflective essays. Based on our quantitative analysis, we chose a diverse and representative subset of the essays for qualitative content analysis for emergent themes (Williams, 2008). Please note that these essays were written by college freshmen. Therefore, some quotes have been lightly edited for clarity, but not grammar.

Previous Preconceptions

Several participants clearly described watching the arrival and growth of the New Latino Diaspora in their communities. Matt, a self-described conservative "American" explained, "I grew up in Dalton, Georgia. Dalton is known as the carpet capital of the world. My town in the past few decades has drawn tons of immigrant workers to do labor work in the carpet factories. Also, my high school was about 60% Mexican and Latin American."

Similarly, African American liberal Zora, who shifted to an even more pro-immigrant stance, wrote, "I [have] had a lot of Latino classmates and I always thought they were legal citizens like everybody else. I've watched cities in Georgia transform more and more each year by the increasing amounts of foreign migrants and their influences."

Like Zora, many students began their essays by reflecting on earlier ignorance about immigration and migrancy, and some directly confessed the falsehoods and stereotypes that they believed before the course. White American Layla stated,

> Growing up in a rural town, I thought myself to be very familiar [with] migrant workers and their hardships . . . I looked at migrants as a part of everyday life, a normalcy. I grew up surrounded by cotton and blueberry fields. Every day, I walked outside and saw the Mexicans working the fields . . . The beliefs I had before these readings and discussions disgust me with how blasé they were.

Layla had started as a moderate but demonstrated a progressive shift.

African American Bernie started pro-immigrant and shifted further in that direction. Nonetheless, he stated that he had previously accepted what he "was always told—that immigrant and migrant farmworkers that hadn't become citizens were living and working here without paying taxes." Mixed Black-White Channing began as a relative centrist and displayed progressive shift. He wrote that "The only things I knew about immigration were the bits of information that I had gathered from overhearing random conversations in life . . . I thought that illegal aliens cost the US more than they contribute."

Effects of Young Adult Novels on Students' Perceptions

Although this study does not focus on the participants' responses to individual books, across their essays there was clear evidence that the YA novels had been instrumental in shifts in their thinking. Laura, a White American, started relatively pro-immigrant and moved further in that direction. She said that while:

> . . . reading the novel *Illegal* by Bettina Restrepo, my thoughts were turned . . . I now strongly agree that a foreigner [who] is willing to work hard at a job most Americans are unwilling to do [should be allowed] to legally immigrate to the USA. If anything, migrant farmworkers are benefiting the U.S. more than some U.S.-born citizens are.

Moderate American Mark read *The Circuit* and shifted his opinion about migrants and education. He had previously thought that

> . . . migrant farmworkers do not value education because they frequently bring their children into the fields with them . . . They do value education. The parents of these children move their families to our country to be given opportunities that they would not get in their home country . . . When a family is struggling as bad as migrant families do, sometimes they rely on their children to help them so food can be put on the table.

Asian/White credited her change to *Arly*:

> [M]y viewpoints changed to migrant farmers are not treated fairly and that the[ir] children should be [allowed] an education . . . It breaks my heart that these children . . . give up their education to help their parents or give their younger siblings an opportunity to learn. No child should have to choose between family or education.

Economics

Many participants described substantial changes regarding the economic impact of immigration and migrants. Conservative White American Wes had one of the larger progressive shifts in the dataset. He stated,

> Coming into this class I have to say that I had a very negative view of all immigrants. . . . Many of my views have changed because of the books that I have read that take you into the world of a migrant farmworker . . . [I] thought that illegal immigrants cost more to our economy than they contribute. [Instead,] they actually contribute a great deal.

Multiple participants explained comparable shifts by referring to how although "Many Americans are complaining that immigrants take jobs, in actuality immigrants do jobs most Americans don't want to do," as asserted by Deborah, a conservative suburban Black who shifted substantially toward support of immigrants.

Rachel, a White/Native American suburban conservative who also shifted quite substantially in part because "before this class, I disagreed that we needed immigrants to sustain our country. Now, I completely agree that our economy would collapse without the hard work of these people."

Political Engagement

In the context of our current national crisis of polarization, some of the most remarkable commentaries of the participants were regarding broader changes in their understandings of immigrants, our nation, and sometimes even their own responsibilities. Moderate African American Megan stated the spirit of many of the students who previously did not understand their privileges: "This course has made me view life different. I am more grateful about the life I lived."

Colbie, a White American moderate, wrote,

> Before taking this class, I viewed immigrants as a threat to the United States. [Now,] I believe that immigration is necessary in America. Immigration and different cultures have helped make America what it is today. America is known as "land of the free" and I believe that all people should be allowed the opportunity [for] a better life.

Channing, quoted earlier, also described a shift in his awareness of political issues:

> My opinions have definitely changed since the beginning of the semester. I'm actually starting to form opinions . . . I've been keeping up with the news. I'm not saying that I've become completely aware of all the problems this country and its people face, but I have become more aware in certain areas. This class has definitely opened up my eyes.

Multiple participants went a step further and pledged themselves to political advocacy. Strong liberal White American Stephanie wrote, "The knowledge I have gained on this topic has strengthened my liberal standpoint and will likely influence my votes regarding immigration policies."

Layla, quoted earlier, stated that

> . . . reading of the struggles of migrants in *Small Town Browny* and *Devil on My Heels* has made my views stronger . . . Now that I was able to see into the mind of

the worker and [be] someone who ha[s] the willpower to stand up for that worker, I know that I can and will. I know my viewpoints on the issue and will finally be able to stand by them.

Angelina, an American, started as a moderate but made a noticeable shift toward the left because she connected with the White male protagonist of *Joyride* and "Like Jeff, I am now able to bring awareness to those who do not understand migrant farmers while working towards creating a new level of acceptance."

IMAGINEERING

The Hippocratic Oath calls doctors to "first, do no harm." Experienced advocates and educators seeking to cultivate cross-cultural understanding and goodwill generally acknowledge this dictum in their teaching and work—even if it is not always possible to achieve given the powerfully polarized discursive divisions with our nation. However, college administrators, who often do not understand the challenges of these efforts, are going to perpetually ask, "Can't we do this more efficiently?" This is especially true post-COVID-19, due to economic contraction and reduced university budgets. In this context, and during inevitable future rounds of budget cuts, our experiences at Georgia Southern can serve as both a powerful cautionary tale of how quickly things can go wrong when the belt is tightened a notch too far, but also a model for how to do it right for not much more money.

As our data demonstrate, many Georgia Southern freshmen come to their FYE course with nativist and stereotype-laden attitudes and ideas about immigrants and diversity in general. Our findings demonstrate that a well-developed course, taught by qualified faculty with knowledge of the dynamics and relationships of race, diversity, and power in the United States, can successfully change hearts and minds. We demonstrated a 10:1 ratio of substantial progress versus backlash without an eruption of counterproductive resistance or protest.

Reflecting on the effectiveness of the previous FYE courses described here versus the backlash against Capó Crucet's speech, we believe that it might have been possible for Georgia Southern to successfully shift toward a Common Read model without inciting protests, reinforcing intolerance, and severely damaging our institution's reputation as a site of prospective welcome. Moreover, this was possible without busting the budget; however, another text would likely have a better chance at success. Capó Crucet's Miami Cuban home culture and Ivy League privilege are both unfamiliar and potentially alienating to most of our university's freshmen. Even though her own/protagonist's experiences of divided loyalties and identity struggles are relatable, a text rooted in histories, cultures, and experiences more familiar to our institution's freshmen would have been a better place to start. We would suggest, for example, *The Land*, by Mildred Taylor; *Day of Tears*, by Julius Lester; *Cy in Chains*, by David Dudley; *Praying for Sheetrock*, by Melissa Greene; or *March*, by John Lewis. Our experience teaching with these books in other courses has shown that our students generally make personal connections with the characters easily. However, as research has shown, mandatory structures for diversity training are often counterproductive. Allowing student choice, at least from among a menu of books, would have been preferable.

It is likely that if the new FYE structure had been built on experienced instructors mentoring adequately trained newcomers, much of the fear and uncertainty could have been avoided. If the course had provided the students with incentives for reading the Common Read, instructors could have built from a shared knowledge of and empathy with the characters. If the instructor training and syllabus had not emphasized study skills over controversial concepts like White privilege and systemic racism, the students would likely have taken the content more seriously. If the administration and instructors had known ahead of time that the speech would be challenging and at times provocative, they could have prepared the students to listen with open minds. If difficult concepts had been developed and discussed before the speech, using materials appropriate to the skills of knowledge of Georgia Southern freshmen, they would have been better prepared to understand Capó Crucet and receive her and her book more positively. And if all this had happened, many would have likely positively shifted some of their preconceptions about immigration, immigrants, and race in America, as most of our participants did.

Of course, this is all speculation, but it is speculation based on experience and research, and thoughtful and informed speculation, planning, and flexible implementation, or more agentively, imagineering, is a core charge of this volume. Acknowledging that universities are in the business of producing and conveying knowledge, including research about how best to address diversity issues, we propose a redoubling of efforts like those that guided Beck's experiences welcoming first-year students in the studied 2012–2015 period and subsequently until 2018. When administrators are singularly focused on the business of budgets and top-down mandates, they often do not look for guidance from their own experts. Yet in this instance, the cost to the university was financial, social, and semiotic.

The rushed changes to the FYE program during 2019 "set this up to fail" (Ellis, 2020, para. 7), but that does not mean Georgia Southern is inevitably trapped in being unwelcoming and reactionary. Indeed, from a diversity standpoint, our institution starts ahead of several of our state peers in who we get through our doors (although a moral necessity for further progress remains). However, we must attend to what all three of Herrera and Holmes's (2015) "new 3 R's" for education in the New Latinx Diaspora. We cannot just focus on *recruiting* a more diverse enrollment. We have a subsequent responsibility to assure that our institutional sphere's *rhetoric* and practices *retain* such students, supporting, encouraging, and empowering them to feel welcome, be visible, and act openly in support of further progress.

Appendix. Young Adult Novels Included in the Study

J. Alvarez's *Return to Sender*
P. Beatty's *Lupita Manana*
J. Betancourt's *Not Just Party Girls*
S. Bridgers's *Home Before Dark*
P. Cochrane's *Purely Rosie Pearl*
C. DeFelice's *Under the Same Sky*
W. Durbin's *Journal of C.J. Jackson*
D. Gates's *Blue Willow*
G. Gonzalez's *So-Called Vacation*
W. Hobbs's *Crossing the Wire*
A. Jaramillo's *La Linea*
F. Jiménez's *Circuit, Breaking Through & Reaching Out*
C. Kadohata's *Kira-Kira*
J. McDonald's *Devil on my Heels*
M. Mulder's *After Peaches*
P. Muñoz Ryan's *Esperanza Rising*
G. Olson's *Joyride*
G. Paulsen's *Beet Fields*
R. Peck's *Arly & Arly's Run*
T. Rivera's *. . . y no se trago la tierra*
Z. Snyder's *Velvet Room*
G. Soto's *Jesse*
J. Steinbeck's *Of Mice and Men*
C. Strang's *Foster Mary*
T. Taylor's *Maldonado Miracle*
L. Travis's *Jean Marie and the Runaways*
H. Viramontes's *Under the Feet of Jesus*

REFERENCES

Beck, S. A., & Allexsaht-Snider, M. (2002). Recent language minority education policy in Georgia: Appropriation, assimilation, and Americanization. In S. Wortham, E. G. Murillo, Jr., & E. T. Hamann (Eds.), *Education in the new Latino diaspora: Policy and the politics of identity* (pp. 37–66). Ablex.

Beck, S. A., & Bodur, Y. (2015). Migrants, farming, and immigration: Beginning a dialogue in agricultural education. *Journal of Southern Agricultural Education Research, 65*(1), 19–37.

Beck, S. A., Bodur, Y., Walker-DeVose, D., Town, C., & Smith, T. (2018). Reading about what it is really like is eye-opening: Literature for youth and college-level critical pedagogy. *Transformations, 28*(1), 19–37.

Beck, S., & Stevenson, A. (2015). Migrant students scaffolding and writing their own stories: From socio-culturally relevant enabling mentor texts to collaborative student narratives. *Voices From the Middle, 23*(1), 59–67.

Beck, S. A., & Stevenson, A. D. (2016). Shifting racialized identities among Mexican heritage women of the rural south: Brown faces in black and white places. *Hispanic Journal of Behavioral Sciences, 38*(1), 31–54.

Board of Regents. (2020). *Semester enrollment report: Spring 2020*. University System of Georgia. https://dlg.usg.edu/record/dlg_ggpd_i-ga-bu500-pr4-bp1-be5-b2020-sspring-belec-p-btext#text

Brooks, F. E. (2006). *Pursuing a promise: A history of African Americans at Georgia Southern University*. Mercer University Press.

Cannady, D. (2017, December 27). *A look back at the Georgia Southern, Armstrong State consolidation process*. WTOC. https://www.wtoc.com/story/37148354/a-look-back-at-the-georgia-southern-armstrong-state-consolidation-process/

Cannady, D. (2019, April 5). Georgia Southern to make budget cuts next school year to balance drop in enrollment. WTOC. https://www.wtoc.com/2019/04/05/georgia-southern-make-budget-cuts-next-school-year-balance-drop-enrollment/

Capó Crucet, J. (2015). *Make your home among strangers*. St. Martin's.

Capó Crucet, J. (2019, October 9). *Common Read lecture*. Georgia Southern University.

Cary, N., & Motsinger, C. (2019, August 29). *Falsely charged for cocaine that was bird poop, college QB speaks as case handling is investigated*. Greenville [SC] News. https://www.greenvilleonline.com/story/news/local/south-carolina/2019/08/29/shai-werts-georgia-southern-quarterback-falsely-charged-during-sc-traffic-stop/1981034001/

Creswell, J., & Plano Clark, V. (2011). *Designing and conducting mixed methods research* (2nd ed.). Sage.

Daniels, H. (2002). *Literature circles: Voice and choice in book clubs*. Stenhouse.

Davis, J., & Stirgus, E. (2012, September 3). Which party has more supporters? AJC PolitiFact. http://www.politifact.com/georgia/statements/2012/sep/10/mikeberlon/which-party-has-more-supporters/

Dobbin, F., & Kalev, A. (2018). Why doesn't diversity training work? The challenge for industry and academia. *Anthropology Now, 10*(2), 48–55.

elainaaan. (2019, October 9). "so after our FYE book's author came to my school to talk about it . . ." [Tweet]. Twitter. https://twitter.com/i/status/1182136933754929152

Ellis, L. (2020, January 17). Racist incidents, budget cuts, and faculty warnings: Inside the run-up to a campus book-burning. *Chronicle of Higher Education, 66*(17). https://www.chronicle.com/article/Racist-Incidents-Budget-Cuts/247845

Georgia Department of Education. (2024, March 7). *Enrollment by Race/Ethnic and Gender - Fiscal Year 2024-3 Data Report: ALL Districts-Schools*. https://oraapp.doe.k12.ga.us/ows-bin/owa/fte_pack_ethnicsex_pub.entry_form

Georgia Southern University. (2011). *Catalog 2011–2012*. https://em.georgiasouthern.edu/registrar/resources/catalogs/

Georgia Southern University. (2015). *Course search*. https://georgiasouthern.gabest.usg.edu/B390/bwckschd.p_disp_dyn_sched

Georgia Southern University. (2019a). *Inclusive excellence*. https://www.georgiasouthern.edu/inclusive-excellence/

Georgia Southern University. (2019b). *Student enrollment data*. https://em.georgiasouthern.edu/ir/enrollment

Georgia Southern University (2020a). *Our history*. https://www.georgiasouthern.edu/history/

Georgia Southern University. (2020b). *Fact books, IPEDS reports and interactive dashboards*. https://em.georgiasouthern.edu/ir/facts-and-figures/factbook/

Guerrero, P. M. (2017). *Nuevo South: Latinos, Asians, and the remaking of place*. University of Texas Press.

Habersham, R. (2016, September 9). *Ga. Southern baseball player accused of throwing bottle at cheerleader*. Atlanta Journal-Constitution. https://www.ajc.com/news/local/southern-baseball-player-accused-throwing-bottle-cheerleader/7RnCKldk8FEsfya9yS5qoO/

Hackle, A. (2019, August 14). *"Never in enrollment decline again!"* Statesboro Herald. https://www.statesboroherald.com/local/never-in-enrollment-decline-again/

Hamann, E. T. (2003). *The educational welcome of Latinos in the New South*. Praeger.

Herrera, S. G., & Holmes, M. A. (2015). The 3 R's: Rhetoric, recruitment, and retention. In E. T. Hamann, S. Wortham, & E. G. Murillo, Jr. (Eds.), *Revisiting education in the new Latino diaspora* (pp. 225–243). Information Age Publishing.

Horton, A. (2019, October 11). *Students burn Latina author's book after she discusses white privilege*. The Guardian. https://www.theguardian.com/books/2019/oct/13/students-burn-book-latina-author-jennine-capo-crucet

Howell, K. (2015, November 19). *College student fired from job after criticizing Mizzou, Black Lives Matter online*. Washington Times. https://www.washingtontimes.com/news/2015/nov/19/emily-faz-georgia-student-fired-from-her-job-after/

Jamison, C. (2019). *10-23-2019 Faculty Senate minutes*. Georgia Southern University. https://digitalcommons.georgiasouthern.edu/faculty-senate-minutes/55/

Johnson, F. (2019, October 11). WAIT A MINUTE | Folks are actually surprised [Status update]. Facebook. https://www.facebook.com/photo.php?fbid=10157699260962171

Kim, Y., Dykema, J., Stevenson, J., Black, P., & Moberg, D. P. (2019). Straightlining: Overview of measurement, comparison of indicators, and effects in mail–web mixed-mode surveys. *Social Science Computer Review, 37*(2), 214–233.

Lakoff, G. (2007). *Whose freedom? The battle over America's most important idea*. Picador.

Logan, E. B. (2018, July 25). *She was eager to meet her college roommate—until the racist text arrived, screenshots appear to show*. Washington Post. https://www.washingtonpost.com/news/grade-point/wp/2018/07/24/she-was-excited-to-meet-her-college-roommate-until-the-racist-text-arrived-screenshots-show/

Lynn, C. (2015). A cultural political economy of public schooling in rural South Georgia. In E. T. Hamann, S. Wortham, & E. G. Murillo, Jr. (Eds.), *Revisiting education in the new Latino diaspora* (pp. 115–131). Information Age Publishing.

Marrow, H. (2011). *New destination dreaming*. Stanford University Press.

Meacham, S., & Meacham, S. (2016). Pre-service teachers' cultural competence and development using multicultural children's literature. In J. Kitchen, D. Tidwell, & L. Fitzgerald (Eds.), *Self-study and diversity II: Inclusive teacher education for a diverse world* (pp. 193–206). Sense Publishers.

Rhone, N. (2017, July 4). *Georgia Southern professor threatened for reporting antisemitic posts of the man behind the Trump/CNN wrestling meme*. Atlanta Journal Constitution.

https://www.ajc.com/blog/talk-town/georgia-southern-professor-threatened-for-reporting-antisemitic-posts-the-man-behind-the-trump-cnn-wrestling-meme/ajDtQQOAxvKP34xqoobaTN/

Rosenblatt, L. M. (1938/1995). *Literature as exploration*. Modern Language Association.

Sexton, J. Y. (2016, June 22). *I told the truth about a Donald Trump rally. Then the trolls threatened my life*. The New Republic. https://newrepublic.com/article/134534/told-truth-donald-trump-rally-trolls-threatened-life

Sowell, E. R., Peterson, B. S., Thompson, P. M., Welcome, S. E., Henkenius, A. L., & Toga, A. W. (2003). Mapping cortical change across the human life span. *Nature Neuroscience*, 6(3), 309–315.

Stacy, J., Hamann, E., & Murillo, E. G., Jr. (2015). Education policy implementation in the new Latino diaspora. In E. T. Hamann, S. Wortham, & E. G. Murillo, Jr. (Eds.), *Revisiting education in the new Latino diaspora* (pp. 335–347). Information Age Publishing.

Stuesse, A. (2016). *Scratching out a living: Latinos, race, and work in the Deep South*. University of California Press.

Sumara, D., Davis, B., & Iftody, T. (2006). Normalizing literary responses in the teacher education classroom. *Changing English* 13(1), 55–67.

Taxel, J. (2007). Reading multicultural children's literature: Response, resistance, and reflection. *Transformations* 17(2), 106–116.

The Harvest/La Cosecha. (2010). Directed by U. Roberto Romano. Shine Global.

Todres, J., & Higinbotham, S. (2015). *Human rights in children's literature: Imagination and the narrative of law*. Oxford University Press.

U.S. Census Bureau. (1913). *1910 census: Volume 1. Population, general report and analysis*. https://www.census.gov/library/publications/1913/dec/vol-1-population.html

U.S. Census Bureau. (1983). *Persons by Spanish Origin, Race, and Sex (Table 59)*; General Social and Economic Characteristics, Georgia. https://www2.census.gov/prod2/decennial/documents/1980a_gaABC-05.pdf

U.S. Census Bureau. (2020). QuickFacts: Georgia. https://www.census.gov/quickfacts/GA

Visser, M. A. (2014). Two plus two equals three: Classification error and the Hispanic undercount in United States census surveys. *The American Review of Public Administration*, 44(2), 233–251.

Walker-DeVose, D. C., Dawson, A., Schueths, A. M., Brimeyer, T., & Freeman, J. Y. (2019). Southern assumptions: Normalizing racialized structures at a university in the Deep South. *Race Ethnicity and Education*, 22(3), 355–373.

Weber, J. (2015). *From south Texas to the nation: The exploitation of Mexican labor in the twentieth century*. University of North Carolina Press.

Williams, J. P. (2008). Emergent themes. In L. M. Given (Ed.), *The Sage encyclopedia of qualitative research methods* (pp. 248–249). Sage. https://doi.org/10.4135/9781412963909

CHAPTER 4

Reengineering Professional Development for Educational Leaders in the New Latinx Diaspora of the U.S. Midwest

Lisa M. Dorner and Emily R. Crawford

THE CHALLENGE

In 1990, the small town of Carthage, like much of Missouri, was predominantly White and English-speaking: only 1.6% of citizens spoke a language other than English at home, and only 200 were foreign-born. Fast-forward 30 years; with the growth of the meat-processing industry and new immigrant settlement, by 2020, some 40% of Carthage public school students spoke Spanish upon enrolling in school; 80% of foreign-born students were from Guatemala and 10% from El Salvador or Honduras. Meanwhile, in the northwest area of the state, Kansas City has remained home to third- and fourth-generation immigrants from Mexico, at the same time increasingly integrating new neighbors, refugees, and asylum seekers from Central America, Western Asia, and Africa. And mid-state, in the college town of Columbia, the relatively small foreign-born population has grown from 2% to 8% over the past 30 years to include over 70 languages in their public schools, the top ones being Spanish, Arabic, and Swahili.

While Missouri is changing and becoming a clear part of the New Latinx Diaspora (NLD), it is difficult to categorize. As demographics have shifted across rural and urban areas, the state has grown increasingly politically conservative. Once known as a bellwether for presidential elections, the majority of voters have picked only Republicans in presidential, gubernatorial, and Senate races since 2008. Anti-immigrant and English-only legislation are consistently under discussion (Dorner et al., 2017); public universities do not allow in-state tuition for undocumented students (National Conference of State Legislatures, 2021); and K–12 public school districts across the state are unsure how to support undocumented students, even though it is their legal responsibility (*Plyler v. Doe*, 1982). At the same time, in 2017, the state department of education created a Seal of Biliteracy primarily for students designated as English learners (Missouri Department of Elementary & Secondary Education, n.d.). This is the NLD in Missouri: diverse, dynamic, yet disconnected—and it presents a challenge for educational leaders as well as for those of us who prepare them.

For many of our communities, fostering a welcoming school environment and adapting pedagogical practices to meet the needs of immigrant-background students and families is still a relatively new proposition that has become increasingly difficult in our politicized times (Crawford, 2017a; Lowenhaupt & Hopkins, 2020). Especially concerning in an anti-immigrant policy environment is how school leaders respond to undocumented students, a challenging topic that educators may shy away from raising in schools for fear it is too controversial (Crawford & Hairston, 2020; Dabach et al., 2018). As two professors in a university department that prepares educational leaders in a state that is diverse but still predominantly White and rural, we have asked: What kinds of professional development (PD) praxis do we need in our NLD? More specifically, what kind of equity- and community-focused PD engages educational leaders in a way that contributes to the development of mutually trusting relationships with transnational community members, especially those from families with uncertain legal status? These questions situate our exploration of the complexities of the relationships among immigration status, immigration enforcement, and leadership in the NLD.

This chapter analyzes our leadership PD practice in Missouri (Crawford, 2017b). Specifically, we detail how we framed and navigated a PD workshop where we utilized a case study approach to encourage leaders' praxis, or their interrelated reflection and action (Freire, 1970), across different NLD contexts. Then, mindful of the educational challenges facing immigrant-rich schools and theoretical constructs of social justice leadership, we provide recommendations for professional development that consider the different needs and circumstances across Missouri's diverse NLD. We provide an example of the kind of praxis that can happen in the U.S. Midwest, and also critique our own approach, in order to *reengineer* best practices in educational leadership for the NLD. Ultimately, we share a vision for the design of PD in similar NLD spaces.

CHALLENGES TO INCLUSIVE SCHOOLING PRACTICES FOR IMMIGRANT-BACKGROUND STUDENTS

Educational leaders—broadly including formally assigned central office administrators, school principals, department chairs, as well as a range of teacher leader positions—play integral roles in schools and have the potential to impact a variety of stakeholders. Principals in particular influence school culture, act as instructional leaders who also determine how education is delivered, are responsible for budgets, and shape student expectations and family engagement practices (DeMatthews & Izquierdo, 2016, 2018; Scanlan & López, 2012). Given their prominence within organizations and in communities and spheres of influence, leaders must consider how their actions and decisions affect diverse constituents whose experiences of schooling may widely vary. This includes considering the variable and often inequitable educational experiences of immigrant and undocumented students, designated English Learners (ELs), refugees, and asylees.

By 2065, it is expected that 88% of the country's population growth will be attributable to immigrants and their children (Radford, 2019). This means definitive change in the demographic makeup of schools, and schools and leaders must be prepared and adapt. However, the U.S. schooling system was initially set up to serve White upper- and middle-class children and families (Rury, 2016), and schools have continued to center their values and needs, excluding and marginalizing students from various racial/ethnic, linguistic, low socioeconomic, and immigrant-heritage backgrounds (Dorner et al., 2021). Deficit views of the cultures, languages, and educational abilities of immigrant-background students and those identifying as Latinx and/or designated as ELs persist, as does unequal access to quality teaching, resources, and welcoming school climates (Abu-El Haj, 2015; DeMatthews & Izquierdo, 2018; Gándara & Contreras, 2009; Hamann & Harklau, 2015; Valencia, 1997). Immigrant-background students have less access to experienced teachers and are more likely than their White peers to go to schools that are segregated economically and racially (Gándara et al., 2003; Orfield & Lee, 2006). Pedagogical strategies may not mirror the diversity in schools if a community is more homogenous racially and ethnically (Berubé, 2000).

For students designated as recently arrived or as newcomers to the United States, there are also heightened needs, such as acquiring English and adjusting to new cultural and schooling norms (Hamann & Harklau, 2015; Hamann et al., 2012). Refugee students may come with trauma and interrupted schooling (Arar, 2020). Undocumented students and those from mixed legal status families often carry additional concerns, such as fear of Immigration and Customs Enforcement (ICE), family separation, and deportation, particularly as myriad, increasingly restrictive immigration policies were normalized under the Trump administration (Gonzales, et al., 2018). Moreover, during the COVID-19 pandemic, there were extra challenges with declining enrollment, declining graduation rates, increased work hours, and increased anxiety among children from immigrant families (Internationals Network for Public Schools, 2021). Anti-immigrant policies and practices persist across changes in presidential administration (Kumar, 2021).

Unfortunately, studies have suggested the United States lacks school leaders who have the knowledge, capacity, or sense of urgency to address these challenges and needs (Jaffe-Walter, 2018; Lowenhaupt, 2015). Research has highlighted the need for better two-way communication (Umansky et al., 2020) and understanding (Koyama & Kasper, 2020) between district leaders, staff, and immigrant-background students and families. Further, regarding schooling for undocumented students or those from mixed legal status families, research suggests that even if leaders hold inclusive attitudes, they lack awareness of specific laws and policies pertaining to students and their educational rights (Crawford,

2017a; Rodriguez & McCorkle, 2019). Others may stay silent about immigration policy changes affecting their students—believing it too controversial to discuss—which students may interpret as educator support for those policies (Jaffe-Walter et al., 2019; Jefferies & Dabach, 2014). Such conditions suggest we need enhanced PD for school leaders to create socially just, inclusive education for immigrant-background students in the NLD.

SOCIALLY JUST, INCLUSIVE LEADERSHIP AND PROFESSIONAL DEVELOPMENT

In our ever-changing educational landscape affected by climate change, wars, and a global pandemic like COVID-19, which all intersect with migration, it goes without saying that school leaders need to be prepared for complex, inequitable conditions. Leaders must have a vision and plan to actively combat injustice across various schooling, community, and policy contexts. That is, leaders must be divergent thinkers (Robinson, 2010) who can envision multiple paths to address educational and often societal conundrums. Building on this book's theme, leaders need the capacity to *reengineer* education, operating with an eye and heart toward what may strike them as (im)possible but decide to proceed anyway. To reengineer education, leaders must first commit to socially just leadership practice, as do those who develop PD to facilitate leaders' reengineering of schools for immigrant schooling.

Many education scholars have sought to conceptualize social justice leadership. While no singular definition exists, scholars cohere around the idea that socially just leaders are concerned with the inequitable treatment of marginalized students and take action to address those concerns (Bogotch, 2002; Dantley & Tillman, 2010; Furman, 2012; Theoharis, 2007). Socially just leaders challenge the status quo (Anderson, 2009) and work to dismantle oppressive schooling practices (Dantley, 2003). They are "... action oriented and transformative, committed and persistent, inclusive and democratic, relational and caring, reflective, and oriented toward a socially just pedagogy" (Furman, 2012, p. 195).

Yet, as Furman (2012) suggests, more work is needed to see what socially just leadership looks like *in practice* and how leaders are prepared for the work. While we have a small but growing literature on combating racism and building equitable programs for Latinx students and families (see Callahan et al., 2019; DeMatthews & Izquierdo, 2018), there are few explicit approaches for developing socially just educational leaders, *especially for the NLD*. Educational leaders in such spaces need to be equipped to address nativist attitudes toward Latinx, immigrant, and immigrant-heritage families, and be ready to critique xenophobic policies and practices in schools and the structures that keep them in place. We must come to this work understanding that local contexts shape responses (Brooks et al., 2007). From our perspective, this means leadership preparation programs and PD must develop educational leaders' knowledge and capacity, and then marry reflection to action. As Furman (2012) highlights, socially just leadership is praxis, which consists of both reflection and action. This praxis stretches over five critical dimensions: the "personal, interpersonal, communal, systemic, and ecological" (p. 193). Ultimately, the task of leadership programs is to foster capacities for reflection and action in each of these five dimensions. However, in leadership PD, building capacities and taking action *together* remains underemphasized, but it is a challenge we took up as we tried to *reengineer* a way forward in Missouri's NLD.

CONTEXT FOR PROFESSIONAL DEVELOPMENT IN MISSOURI'S NLD

In July 2019, we co-facilitated a workshop for a group of 17 educators as part of a Summer Institute focused on strengthening equity, enhancing multilingual instructional practices, and devising new family engagement activities for students designated as ELs. The Summer Institute was a 3-day conference that brought together school leaders, teachers, and community leaders from four school districts across the state of Missouri (district names used in this chapter are pseudonyms). The districts were urban (Crow City), suburban (Beauton), rural (Tunis), and a diverse metropolitan with schools across rural and urban contexts (Midtown). Each district has its own unique history of Latinx and immigrant settlement (see Table 4.1). In urban Crow City, Mexican immigrants have settled for over 100 years, while rural Tunis saw a sharp increase with the opening of nearby meat-processing plants in the 1990s. Midtown's largest percentage of designated ELs were from Spanish-speaking families at the time of our PD, but like Beauton, many of their students came from refugee communities across the world.

Table 4.1. District Demographics in Year 1

District	Number of ELs Receiving Services	Percentage of Designated ELs	Number of Languages	Top 3 Languages
Beauton, Suburban	350	20%	30	Bosnian, Vietnamese, Arabic
Crow City, Urban	4,000	25%	55	Spanish, Swahili, Somali
Midtown, Metropolitan	1,250	10%	60	Spanish, Arabic, Swahili
Tunis, Rural	1,200	25%	5	Spanish, Micronesian languages

Note. Numbers are rounded to preserve anonymity.

WORKSHOP DESIGN

Prior to meeting in person, we created four groups of 3–5 participants to intentionally include a mix of teacher leaders, principals, and district leaders across contexts. Each group read two case studies from a book we edited intended as a professional development resource (Crawford & Dorner, 2020), the heart of which was to present ethical dilemmas in immigrant education for leaders to consider. These case studies focused on various NLD issues such as language brokering, college access, student identification and placement, and ICE raids. Each case narrative, authored as a realistic but hypothetical scenario that educational leaders have experienced, included key information about policy and practice in education and immigration. Discussion questions and activities followed each case to generate thinking.

Our agenda was relatively straightforward. Participants were grouped at tables with others who had read the same two chapters. Groups chose one case to discuss, making sure all members understood the actors involved in each case and could pinpoint the critical incidents that posed a dilemma for the educational leader(s) in that context. Relating their fictional case to their reality, participants then discussed possible responses. One group chose a chapter titled, "When ICE Came to Town: Separating Families and Disrupting Educational Trajectories" (Castrellón et al., 2020). This chapter presented a scenario detailing the many immigration policy changes after the 2016 election, particularly the Trump administration's "high-profile worksite enforcement operations" (Chishti et al., 2018). The scenario aimed to capture the disparate impact of immigration raids on students and school communities of color in a historically White city that had undergone significant demographic change—similar to many of our Missouri district contexts. It described the experience of a high school student whose parents were detained after a raid, and he did not know their whereabouts. This high schooler, who aspired to go to college, suddenly became the guardian for his two younger siblings.

As they discussed their case, two participants in the group drew connections between the case study's presentation of how undocumented immigrants can feel vulnerable to ICE and deportation and a real incident that occurred in their own community the night just before the workshop. These participants recounted that, while a mixed legal status family was driving to seek healthcare for their child, law enforcement—reportedly ICE—pulled over the family's vehicle. The driver, who was purportedly undocumented and scared, refused to exit the vehicle despite coaxing. The city police were called, and they ultimately smashed a window and pulled the driver out of the vehicle, greatly alarming the driver's wife and children, who witnessed and recorded the incident. Participants connected this incident to how undocumented *and* documented immigrant families in their school communities feared leaving their homes due to the anti-immigrant climate. They told the group that some even refused assistance or food from local educators, even as the leaders wanted to be trusted as safe allies and assist in any way necessary.

THE DISCUSSION AND PARTICIPANTS' POSITIONALITIES

The chapter discussion and recounting of the previous day's incident sparked unforeseen—but fruitful—tensions over participants' positions on the ICE case and experiences with policing and immigration enforcement. Various discourses about the law and undocumented immigrants surfaced, and these were shaped by the (sometimes unexpected) intersecting identities of each participant.

Of the 17 participants, seven spoke up during this discussion. The active speakers shared the following identify information about themselves throughout the session:

Speakers 1 and 2: White secondary assistant principals (one male, one female) in Crow City urban neighborhood schools near the location of a very recent incident involving ICE, the police, and a purportedly undocumented father from one of the leader's school communities.

Speaker 3: White principal of an immigrant background who led an urban Midtown secondary school that included a newcomer program and who had recently supported a family whose mother had been detained by ICE; Speaker 3 was also a graduate of our university's Education Doctorate (EdD) program, which focuses on social justice and equity.

Speaker 4: Latinx urban district-level program coordinator who was administering Latinx community partnerships; she had previously worked as an immigrant legal advocate and a Crow City police officer.

Speaker 5: White middle school teacher in Midtown; she shared she was the mother of a military police officer.

Speaker 6: White district-level family/community specialist for Crow City, who was an outspoken advocate for Black Lives Matter and racial justice.

Speaker 7: Black assistant principal in a suburban Midtown secondary school, who was also a graduate of our university's EdD program.

The remaining participants included three district EL leaders, four teacher leaders (all White women), one Black early childhood teacher, one Korean-American PD leader, and one Latinx immigrant interpreter who worked in early childhood contexts. Although none of these educators participated verbally, they followed the conversation attentively. When the discussion turned particularly emotional, as described in the next section, the Latinx immigrant interpreter left the room. The Midtown secondary school principal (Speaker 3) caringly followed her and later reported to us that her colleague was tearful as the discussion brought to mind when her adult son had experienced challenging encounters with ICE.

THE DISCUSSION AND UNANTICIPATED TENSIONS

During the workshop, participants wrestled with describing their views on immigrants and the role of law enforcement, as well as the fight for equity for Black people and other people of color. As the conversation progressed, the exchange among participants grew heated and emotional. By providing some of the actual words used within the session, we describe key turning points and discourses of the discussion, highlighting how the figured worlds of "law enforcement/police" and "undocumented immigrants" shifted and how we as facilitators tried to encourage the conversation in certain directions (sometimes successfully, sometimes not).

The conversation began as two White secondary school principals (Speakers 1 and 2) recounted the chapter and connected it to an incident with ICE that had occurred near their schools the previous night. This set the initial tone for the discussion by presenting particular figured worlds of "law enforcement" and "undocumented immigrants." Law enforcement was initially portrayed as an entity meant to take care of "citizens," as opposed to supporting undocumented individuals, who were not "worthy" of that protection. However, subsequently, law enforcement was characterized as to be feared and violent: "[They will] bust out your windows." Meanwhile, in this turn of the conversation, undocumented immigrants were portrayed as kind, caring family members ("gentleman," "daddy," "may I?"). Below, bolded words were emphasized or spoken more loudly by the speakers. In our transcription of this exchange, we decided that the transcription could be readily written as "stanzas." While we do not repeat all the "stanzas" here, we do hold on to our initial stanza numbering so that (a) readers can see that the quoted material transpired chronologically, and (b) readers can differentiate between larger gaps between direct quotations and shorter ones.

STANZA 3—The Banner of National Security
(Recounted by a Crow City Asst. Principal (Speaker 1)

And all this [in the chapter],
what we kind of got from this [case],
especially this first part of the article was,
all of these things were done under this **banner** of national security:
We are **taking** care of our citizens,
we are **keeping** everybody **safe** and **protected**
at the expense of people

who, certain people **felt** were not worthy of that protection
or not worthy of being here in our country.

STANZA 4—This Hit Home
(Recounting the Current Event by Speaker 1)

... (*The speaker describes the beginning of the incident with ICE.*)

And the father was undocumented
um (pause)
and (pause)
In their car, ICE agents, uhh, "get out."
The gentleman asks, "may I see the warrant?"
All of this is on video. Huh (*slight breath out*).
"You don't have to—we don't have to show you a warrant. We don't have to have a warrant." (ICE)
"Yes, my rights say, search of a warrant." (gentleman)
[He]would not [leave his vehicle].
"Get out or we'll bust your windows." (ICE)

... (*The speaker describes that ICE then calls the Crow City Police.*)

Um, so what they ended up doing was busting the window out,
and dragging the gentleman out,
putting him on the ground
cuffing him and taking him away,
while his 11-year-old child is crying and screaming for their daddy.

After explaining the case study and what recently happened in their own community, the two White assistant principals (Speakers 1 and 2) described their reaction and named resources in their community, as well as local PD that they had attended around these issues. Throughout these parts of the conversation, their discourse suggested law enforcement can be dehumanizing. For instance, they took a position that immigrants—or anyone—should "not [be] allowing someone," just "because they have a badge or a uniform" to strip their rights away and "almost dehumanize you" (Stanza 6, Article Reflection).

After this point, one facilitator and coauthor (Emily) spoke up for the first time, asking if other participants had had similar experiences with ICE in their communities. Speaker 3 (a White principal from urban Midtown from an immigrant background) shared what their school did after ICE detained a mother. Emily took another turn at reiterating actions that school leaders could take, including finding certain kinds of support and services in the community. However, the Midtown leader responded that sometimes the community does not want the support from "any government" entity because it's too "dangerous." The Crow City assistant principals (Speakers 1 and 2) agreed, saying that even people who have "been here more than two generations" are "fearful," thereby adding to the figured world on undocumented/immigrants.

At this point, the other facilitator and coauthor (Lisa) called on Speaker 4, the Latinx partnership program coordinator also from Crow City who had appeared to be trying to say something for several speech turns. Speaker 4 explained her previous role as both an immigrant legal advocate and a Crow City police officer. She then asserted that "cops have a job to do," and individuals do not always have the full information on everything happening in a video or engagement with local police. In her discourse, she both justified the police's actions, arguing to respect the rule of law, but also strongly distanced herself from ICE, arguing that we're all "on the same page here," regarding views on federal immigration enforcement practices and in wanting to reform immigration law and policy. In this part of the conversation, and later on, she strongly advocated for understanding multiple perspectives. Finally, she also suggested that we, as educators, need to get control of our emotions, but other participants interpreted her statement as immigrants needing to control their emotions and emotional responses to law enforcement.

STANZA 13—Perspective Taking (Speaker 4)

But it's really important to kind of get control of the emotions because I've been, I have been working with them with their families for many years.
And I was also a Kansas City Missouri police officer.

So when I see that video,
I see it from two perspectives.

I see it from the family perspective,
and I don't see it from the ICE perspective, okay?
But the cops have a job to do.
And if they show up at the scene
And they are told that they need to get that guy out of the car,
They're getting that guy out of the car, right?

After the former police officer and immigrant legal advocate's comparatively long comment, the facilitators took the floor for the fourth time, making their last significant contribution to the discussion. Here, Lisa agreed and highlighted the importance of perspective-taking, saying that in the antiracist neighborhood group she belongs to, they have discussed the importance of remembering that any video or recounting of an event shows only one perspective. She notes that we need to "slow down" and "get to know people," including our immigrant families and others who are "involved in their support or not support." However, Speaker 5, a White teacher from Midtown, did not pick up on these ideas. Instead, shaped by her family experience and her (potential mis) interpretation of Speaker 4's position on law enforcement, she builds upon the law enforcement–figured world that police set the "rules," which undocumented individuals must "follow," as highlighted in this next excerpt.

STANZA 15—Training for Families? Just Do What You're Told—White Middle School Teacher (Speaker 5)

I have a question and a comment.
Is there training for these families—um.
My son's in the military police.
And so, he's been overseas
a couple of times
and he tells stories
about the **easiest** way to deal
is when people just **follow** the police orders
whether you agree with them or not,
because again, he's just doing his job
and he has one job.
And when people follow those orders,
things usually work out a lot **easier**
and a lot **better**
than when they decide to run or fight back.

and if, if we can just train those families to
To try to get out of the emotion
and just, just **do** like the mom
that at our school
that was released.

At this point, for the first time, there was an eruption of overlapping speakers. The facilitators tried to interject a fifth time but could not break into the discussion nor stop it to organize or summarize it. Eventually the Latinx partnership program coordinator (Speaker 4) maintained the floor and repeated her point that these conversations are "polarized," "delicate," and "complicated." There may be times, she said, when it's right for immigrants to "know their rights" and not open a door to ICE, but there may be times when she would advise them to do so. "Not one size fits all," she concluded. Again, the facilitators tried to confirm the conversation, without gaining the floor until Lisa called on the Black assistant principal from Midtown (Speaker 7), who had been trying to talk throughout this final section of overlapping speech.

Lisa and Emily suggested this would be the last comment before moving to the next group. Speaker 7, then, returned the conversation to a humanizing discourse about undocumented immigrants, focused on the idea that fear and anxiety is real. Instead of depending upon immigrant families to control their emotions, she also suggested a new figured world for law enforcement: that they have some learning to do and should treat undocumented immigrants with dignity.

STANZA 20—Emotions Are Real and Immigrants Are Human (Speaker 7)

The only thing that I will say in response to that is,
yes,
there is a way of educating.
But (pause) you have to educate
from the standpoint of not creating (pause)
a hierarchy,
or some kind of—
when you say, for example,
teach the, tell them to calm down their emotion?
That is, if—this is all about emotion,
this is about fear.
This is about losing
me having a whole lot to lose
and seeing
a person as the person who's going to take it away from me.
So to say, to take the emotion out,
is
that's not educating them.
They're not going to be able to take the emotion out,
and I think that's what you were saying.

... (*Speaker 7 suggests that part of "educating" immigrants should not be to tell them to take their "feelings out of it." Their fear and anxiety are real. She continues, perhaps it is law enforcement that needs education on how to handle such fear and anxiety.*)

It could be helpful that the law enforcement
or the, whomever, ICE,
with understanding that
my cortisol level is going to be high,
...
do it with that in mind,
they can carry out their jobs,
without heightening or exacerbating my fear
or making me feel **less** than

because I am in a situation
that is different from theirs.
That's my only response to that.

But there is a way to do things
with dignity and respect
for a human being
because that's what we're talking about.
We're not talking
they made a decision
to try to come somewhere
to better themselves,
somehow or another,
politically or **whatever**,
we have made them think
they're wrong,
that **that** choice to do better for our family.
Is wrong.

At the core of it, they're **right.**
They're not better than or less than,
they're different.
And we should treat them like **humans,**
and educate them. Yes.
But not educate them from that
the
from our lens.
Trying to understand it
from their lens
is how you get them
to do
maybe open their door
because it's inevitable.
You're gonna go
But you don't have to go with **violence.**
You don't have to go
feeling less than.

Speaker 7 highlighted key discourses, concluding with a description of a humane and socially just world for educators to contemplate, where immigrants are humans with real fear and emotions, and "we" (both educators and law enforcement) should treat them with dignity and respect.

While there were tensions throughout the discussion, we (facilitators) summarized the points that perspective-taking is important and that we must recognize the dignity of all human beings and none of the participants dissented. Overall, the conversation provided resources, as well as new knowledge and capacity for educators. That said, within this part of the PD, we were less adept at connecting and deciding on actions for school leaders to take away from this training, which they could put into practice in their places of work, as we further discuss in our conclusion.

RECOMMENDATIONS FOR REENGINEERING PD IN THE NLD

We appreciated participants' honesty and identity-grounded contributions, and especially how the strongest—and concluding—ideas matched our goals for the session: how to develop socially just leadership in the NLD. That said, as facilitators, we felt uncertain at times how to continue the PD praxis as we observed some participants grow visibly uncomfortable with the dialogue, as they engaged in back-and-forth dialogue about systems of power and their embeddedness in social institutions, and how historically marginalized and oppressed peoples respond to law enforcement. Our challenge became navigating the emotions brought out by participants who connected elements in the case study narrative to their deeply personal and felt real-life experiences and then finding interstices to enhance capacity for reflection and common ground for collective action. We were forced to think on our feet and try to work through the complexity of participants' identities, emotions, and experiences.

USE REALISTIC CASE STUDY SCENARIOS

The case studies provided complex scenarios intended to encourage readers like our participants to wrestle with their identities, biases, and figured worlds as they sought solutions to ethical dilemmas. Participants were given time to make sense of the case studies prior to the workshop, before continuing to process them and share their experiences and opinions with others during the session, first as part of a small group and later with all session participants. Together, teams came up with insights, resources, and practical actions they could apply to engage more closely with immigrant families and students and support them. For one small group, presenting to the larger group to elicit feedback led to unanticipated tensions that perhaps neither the presenting team nor facilitators expected. We had been unaware as facilitators, for example, that such a recent, real event would resonate with their chosen reading; that a Latinx cop was a session participant; and that another participant had a child who had been detained by ICE. The presenters, too, may have assumed more points of connection across school communities and personal and professional experiences than existed practically. The whole-group conversation revealed other participants' recognition of the obstacles the Crow City presenters faced in maintaining trusting relationships with immigrant families. This was a mirror into how each individual carries multilayered identities, histories, and roles that shape their figured worlds. This PD session served as a powerful reminder for us as facilitators, and hopefully for participants to be careful about ascribing a particular political position, set of beliefs, or affinities to any person or group based on one's own assumptions.

CREATE INTENTIONALLY DIVERSE GROUPS ALONG VARIOUS POSITIONALITIES

However unplanned the extent of conflict among participants' figured worlds in exploring the intersections among immigration status, school leadership, and law enforcement, we believe that the presence of differences in opinion and viewpoints, coupled with the opportunity to work through similar and contrary perspectives, proved essential to the session. Engaging in differences of perspective is critical to reengineering PD in the NLD and beyond—and should be intentionally pursued. The dynamic session resulted from having participants with multiple, racially and culturally diverse experiences, histories, and perspectives. This included a Latinx immigrant advocate who was a former police officer, a teacher with a son in the military police, an African American assistant principal, and several multilingual, White, district and school-level leaders. In addition, the session gained from making groups of people from different geographical contexts. The intent was for leaders to learn new ideas to implement from other leaders who are taking action.

ENSURE TIME AND SPACE FOR ACTION PLANNING AND CARE WITHIN AND BEYOND PD

Even so, identifying concrete opportunities for action remained difficult. Creating action plans and identifying practical courses of action as tasks that leaders invested in reengineering socially just practices for immigrant education must consider. The session offered additional time for participant reflection but might have included time set aside for intentional action planning. Such action planning can occur within PD sessions and should also include time for facilitators to "check in" with leaders over the coming months to provide support and discuss how their actions are being implemented.

Finally, although participants strongly disagreed with one another at times, they displayed bravery in speaking about their varied perspectives on a complex topic. While we cannot claim the discussion led to anyone shifting their position or viewpoint on law enforcement or undocumented immigration/immigrants, we hope that having a space to discuss challenging topics, to be exposed to differing viewpoints, and to try to work through them to find common ground is a starting point. Moving forward, it would be beneficial when engineering PD in the NLD not only to follow up with participants about the actions they took, but also to show care for participants, especially those for whom the topics touched close to home and caused pain.

To conclude, revisioning PD and reengineering education for immigrant students requires making the time and space to continue important conversations like those that happened in our workshop. Opportunities for coordinating reflection and action across complex, distinct, but related contexts—where educational leaders' diverse backgrounds and identities, schooling contexts, and levels of experience working with Latinx and immigrant populations shape their responses to demographic change—must be intentional. For socially just praxis, consisting of reflection and action together, leaders must interweave the "personal, interpersonal, communal, systemic, and ecological" to create equitable and sustainable changes in the education of immigrant students (Furman, 2012, p. 193).

REFERENCES

Abu-El Haj, T. (2015). *Unsettled belonging: Educating Palestinian American youth after 9/11*. University of Chicago Press.

Anderson, G. L. (2009). *Advocacy leadership: Toward a post-reform agenda in education*. Routledge.

Arar, K. (2020). *School leadership for refugees: Social justice leadership for immigrants, migrants and refugees*. Routledge.

Berubé, B. (2000). *Managing ESL programs in rural and small urban schools*. Teachers to Speakers of Other Languages, Inc.

Bogotch, I. (2002). Educational leadership and social justice: Practice into theory. *Journal of School Leadership, 12*, 138–156.

Brooks, J. S., Jean-Marie, G., Normore, A. H., & Hodgins, D. W. (2007). Distributed leadership for social justice: Exploring how influence and equity are stretched over an urban high school. *Journal of School Leadership, 17*, 378–408.

Callahan, R. M., DeMatthews, D., & Reyes, P. (2019). The impact of *Brown* on EL students: Addressing linguistic and educational rights through school leadership practice and preparation. *Journal of Research on Leadership Education, 14*(4), 281–307.

Castrellón, L. E., Rivarola, A. R. R., & López, G. R. (2020). When ICE came to town: Separating families and disrupting educational trajectories. In E. R. Crawford & L. M. Dorner (Eds.), *Educational leadership of immigrants: Case studies in times of change* (pp. 58–70). Routledge.

Chishti, M., Pierce, S., & Bolter, J. (2018, January 24). *Shifting gears: Trump administration launches high-profile worksite enforcement operations*. Migration Policy Institute. https://www.migrationpolicy.org/article/shifting-gears-trump-administration-launches-high-profile-worksite-enforcement-operations

Crawford, E. (2017a). When boundaries around the 'secret' are tested: A school community response to the policing of undocumented immigrants. *Education and Urban Society, 50*(2), 155–182.

Crawford, E. (2017b). The ethic of community and incorporating undocumented immigrant concerns into ethical school leadership. *Educational Administration Quarterly, 53*(2), 147–179.

Crawford, E. R., & Dorner, L. M. (2020). *Educational leadership of immigrants: Case studies in times of change*. Routledge.

Crawford, E. R., & Hairston, S. (2020). (Mis)Recognizing undocumented students and families in a rural school. *Leadership & Policy in Schools, 21*(3), 635–656. https://doi.org/10.1080/15700763.2020.1827268

Dabach, D. B., Merchant, N. H., & Fones, A. K. (2018). Rethinking immigration as a controversy. *Social Education, 82*(6), 307–314.

Dantley, M. (2003). Purpose-driven leadership: The spiritual imperative to guiding schools beyond high-stakes testing and minimum proficiency. *Education and Urban Society, 35*(3), 273–291.

Dantley, M., & Tillman, L. C. (2010). Social justice and moral transformative leadership. In C. Marshall & M. Oliva (Eds.), *Leadership for social justice* (2nd ed., pp. 19–34). Allyn & Bacon.

DeMatthews, D., & Izquierdo, E. (2016). School leadership for dual language education: A social justice approach. *Educational Forum, 80*(3), 2778–2293.

DeMatthews, D., & Izquierdo, E. (2018). The importance of principals supporting dual language education: A social justice framework. *Journal of Latinos and Education, 17*(1), 53–70. https://doi.org/10.1080/15348431.2017.1282365

Dorner, L. M., Cervantes-Soon, C. G., Heiman, D., & Palmer, D. (2021). "Now it's all upper-class parents who are checking out schools": Gentrification as coloniality in the enactment of two-way bilingual education policies. *Language Policy, 20*, 1–27.

Dorner, L. M., Crawford, E. R., Jennings, J., Hager, E., & Sandoval, J. S. O. (2017). I think immigrants "kind of fall into two camps": Boundary work by US-born community members in St. Louis, Missouri. *Educational Policy, 31*(6), 921–947.

Freire, P. (1970). *Pedagogy of the oppressed*. Herder & Herder.

Furman, G. (2012). Social justice leadership as praxis: Developing capacities through preparation programs. *Educational Administration Quarterly, 48*(2), 191–229. https://doi.org/10.1177/0013161X11427394

Gándara, P., & Contreras, F. (2009). *The Latino education crisis: The consequences of failed social policies*. Harvard University Press.

Gándara, P., Rumburger, R., Maxwell-Jolly, J., & Callahan, R. (2003). English learners in California schools: Unequal resources, unequal outcomes. *Educational Policy Archives, 11*(36), 1–54.

Gonzales, R. G., Ellis, B., Rendón-García, & Brant, K. (2018). (Un)authorized transitions: Illegality, DACA, and the life course. *Research in Human Development, 15*(3–4), 345–359.

Hamann, E. T., & Harklau, L. (2015). Revisiting education in the new Latino diaspora. In S. Wortham, E. G. Murillo, Jr., & E. T. Hamann (Eds.), *Education in the new Latino diaspora: Policy and the politics of identity* (pp. 3–28). Ablex Press.

Hamann, E. T., Wortham, S., & Murillo, E. G. (2002). Education and policy in the new Latino diaspora. In S. Wortham, E. G. Murillo, & E. T. Hamann (Eds.), *Education in the new Latino diaspora: Policy and the politics of identity* (pp. 1–16). Ablex Press.

Internationals Network for Public Schools. (2021). *Re-engaging multilingual learners post-pandemic: Lessons from Internationals Network for Public Schools*. https://www.internationalsnetwork.org/wp-content/uploads/2021/07/Re-Engaging-Multilingual-Learners-Post-Pandemic.pdf

Jaffe-Walter, R. (2018). Leading in the context of immigration: Cultivating collective responsibility for recently arrived immigrant students. *Theory Into Practice, 57*, 147–153.

Jaffe-Walter, R., Miranda, C.P., & Lee, S. (2019). From protest to protection: Navigating politics with immigrant students in uncertain times. *Harvard Educational Review, 89*(2), 251–276.

Jefferies, J., & Dabach, D. B. (2014). Breaking the silence: Facing undocumented issues in teacher practice. *Association of Mexican-American Educators, 8*(1), 83–93.

Koyama, J., & Kasper, J. (2020). Pushing the boundaries: Education leaders, mentors, and refugee students. *Educational Administration Quarterly, 57*(1), 1–33.

Kumar, A. (2021, September 6). *Biden mulls 'lite' version of Trump's 'Remain in Mexico' policy*. Politico. https://www.politico.com/news/2021/09/06/biden-remain-in-mexico-policy-509436

Lowenhaupt, R. (2015). Bilingual education policy in Wisconsin's new Latino diaspora. In E. T. Hamann, S. Wortham, & E. G. Murillo, Jr. (Eds.), *Revisiting education in the new Latino diaspora* (pp. 245–262). Information Age Publishing.

Lowenhaupt, R., & Hopkins, M. (2020). Considerations for school leaders serving US immigrant communities in the global pandemic. *Journal of Professional Capital and Community, 5*(3/4), 375–380.

Missouri Department of Elementary & Secondary Education. (n.d.). *Missouri Seal of Biliteracy*. https://dese.mo.gov/college-career-readiness/curriculum/missouri-seal-biliteracy

National Conference of State Legislatures. (2021). *Undocumented students tuition: Overview*. https://www.ncsl.org/research/education/undocumented-student-tuition-overview.aspx

Orfield, G., & Lee, C. (2006). *Racial transformation and the changing nature of segregation*. Civil Rights Project.

Plyler v. Doe, 457 U.S. 202 (1982).

Radford, J. (2019, June 17). *Key findings about U.S. immigrants*. Pew Research Center. https://www.pewresearch.org/fact-tank/2019/06/17/key-findings-about-u-s-immigrants/

Robinson, K. (2010, October 10). *Changing education paradigms* [Video]. Ted. https://www.ted.com/talks/sir_ken_robinson_changing_education_paradigms

Rodriguez, S., & McCorkle, W. (2019). Examining teachers' awareness of immigration policy and its impact on attitudes toward undocumented students. *Harvard Kennedy School Journal of Hispanic Policy, 31*, 21–44.

Rury, J. L. (2016). *Education and social change: Contours in the history of American schooling* (5th ed.). Routledge.

Scanlan, M., & López, F. (2012). ¡Vamos! How school leaders promote equity and excellence for bilingual students. *Educational Administration Quarterly, 48*(3), 583–625.

Theoharis, G. (2007). Social justice educational leaders and resistance: Toward a theory of social justice leadership. *Educational Administration Quarterly, 43*(2), 221–258.

Umansky, I. M., Hopkins, M., & Dabach, D. B. (2020). Ideals and realities: An examination of the factors shaping newcomer programming in six U.S. school districts. *Leadership and Policy in Schools, 19*(1), 36–59.

Valencia, R. (Ed.). (1997). *The evolution of deficit thinking: Educational thought and practice. The Stanford series on education and public policy*. Falmer.

CHAPTER 5

Reframing Emergent Multilinguals as "First-Class Citizens" in the New Latinx Diaspora of New Jersey

Meredith McConnochie

> We are always gonna be second-class citizens no matter what. It's true ... why do I have these kids in my classroom. Can't you give me a break. They are always complaining about them. Like they are misfits. Why do we always get them. I hear it all the time. Everyone wants to teach up here. Everyone has a certain standard. You're never gonna get to that level, that high level.
>
> —Ms. Dara, ESL teacher

In this opening quote, Ms. Dara, one of the English as a Second Language (ESL) teachers, describes her feelings that ESL and bilingual teachers in the building were treated as second-class citizens in Warner Elementary School, where she worked. She linked the perceived inferior status of ESL/bilingual teachers to deficit views among other teachers about English learners (ELs).[1] As Ms. Dara discussed frustrations about the treatment of ESL/bilingual teachers and emerging bilinguals as second-class citizens, she pointed to a prevalent concern among administrators and ESL/bilingual teachers regarding the acceptance of the English learners in the school district of Smithtown,[2] New Jersey. Smithtown is one of several suburban New Latino Diaspora communities in New Jersey that only recently have experienced a drastic increase of Latino residents. Administrators and teachers in the Smithtown ESL/bilingual program consistently expressed frustrations over the ways that funding inequities, overcrowding, teacher shortages, assessment inadequacies, and inadequate support from non-ESL/bilingual teachers had combined to restrict the space and time granted to the instruction of English learners.

Yet, as they voiced their support for policies and practices that invest in English learners, they also legitimized *raciolinguistic ideologies* that position White family language practices as the norm (Flores & Rosa, 2015). In the opening quote, Ms. Dara revealed a contradictory trend in that she critiqued other teachers' views of English learners as "misfits" while calling for acceptance that English learners were "not gonna get to that level—that high level." By accepting an objectified notion of "a high level" that was unattainable for the English learners, she implied that school improvement demanded that teachers lower expectations. This statement is noteworthy in that, although the ESL/bilingual teachers held bilingual proficiency and explicitly stated their support for multilingualism, they had also accepted and occasionally justified English-dominant policies, raciolinguistically discriminatory beliefs, and monoglossic ideologies that positioned themselves, their students, and families as inferior citizens.

Concerned with these ideological trends and pervasive deficit discourses but inspired by the call to "reengineer" equity in the New Latino Diaspora (NLD), this chapter offers a discursive approach for reframing English learners and their families as "first-class citizens." To propagate an ideological shift in discourses about language and citizenship in the NLD, for remainder of this chapter I refer to English learners, and other students who speak one or more languages other than English at home, as *emergent multilinguals*. Building on the term emergent bilinguals, first coined by García and Kleifgen (2010) to be used as an asset-based label for English learners, this chapter uses emergent multilinguals to represent an encompassing group of students who have already begun learning one or more languages at home and have acquired varying levels of English proficiency. By demonstrating how language ideologies similarly position students and families with dominance in Spanish and other languages as second-class or noncitizens regardless of English proficiency levels, this chapter argues for an ideological shift in school discourses that reconceptualizes citizenship in terms of the multilingual potential and capacity of all Latinx families.

Integrating theories of *cultural citizenship* (Ong, 1996; Rosaldo, 1994) and *raciolinguistic ideologies* (Flores & Rosa, 2015), the chapter reimagines administrator and teacher discourses and ideologies that frame the cultural citizenship of Latinx emerging multilinguals as first-class. As defined by Ong (1996), cultural citizenship is "the cultural practices and beliefs produced out of negotiating the often ambivalent and contested relations with the state and its hegemonic forms that establish the criteria of belonging within a national population and territory" (p. 738). In turn, raciolinguistic ideology theories interrogate the relationship between language and race in the production of inequality. The chapter begins with an analysis of school-based ideologies about language and citizenship that administrators and teachers revealed regarding the ESL/bilingual program. I examine how their ideologies imply different theories of action (Hatch, 1998) for existing language education and language education reform in the NLD.

To help to reimagine a notion of cultural citizenship rooted in the language competencies of families, I introduce the case of one emerging multilingual family of Mexican origin and analyze their participation during a community-wide letter-writing campaign in order to demonstrate how a shift in language ideologies can help to reframe emergent multilinguals as first-class citizens. I argue that the language ideologies conveyed through the family's civic engagement in a multilingual and collaborative letter-writing campaign provide a model for reconceptualizing the citizenship of Latinx emerging multilingual students and families. Informed by emerging critical and multilingual ideologies about family citizenship, I hope to inspire language education reform initiatives that (a) treat the education of emergent bilinguals as a financial investment in the future of the local and global community through equitable funding policies and the instatement of a dual immersion program in which dynamic bilingualism and biliteracy is treated as the goal; (b) construct and implement approaches to parent involvement that validate parents' epistemic, linguistic, and moral dispositions through everyday interactions with children and parents; and (c) inform a democratic approach (Shohamy, 2001) to assessment for the purpose of engaging students in self-reflection, supporting student autonomy in learning, and scaffolding students into meaningful, rigorous, multilingual, and digital literacies across content areas.

ENGAGING IN THE SMITHTOWN COMMUNITY AND SCHOOL

I first became acquainted with Smithtown in 2013 when I volunteered to support the immigrant rights community organization, ALMA, as an English teacher for adults and as a leader for their membership campaign.[3] Upon building relationships with families at ALMA, I started visiting the homes of families to learn more about language learning in families. This initial involvement led to a 2.5-year ethnographic study of language learning in Smithtown through participant observation in homes and at school. Over the course of the 2.5-year period, I engaged in participant observation during 8–10 visits to the homes of seven families of Mexican origin and during 26 visits to a 2nd-grade bilingual classroom in Warner Elementary School. I also conducted interviews with teachers and administrators during the days I visited the school.

Data consists of over 200 hours of audio-recorded interactions in the home and school that occurred naturally, field notes written about every visit, and interviews with various education stakeholders. I recorded and transcribed informal interviews with seven mothers, eight K–2 children, the district superintendent, the ESL/bilingual coordinator, two ESL/bilingual teachers, and two general education inclusive teachers. While the overarching purpose of the study was to examine how language ideologies were interpreted and conveyed through everyday schooling routines, early in the study it became apparent that a central focus of school and community discourse revolved around debates over the citizenship and belonging of Latinx families in the district. Tensions within and outside of the school building were grounded in various beliefs about who is a citizen, who belongs in the community and school, and how language abilities and linguistic forms of expression signified kinds of citizenship. Acknowledging these existing tensions, this chapter focuses specifically on ideologies about families' languages of citizenship and their role in reforming the educational context of the NLD.

To get a sense of various perspectives within the school, I first talked with Dr. Tomatelli, the superintendent of the district; Ms. Paulina, the ESL/bilingual coordinator; Ms. Dara, an ESL teacher; Ms. Nixon, an ESL teacher; and Ms. Small, a 2nd-grade bilingual teacher. In each of these interviews, I asked them to talk about their concerns about the education of emergent bilinguals in the district. The analysis demonstrates how their discourse focuses largely on advocacy for more spaces for English instruction for emergent bilinguals—spaces infringed upon by a lack of funding. However, when asked more about the approach to language education in the district, administrators and teachers gave a range of rationales for why they supported the continued use of a subtractive model that privileges English, despite being general advocates for multilingual learning. Each rationale connected to views about cultural citizenship of families in this community.

Recognizing the importance of theories of action for educational reform, I argue that the administrators and teachers' *theories of action* (Hatch, 1998) about how to reform the ESL/bilingual program were predicated on a raciolinguistic notion of societal citizenship that requires English monolingualism and a school notion of citizenship linked to English instruction. But I argue that this view of citizenship will continue to disadvantage and marginalize the Latinx families and emerging multilinguals in this district who have linguistically distinct but rich backgrounds. Drawing from the voices of Latinx families and emerging multilinguals, I offer an alternative construction of cultural citizenship that privileges their linguistic and cultural knowledge. My belief in the potential of schooling experience to support multilingual learners is undoubtedly influenced by my own training and background as a bilingual-certified teacher. As a former kindergarten and 1st-grade teacher in multilingual settings, I see the potential of creating a more inclusive society if administrators and teachers work effectively with students and families. I hope that insights from this chapter support policymakers, administrators, and teachers in creating more spaces for the critical multilingual voices of Latinx students and families in schools.

SETTING: THE NEW JERSEY NEW LATINO DIASPORA OF SMITHTOWN

The context of this study is the community of Smithtown, a New Latino Diaspora suburb located within the state of New Jersey. In *Lady Liberty's Shadows: The Politics of Race and Immigration in New Jersey*, Rodriguez (2017) describes the history of racist exclusionary policies in the suburbs of New Jersey. She analyzes the prevalence of exclusionary racist housing practices that date before 9/11 and the increase of racist and anti-immigrant policies post-9/11 intended to maintain the whiteness and privilege of the suburbs. She argues that the suburbs of

New Jersey continue to be spaces where politics of citizenship and belonging are negotiated. Common practices in these communities include racist practices by rental and housing associations and citizens seeking to preserve the status of the suburbs. Driven by fear of immigration, New Jersey suburbs also serve as Homeland Security states in which police officers commonly work with U.S. Immigration and Customs Enforcement (ICE) to turn in residents suspected to be undocumented and create fear among Latino residents. Smithtown represents one of the suburbs whose racial politics are examined in this book.

From 1980 until 2010, the Hispanic or Latino population in Smithtown grew from only about 5% of residents and 0.2% as Mexican to 43% Hispanic or Latino and 30% Mexican. Between 2009 and 2013, approximately 37% of residents reported being foreign-born. The rise of Latino immigrants in Smithtown and in New Jersey suburbs correlates with the construction boom in the United States. Many Latino immigrants in the community worked as day laborers to work in construction or landscaping. Given this recent influx of Latino immigrants to the region of Smithtown and others throughout New Jersey, the suburbs resemble other parts of the NLD defined by an "increasing numbers of Latinos (many immigrants and some from elsewhere in the United States) [that] are settling both temporarily and permanently in areas of the United States that have not traditionally been home to Latinos" (Hamann et al., 2002, p. 1). Thus, although the state of New Jersey has a history of Latino immigrants, communities such as Smithtown are similarly in the process of reconstructing education policies to meet the needs of a new demographic.

CITIZENSHIP AND THE RIGHT TO INSTRUCTIONAL SPACE

As Smithtown's student population shifted and grew, tensions mounted among school district employees and community residents regarding who is responsible for addressing the overcrowding and underfunding of schools. In 2015, the district reported enrolling 600 students over the recommended capacity. Exacerbating the problem, in 2010 the state governor imposed a flat funding rate, which prevented Smithtown from receiving additional state funding despite the dramatic increase in student enrollment. In September and December of 2014, the Board of Education and the superintendent proposed a referendum that asked voters to support the construction of additional classroom space. Many Smithtown residents and parents of Smithtown with whom I talked expressed support of the expansion but lacked the citizenship papers required to vote. However, voters rejected the referendum on both occasions, citing objections to a housing tax increase and a lack of desire to fund the education of children from immigrant families. But immigrant families' voices and opinions remained invisible in the voting process. In this way, these families' legal citizenship granted or denied access to cultural citizenship symbolized by the expression of civic identities in major decisions related to their children's education.

The Smithtown school district adopted several coping strategies to ease the strain of overcrowding. They moved the kindergarten classes to a separate building on the other side of town, partitioned the library using portable dividers to create space for ESL classes and basics skills instruction, and arranged for the elementary and middle school students to share the cafeteria and gymnasium. From the perspectives of the ESL teachers at Warner Elementary School, a lack of classroom space was problematic for two primary reasons: (a) their classroom sizes were too large to attend to the needs of ESL students, and (b) the library classroom space was too noisy and distracting for students to concentrate, given the lack of walls to divide the designated instruction areas from the rest of the library. Consequently, the students in the ESL program were particularly impacted by the strain in resources.

In their talk about educational issues pertaining to emergent bilinguals, district administrators and teachers highlighted how first-class citizenship was linked to the time and space allowed for high-quality instruction. They consistently implied that cultural citizenship was granted through policies that place a financial and social investment in their students. As the superintendent, Mr. Tomatelli, explained, "The big issues in this district are the overcrowding of students and underfunding of state aid. They work together to create overcrowded classrooms and lack of services that states require of us." In addition to the consequences of the funding strain mentioned earlier, such as the insufficient gym space or a library to support instruction, he explained that 87% of class sizes are too large according to state requirements for students at our poverty level. There were insufficient resources for special education pullout in language and math, and this lack of resources was directly impacting ELs and Hispanic students. Tomatelli stated:

> Specifically, the EL students are affected. We are supposed to pull them out two times a day; we only pull them out one. We should have intervention teachers. We have no basics skills mathematics program. There's a disparate effect on the Hispanic students when we look at their access into the honors programs. We find that Smithtown is last in feeding to the high school district. The Hispanic students have the least access into the district.

The ESL teachers further delineated the impact of their lack of funding and space on their ability to collaborate with other teachers and their ability to provide quality instruction. Ms. Nixon, an ESL/bilingual teacher, explained:

> It's very difficult. We don't have any common planning time with any teachers. I have it with no teachers. I don't have it with the other ESL teachers. And that's again a space issue. And the fact that's a space issue. And the fact that we share specials teachers. I don't know if you realize that we share specials teachers . . . with the

[middle] school. So the [middle] school has to make their schedule first and we have to fit around that. That makes common planning time very difficult.[4]

Ms. Paulina, the ESL/bilingual coordinator, corroborated that idea, saying:

> The biggest challenge is I don't have enough teachers. The district is understanding that we are doing with what we have. We are overcrowded. If we hire more teachers, where do we put more teachers? Programmatically we have grown. What we institute through Title 3 funds—every year we try to do more. But what keeps us from getting traction is teacher turnover. Not enough space.

She later explained that ESL teachers were in demand, and many will go to districts where they can get paid better.

When I asked Ms. Dara about the biggest challenge in the district, she answered:

> I think we have too many kids. in the classroom because when you're looking at a pullout—when you're talking about a resource program, it's designed to pull out 3–4 kids at a time. It's small-group instruction. I have 19 kids in here. This is a classroom size. This is by no means small-group instruction.

She later expanded on this point when she explained how she had been put in the library: "Those are the children that have the most needs. And they're squished. They're hearing what's going on in the other classrooms." From Ms. Dara, we see the need for space that will allow for smaller-group instruction.

I also inquired about why it was so difficult to get the referendum passed in the district. Ms. Nixon responded that:

> There is a lot of resentment and a lot of the people in the borough are not going to vote something up that is going to increase their taxes when they feel that there is a certain population that is not holding their own in terms of supporting the schools. And that has been snowballing for the past 15 years. So even when I started so long ago that sentiment is getting worse and worse—now that we are so uber crowded.

She explained that she heard this kind of thing from parents at parent-teacher conferences or when reading comment sections about articles regarding the issue.

Ms. Paulina similarly shared that she had heard this discourse about concern for taxes. They also both articulated the perspective that they reported the union and superintendent had been spreading:

> Really, it's saying you are cutting off your nose to spite your face. If you're not supporting your schools, your property taxes [will go down]. If you are supporting the

schools, the taxes are going to go up a little bit, but your property values are going to go down if you don't have a school district that can sustain itself.

Teachers' and administrators' talk demonstrates how community members treated the Latinx students and families as not "belonging" or as citizens who are not deserving of investment. Because of this communitywide discourse, the school lacks the teachers and spaces to ensure that Latinx students and emerging bilinguals receive high-quality instruction. Through their discourse, the administrators and teachers of the ESL/bilingual program emphasize the importance of greater state and local funding for teachers and districts to be able to grant the amount of space and time that first-class citizens are granted. However, as I describe below, by focusing advocacy efforts on citizenship as physical space and time, and not on advocating for cultural citizenship that values student and family languages, they push reforms that will continue to render their students, families, and themselves as second-class citizens.

Citizenship and the Right to Language Instruction

To respond to the language demands of the new population, the district established an ESL program and a transitional bilingual program. Rooted in the Bilingual Education Act passed in 1974, New Jersey Administrative Code (NJAC) 6A:15 requires that districts create a bilingual program when there are more than 20 students with limited English proficiency per grade from a single language group, and to offer an ESL program when there are more than 10 students identified as limited in English. New Jersey's Bilingual Education Code was aligned with expectations for English language learners outlined in Title 3 of No Child Left Behind (NCLB), which states that schools must provide language instruction that is grounded on scientifically based research. Aligned with the law, Smithtown established a bilingual program in grades K–2 and ESL pullout services for students whom the school has not yet determined to be proficient in English. According to the district website, the goal of Smithtown's bilingual program is to use the home language of students identified as ELs to support the acquisition of academic content while they simultaneously learn spoken and academic English. As EL students transition through grade levels, bilingual teachers are expected to gradually use less Spanish in their classrooms.

Title 3 also provided funding for additional services intended to support EL students' learning. The Smithtown school district uses Title 3 funds to support the implementation of a biweekly afterschool program. The program was offered to EL students whose teachers had identified them as students who would benefit from additional academic support. During the afterschool program, teachers with various certification backgrounds (not solely those certified as ESL/bilingual teachers) facilitated small-group instruction in exchange for extra pay. Additionally, the Smithtown school district used Title 3 funding to create a "parent academy." During the 2014–2015 school year, ESL and bilingual teachers organized and facilitated parent academy workshops that focused on topics such as "preparing your children for the PARCC and ACCESS tests" (state-required annual standardized tests), "reading with your child at home," and "enrolling your child in educational summer programs." While only parents with children enrolled in ESL or bilingual programs were formally invited to these meetings, the ESL/bilingual coordinator and teachers informally encouraged parents of ESL students to invite their friends, even if they did not have children enrolled in ESL/bilingual classrooms.

Educational assessment policies are also widely viewed as implicit language policies in schools as they convey certain ideologies about what kinds of language usage are ideal (Menken, 2006, 2008; Shohamy, 2003, 2007). During the 2014–2015 academic year when this study was conducted, New Jersey began administering the PARCC exam to fulfill NCLB's national requirement for states to annually evaluate students' academic development using a standardized assessment. Based on regulations established by the PARCC consortium, "Limited English proficient students" (to use the then-extant terminology) were permitted to take the PARCC mathematics examinations in their native language. The instructions of the language arts exam may be translated to students in their native language, but the test must be taken in English.

In addition to the PARCC examination, "Limited English proficient" students were also expected to take the ACCESS examination. New Jersey uses the ACCESS exam to monitor the language development of these students. Title 3 of NCLB requires states to adopt an English assessment for schools to use to evaluate English language development. During the spring of 2015, when I visited Warner Elementary School, the emergent bilingual students in the 2nd-grade bilingual class took the PARCC and ACCESS tests. An additional source of tension in the district pertained to the staffing required to administer these assessments, taking instructional time away from students, and concerns that the emergent bilinguals were being over-tested for language given the linguistic demands of the PARCC exam.

In addition to concerns about space, ESL/bilingual administrators discussed their language programs. In their discussion, they frequently advocated for ways to improve English language pedagogy. Through this discourse, they revealed the way they associated citizenship with English language competency and that granting access to first-class citizen status was achieved through high-quality English instruction. This belief was clear when they talked about various components of their language program. In their interviews, bilingual/ESL school staff justified the prioritization of English in their ESL and transitional bilingual programs and described it as preferable to the use of dual-language programs. Despite acknowledging the benefits of dual-language programs for preserving and developing bilingualism, they rationalized the continuation of an ESL and transitional bilingual program for their community. While a bilingual administrator argued that Smithtown needed to focus on English because it was surrounded by English-speaking townships, a bilingual teacher suggested that the Latinx family members residing in Smithtown lacked the academic Spanish necessary to provide sufficient foundations for biliteracy. They both positioned the families as responsible for the Spanish development of their children in their district language education model and obscured the ways that their education policies and practices framed Latinx emergent bilinguals and their families and their language practices as perpetual "second-class citizens."

In the opening quote from Ms. Dara, we get a sense of how she sees other teachers as contributing to the lack of instruction. Ms. Dara, for example, explained that she didn't think many of her students were ready to exit the program even after 3 years in the program. When I asked what the difference was between students who were ready and who were not, she said: "I think it has to do with the general ed teacher—if they get the support from me and from them—I think that's the biggest factor really." She also explained that they do not collaborate. This is when she made the statement presented at the beginning of the chapter, saying, "I think it's the way that they look at our population is a big factor. We are always gonna be second-class citizens no matter what. It's true."

Ms. Small reiterated this idea about the deficiency of other teachers when narrating what she had told the principal about what she was doing that other teachers were not:

> I said to him teachers don't understand the bilingual child in this building. When they hear they have to have an ESL student in their class, they panic. It's not SIOP [Sheltered Instruction Observation Protocol] trained. They have SIOP strategies. And you have people saying I don't want the kids. I can't speak Spanish.

She explained how she showed the principal the success that she had with one of her students because of the high-quality instruction she had provided.

Similarly, when discussing their views of assessments, ESL/bilingual administrators and teachers expressed concerns pertaining to the quality of required assessments. For instance, Ms. Paulina, the ESL/bilingual coordinator, spoke more highly of the ACCESS exam (used to determine English proficiency and qualifications to "exit" ESL/bilingual programming) than the PARCC exam (content knowledge). She suggested that the ACCESS exam was a fair examination of all domains by language and had the benefit of being developed by linguists. However, when asked about the PARCC, Ms. Paulina responded:

> My knee-jerk reaction is that it's being treated as a language assessment more than a skills assessment if you don't offer it in Language Arts in Spanish. Those students were able to do so for up to two years. But there's no opportunity to do that through PARCC. My observation is that if PARCC isn't willing to be translated into Spanish for Language Arts, then you are testing what kinds of language they know, not skills they know in Language Arts and we already have a language test—the ACCESS—so it's really double-testing in one domain, the language domain.

When asked to elaborate on what she thought made the PARCC exam too difficult, Ms. Paulina explained that it was designed for the native English speaker, that there were multistep questions that ask students to find evidence in the text, and that the text itself has a lot of passive language.

While the administrators and teachers expressed concern about English instruction and assessment, I was interested in their perspectives about the language program and its emphasis on English. When I asked Ms. Paulina what I should know about the district, she answered in the following way:

> First my role. Also, the population here is predominantly Spanish speakers of Mexican origin. If I were a teacher. I would have to rely on my ESL strategies because my Spanish would kick in too strong. and that's not the goal of the ESL program. The goal is to get them to speak English. At Cannon (where I also teach), my ESL strategies were in full effect because I didn't speak Punjabi.

She extended her thinking later in the interview by explaining the rationale of transitional bilingual education in the following way:

> It's not a goal to have them learn two languages. I am a proponent of bilingual education. but these kids live in the borough and it's surrounded by [names community] where it's not a requisite to speak Spanish. So, at a place like [names another school], bilingual education works well from there because you have to learn Spanish there. Whereas our kids here, if they speak only Spanish, it's a problem. They still have the bilingual background. So the bilingualism is more dependent on the parent.

In her talk about the program, Ms. Paulina positions her own Spanish ability as a potential problem if she were teaching in this district when she states that her Spanish would "kick in too strong" because she knows that the students are Spanish speaking. She suggests that this would be an issue, particularly because the goal of the program is to get students to speak English. Interestingly, she is implying that Spanish could not be an asset in learning English despite what research suggests about the effectiveness of translanguaging and dynamic views of bilingualism, whereby students switch between languages for purposes of developing their understanding of disciplinary content. By doing so, Ms. Paulina positions herself in alignment and support of the program goals. When I later asked her about the goal of the bilingual program, she explained that it was to "give students support to succeed while they learn English. The schedule is a driver of the program. Also, teacher availability. I have an issue of teacher turnaround here, and that doesn't seem to stop. So, there are different things." Moreover, by explaining the rationale for their model in Smithtown, she implicates the surrounding communities as influential in determining the appropriateness of the program. With this explanation, she implies that this goal of citizenship is specific to this particular region rather than any other country or community in which they may seek to hold membership in the future. She contrasts the needs of Smithtown with the towns in northern New Jersey where she views Spanish as important. Also noteworthy is the way she suggests that parents are responsible for Spanish development.

Given the emphasis on English in school and concern for English development among Latinx emergent bilinguals, we can see how this logic holds families responsible for deficits in both English and in Spanish. The work of Flores and Rosa (2015) draws attention to the way in which many school districts perpetually frame the linguistic abilities of Latinx families as deficit, and we can see these raciolinguistic ideologies operating in this logic.

The implications for the framing of Latinx families in this model is made even more explicit in the way in which Ms. Small discussed the program model in this district in comparison to other districts. During one of my interviews, I initiated the subject by attempting to elicit Ms. Small's opinion on models of bilingual education. Specifically, I asked what she felt like the most effective model was from a language and literacy standpoint. She explained:

> I think the problem with answering that question is that you have students that are born here and they have siblings that have been to school and already have that social English. They don't have that academic Spanish. I don't think Spanish is always the way to go because I think a lot of times they're not reading—parents don't read to their children in their native language—I used to watch parents change the baby like it was a robot. They're like talking to other people when they're changing the diaper. They are not saying head, shoulder, knees, and toes. They're not saying *papita papito papito nariz*. And even if they are illiterate, they are not sitting down with a picture book saying, look at the pictures. I have watched people here in town, and I think it's their parental background. I've watched people come in with their kids and read three stories on a Saturday; they're showing their kids that books are important. I have seen the pendulum with that. What I have learned is that the board dictates what program you're gonna have. Here there is no difference from my room and another one other than the fact that if they get stuck on a word, I can use Spanish. I am not allowed to use Spanish materials to start off . . . It depended also on what school I was with. I had a Hispanic principal where everything was Spanish. The last position, I had a principal who rejected the concept of bilingualism and never wanted anything, wanted that transition to English as soon as possible.

In this narration of her experiences, Ms. Small suggests that teaching students Spanish may not be a good option because their parents might not have knowledge of academic Spanish. She makes a metapragmatic statement about parents when she says, "They don't have that academic Spanish" and links that statement to observations that parents are not interacting with their children in a way that she deems as the most supportive for academic Spanish learning. Yet, as Zentella (2005) and others have written about, there are many ways in which Latinx families support language learning in ways that may not be recognized by the school. By focusing on traditional parenting language ideologies as signals of citizenship, Ms. Small also conveys parenting language ideologies that link interactions to academic Spanish and traditional parenting ideologies that suggest the ideal parent treats their child as a conversation partner (looks at them), labels body parts or objects to model language, and uses books. We can see from this quote how Ms. Small perpetuates the idea of families' linguistic deficiency and the raciolinguisitic ideologies that prioritize English in her explanation of the program model. Nonetheless, it is important to also highlight how she points to her requirement to accept the program model despite what she believes by preventing her in this model from using any Spanish. This highlights how the role of top-down policy affects decisions about language in the district as well as the thinking teachers have about students and families and the ways that families show citizenship through their family language practices.

In her interview, Ms. Nixon articulated that there had been a lot of district improvements over the past 14–15 years regarding communication with Latinx families. She explained how, in contrast to the past, everything sent home was now translated into Spanish so that families could understand the materials. Additionally, she now played the role of liaison and worked to help translate materials and interpret during conferences. With this explanation, she revealed how the district now viewed families as cultural citizens with a right to understand what is happening in the school and classrooms. Yet, while communication increased with families through translation improvements and incorporation of these family academies, their discourse continued to suggest that families' voices were excluded from contributions. Families, thus, were viewed as having a right to listen but not to be heard. In an order to reframe emergent bilinguals as first-class citizens in the NLD, it is important to have the voices of families involved. To illustrate what this would look like, in what follows I present the discourses of one family about their experiences in the district. I argue that the family offers insights into how to reframe discourses and policies in the district and imagineer a context that values the input, language, and knowledge of Latinx families and students.

IMAGINEERING NLD DISCOURSES THROUGH THE ADVOCACY OF MULTILINGUAL LATINX FAMILIES

With a goal of reimagining the way we think about citizenship and emerging multilinguals in the district, I turn to the insights of one Smithtown family originally from Mexico whose home I visited on 10 occasions over the course of 2.5 years. With the guidance and leadership of a nonprofit community organization dedicated to supporting immigrant rights, I invited the family to participate in a letter-writing campaign to express their opinion about the desire to expand the school and the way in which overcrowding had affected them. The ways in which the families participated in this activity offer us a way to reengineer the link between language and citizenship in the Latino diaspora and position multilingual critical literacies of Latinx families as tools for action.

The letter-writing campaign grew out of a collaboration between the superintendent, the Board of Education, and community organizations who shared concerns over the disparate effects of underfunding and overcrowding on the Latino students in the district, and the exclusion of immigrant families from the voting process. ALMA and the County Latino Coalition (another organization also named by pseudonym) led the organization of the letter-writing campaign to allow residents who were unable to vote to express their opinion to the Commissioner of Education. The hope was that the commissioner would offer a bond that would provide funding for the expansion of the school. To facilitate this advocacy effort, ALMA created several letter templates to assist immigrant children and parents in expressing their support for the referendum and encouraged families to choose a letter template, personalize it, and sign the letter with their name and address.

When I visited the homes of the two families that participated in my study for 2 years, I brought letter templates and asked if they would like to write letters as part of the campaign. From these interactions, I learned that parents and children were concerned that sharing the cafeteria and gymnasium with middle-school students was a safety hazard due to the difference in size and strength between elementary and middle-school students and a lack of caution on the part of the middle-school students. I then explained that this sharing of space was what the referendum was trying to address and then asked if they would like to write letters in support for the expansion. While crediting the letter campaign as *the* reason for change might be overstating it, several months after the hearings were completed, a judge ruled that the state should overturn voters' decision in December 2015 and authorize the bonds for school expansion. By 2016, the bonds and expansion had been approved.

These examples demonstrate how family participation in community advocacy raises the voices of immigrant parents and allows them to articulate the pressures of English monolingualism. I argue that a new approach to pedagogy, curriculum, and instruction in schools requires the integration of ideas regarding a democratic approach to assessment that values multilingualism, multimodalities, student autonomy over topic, family collaboration, and self-reflection—all elements of the interaction that surrounded the letter-writing effort.

NOTES

1. While the Every Student Succeeds Act (ESSA) refers to this population of English learners (ELs), at the time of the study when the governing federal legislation was the No Child Left Behind Act, the population was referred to as "limited English proficient (LEP)" students.

2. Smithtown is a pseudonym used to protect confidentiality. While the opening chapter suggests that New Jersey as a state is not part of the NLD given its comparatively long history of being home to Latinos, suburban towns like Smithtown is new and unprecedented with interethnic interactions often both unequal (e.g., teacher to student) but also improvisational (Hamann et al., 2002).

3. ALMA is a pseudonym for an organization whose title is also an acronym. I liked the idea of using a pseudonym that doubled as a word in Spanish, in this case the word for "soul."

4. "Specials" references teachers, like elementary music, art, and ESL teachers, who work with multiple grade levels for short periods each week. Specials can also be slang for the subject (e.g., art, music, ESL) that these teachers teach.

REFERENCES

Flores, N., & Rosa, J. (2015). Undoing appropriateness: Raciolinguistic ideologies and diversity in education. *Harvard Education Review*, 85(2), 149–171.

García, O., & Kleifgen, J. A. (2010). *Educating emergent bilinguals: Policies, programs, and practices for English language learners.* Teachers College Press.

Hamann, E. T., Wortham, S., & Murillo, E. G., Jr. (2002). Education and policy in the new Latino diaspora. In S. Wortham, E. G. Murillo, Jr., & E. T. Hamann (Eds.), *Education in the new Latino diaspora: Policy and the politics of identity* (pp. 1–16). Ablex.

Hatch, T. J. (1998). The differences in theory that matter in the practice of school improvement. *American Educational Research Journal*, 35(3), 3–31.

Menken, K. (2006). Teaching to the test: How No Child Left Behind impacts language policy, curriculum, and instruction for English language learners. *Bilingual Research Journal*, 30(20), 521–546.

Menken, K. (2008). *English learners left behind: Standardized testing as language policy.* Multilingual Matters.

Ong, A. (1996). Cultural citizenship as subject-making: Immigrants negotiate racial and cultural boundaries in the United States. *Current Anthropology*, 37(5), 732–762.

Rodriguez, R. M. (2017). *In lady liberty's shadow: The politics of race and immigration in New Jersey.* Rutgers University Press.

Rosaldo, R. (1994). Cultural citizenship in San Jose, California. *Polar,* 17, 57–63.

Shohamy, E. (2001). Democratic assessment as an alternative. *Language testing,* 18, 373–391.

Shohamy, E. (2003). Implications of language education policies for language study in schools and universities. *The Modern Language Journal*, 87(2), 278–286.

Shohamy, E. (2007). Language tests as language policy tools. *Assessment in Education*, 14(1), 117–130.

Zentella, A. C. (2005). *Building on strength: Language and literacy in Latino families and communities.* Teachers College Press.

CHAPTER 6

Imagining and Reengineering Inclusive Schooling for All Students in the New Latino Diaspora

Tricia Gray

Washington River, a community of 26,000 residents in the midwestern United States, has experienced demographic change because of immigration from Mexico, Guatemala, El Salvador, and Honduras since the 1990s. As Washington River was not a site of Latinx settlement prior to the 1990s, it became a part of the New Latino Diaspora (NLD) (Hamann et al., 2002, 2015). This change has forced long-standing residents and newcomers to negotiate ways of living together among differences in language, culture, and race, and the resulting growing pains have been vitriolic and polarizing, as well as enduring. Nostalgic pleas from a small but vocal group for a community that supposedly existed before the arrival of immigrants in the 1990s were a code to communicate the nativist and racist desires to return to a mostly White, English-dominant community. While White, English-speaking residents still made up almost 90% of the population at the time of this writing, a city ordinance enacted in 2010 banning landlords from renting to undocumented residents was a xenophobic message of unwelcome.

Located within this polarized community, Washington River High School (WRHS) is tasked with responding to the changing sociopolitical and sociocultural realities that newcomer students make visible. The school places non-English dominant newcomer students into an English learning (EL) program for language instruction and "sheltered" content classes. Sheltered instruction is an approach "that draws from and complements effective methods advocated for regular classrooms but adds specific strategies for developing English language skills" (Short, 2002, p. 18). This chapter draws from a larger ethnographic study exploring how newcomer high school students in WRHS constructed citizen identities in their social studies class, a space where they learned English and American history and engaged in the more abstract work of constructing citizen identities in their daily lives at school. My use of the word "citizen" refers to all people who are guaranteed equal protection of rights under the

14th Amendment of the Constitution of the United States—that is, all people living in the U.S. *regardless of legal status* (Chomsky, 2007; Levinson, 2012).

Ethnographic study in WRHS illuminated the conditions in which newcomer students learned to understand themselves as belonging (or not) in the school, the community, and the country. Evidence demonstrates that schooling structures were incompatible with newcomer students' dual realities of youth and adult, of student and worker, and as realistic and aspirational. Newcomer students largely operated in the margins of the school in order to stay under the radar of the various mechanisms of surveillance, and this location of citizenship construction negated opportunities for newcomers to experience the full realm of public space and to enter the public consciousness. The EL classrooms, located in one far corner of the school, created a space that was both sanctuary and trap for newcomer students, affording them space to negotiate their identities in this new place but also keeping them largely hidden from the rest of the school community. Even with the best of intentions, there were missed opportunities in the sheltered American history class to connect curriculum to students' lives and to integrate them into the school and community in meaningful ways. Newcomer students' experiences of school lacked aspirational guidance and instead focused narrowly on meeting newcomers' immediate needs and perceived deficits (i.e., learning English). This chapter offers useful lessons for building on the opportunities presented to move toward more equitable and inclusive schools for newcomers, and the aim of this chapter is to use those lessons to imagine what "better" might look like and then reengineer the policies and practices that would create those conditions.

Education reform historically has been mandated by a central authority that surveils, rewards, and penalizes the people tasked with making change (Tyack & Cuban, 1995). A "reengineering" design approach to education reform aims to imagine something better and takes deliberate steps to bring "better" into being. This approach assumes that any social actors can be agents of change as a social problem is reframed as an opportunity. At WRHS, newcomers were regarded by some as a problem because of the differences between their experiences and backgrounds and those of longstanding residents. This posture found some echo in the extant formal policies and daily practices of the school. Shifting to a justice-oriented stance, I reframe the social problem as an opportunity: How might newcomers transform this school? In the sections that follow, I offer excerpts from my field notes and interviews to demonstrate three overarching themes that emerged in this research and then propose a recursive framework of questions and ideas to help reimagine what better policies and practices might require.

CONSTRUCTING CITIZENSHIP IN THE MARGINS

Dewey (1916/2001) argued that education is a "midwife" of democracy, a deliberate cultivation of the knowledge and skills required to sustain a robust democracy.

Early advocates of public schooling argued that schools would be makers of citizens, bringing together all young people regardless of race, socioeconomic status, gender, or other socially constructed differences. That is, young people would co-construct the rules by which they would live together in the quotidian practices of their lives at school. Locating the construction of citizen identities in school implies an obligation for all students to experience inclusion and a sense of belonging and to have opportunities to have their voices heard there.

A justice-oriented stance also requires attending to the cultural and racial identities that inform how citizen identities are constructed and practiced (Ladson-Billings, 2004), especially given the historical construction of citizenship in the United States. This dimension of citizen identities acknowledges that whiteness has been used historically as a criterion for citizenship in the United States, and it insists that "full membership in the community" is central to citizenship (Ladson-Billings, 2004, p. 101). Historically minoritized and marginalized groups of people have had to claim their rights to bring their full identities to their practice of citizenship within this context. "Cultural citizenship" in a democracy insists upon equity among all citizens, especially when socially constructed boundaries have oppressed certain groups' claims to and practice of citizenship (Rosaldo, 1994).

Public schools are, however, constructed by social actors with their own ideological values and practices. Due to the dominance of whiteness in the United States, social actors perform "cultural scripts" (Gutierrez et al., 1995) that perpetuate majoritarian stories, thus enacting "evasion pedagogies" that regard social actors as agentive in "evad[ing] solving the fundamental problem of inequity in our schools and society through the project of teaching and learning" (Viesca & Gray, 2021, p. 214). Majoritarian stories are "the description of events as told by members of dominant/majority groups, accompanied by values and beliefs that justify the actions taken by dominants to insure their dominant position" (Love, 2004, p. 228). In the context of WRHS, a central majoritarian story that influenced the lives of newcomer students was that English was the language of learning. This majoritarian story minimized the linguistic repertoire of newcomer students to a single deficit. Given the dominance of this majoritarian story in WRHS, school leaders and teachers performed a cultural script that pathologized and labeled newcomer students' deficits in English and thus segregated them from the wider school community. The evasion pedagogies at play in WRHS offer useful lessons for disrupting them.

The Mismatch of School Policies and Students' Dual Realities

WRHS was a mismatch to newcomer students' realities in many ways (Deschenes et al., 2001), and they largely operated in the margins of the school in order to stay out of trouble. The underlying assumption was that newcomers would adapt to the extant policies and procedures of the school, and these durable structures constructed dual realities for newcomer students. For example, many newcomer students held full-time jobs with very adult responsibilities while navigating the often infantilizing rules dictating students' lives at school. Thus, they were both adult and youth, as well as worker and student. They also experienced exclusion from the rest of the school community due to their placement in the EL program—spending the overwhelming majority of their school day in those classrooms—while, importantly, also experiencing a deep sense of belonging within them, finding cultural and linguistic affinity with their peers in the program. All the newcomer students in the EL classroom I observed spoke Spanish and so the classroom was alive with Spanish all day, assisting students in their learning; however, outside the EL classroom, their Spanish proficiency was a marker of their deficit in English.

Students at Washington River High School had to contend with rules that limited what they could do at school and, therefore, limited how they could function in their adult roles. Students learned either to hide or to overtly break the rules in order to do what they needed to do. The following vignette illustrates one student's dual realities of adult and youth as he quickly made the decision to break a school rule restricting student cell phone use in order to take an urgent phone call from his father's immigration attorney. For Mateo, the no cell phone policy meant that if he wanted to help his father with his immigration case by speaking with his immigration attorney, he needed to frantically gain permission to break the rule or suffer the consequence of having his phone confiscated and withheld from him for the rest of the day.

> Mateo's phone buzzes and he looks pleadingly at his teacher, Mrs. Durham, as he holds up his phone to her. She is busy working with another student and so does not see him trying to get her attention. Mrs. Sánchez, the paraeducator in the classroom, watches him and nods when he mouths that it is his father's immigration attorney calling. Mateo has to translate between his father and the attorney. Sensing the urgency to answer the call, he walks to the back of the room to answer it without having gotten the teacher's permission. Mrs. Durham looks up and seeing him with his phone to his ear, walks toward him and yells, "What the heck, Mateo?!?" Mrs. Sánchez is quick to calm her, "It's his father." This is a game-changer; Mrs. Durham stops abruptly, nods, and walks back to the front of the classroom. Mateo's father's attorney had called him—in school—to discuss his father's immigration case. (Field notes, 11/07/16)

Mateo's cell phone use—even though it was not during instruction—was policed, and he was forced to break the rule or risk missing the opportunity to facilitate the meeting between his father and his attorney. The no cell phone policy and other rules of school were clearly not sensitive to the students who handled adult situations like Mateo did.

Facing challenges in finding translators to help them communicate with attorneys, and especially in the case of Mateo's father in which there were no professional translators in his dominant language in the community, families relied on their school-aged children who were more proficient in English to help. The rigid cell phone policy was more than a way to attempt to control students' focus and attention; it signaled to students that what they saw as an obligation to their families was a problem for the school. Moreover, fulfilling this familial obligation forced students to risk disciplinary action by the school, requiring them to serve detention time after school and often making them late for their afterschool jobs.

Imagining what better might look like in Mateo's situation means centering his and his family's experiences and situating them realistically within the context of the school and community. Mateo and his family were navigating the complicated and often frustrating immigration system in order to secure documentation that would allow them to work legally in the United States, a process that takes years and even decades in some cases (Transactional Records Access Clearinghouse [TRAC], 2021). At the same time, Mateo was required by the compulsory attendance policy to be in school during the hours school was offered, and he was subject to disciplinary policies that neither he nor his family had a voice in establishing. Acknowledging that school as an institution needs rules by which to operate, we can also reimagine what those rules are and grapple with what they are meant to do.

The challenges newcomers experience through the multiple mismatches between school structure and their realities carry implications for how they construct citizen identities. If they learn in overt and subtle ways that their difference is regarded as a problem, not only do they not experience belonging, they risk internalizing the notion of whiteness—including speaking English—as a prerequisite for citizenship. If we can resituate the problem in the fossilized structures and practices of school instead of in people, we honor newcomers' diverse experiences and "funds of knowledge" (Moll et al., 1992) and regard them as worthy of the rights and responsibilities guaranteed all citizens by the U.S. Constitution.

Implications of Different Kinds of Care

The different ways in which different social actors within WRHS demonstrated care implied differing aims for citizenship. The hidden curriculum (Jackson, 1990) newcomers learned through different kinds of care in the EL classroom taught them important lessons about who they are and how they ought to be. In this section, I offer examples to depict how care was expressed differently between students; between Mrs. Sánchez, the paraeducator, and the students; and between Mrs. Durham, the teacher, and the students. Then, I explore how the different kinds of care constructed ideas about newcomers' claims to citizenship.

Care Among Students

Students in the EL program clearly felt an obligation to help newcomers learn the ropes of the new school. They partnered with new students to walk them around the school, help them navigate the chaos of the lunch line and cafeteria, and even offered notes and homework for new students to copy. When I asked Isabel (an EL student) how they know how to help new students, she explained that someone had done the same for her when she was new. She emphasized the importance of showing the new student "how classes go and how things in the school are" rather than just telling them (personal communication, December 13, 2016). Other students echoed this. Sarai recalled that Anyelín had helped her when she was new: "Anyelín showed me how to go through the lunch line and enter my code . . . twice . . . and she explained the rules to me" (personal communication, December 13, 2016).

I routinely saw the students helping new students in the classroom as well. One morning, Alejandro sat down and talked with a new student about Mrs. Durham. He acted out what she does when she gets angry, placing his hands on his hips and talking loudly. The new student smiled and nodded, and when Alejandro sat back down, he offered his paper to the new student, suggesting, "Copy?" The student took his paper and started to copy onto his own paper. I noted as an aside in my field notes, "He's teaching the new guy how to get it done" (Field notes, December 12, 2016).

Care among students was tied to the cultural notion of *respeto*, which has much deeper and more complex implications for behavior than does its English counterpart. Valdés (1996) offers a definition that helps explain how the concept guides interpersonal interactions:

> *Respeto* in its broadest sense is a set of attitudes toward individuals and/or the roles that they occupy. It is believed that certain roles demand or require particular types of behavior. *Respeto*, while important among strangers, is especially significant among members of the family. Having *respeto* for one's family involves functioning according to specific views about the nature of the roles filled by the various members of the family (e.g., husband, wife, son, brother). It also involves demonstrating personal regard for the individual who happens to occupy that role. (p. 130)

This concept provides guidance in understanding the culture of this classroom because the concept of family was purposefully cultivated among the members. Students, drawing on their cultural understanding of family, transferred the notion of *respeto* into the space; in fact, many of them used the word to describe the behaviors they hoped to live out in their daily lives. *Respeto*, in the life of this classroom, mandated kindness and empathy toward one another as well as sharing a collectivist mindset. As such, the implications for how their citizen identities were cultivated within this context point to a shared responsibility to help one another thrive.

Care Between Mrs. Sánchez and the Students

Mrs. Sánchez, a bilingual "para," or paraeducator, who had immigrated to the United States as a young child, demonstrated *respeto* as well, but her care was undergirded by her many years of experience navigating the differences between her home culture and that of institutionalized structures like school that were linguistically and culturally different from home. The ways in which she cared for students leveraged her experience and positioned her as a cultural broker who was "able to straddle both cultures, to take mainstream values and communicate them to the ethnic cultures, and communicate the ethnic culture to the mainstream" (Gentemann & Whitehead, 1983, p. 119). At times, this meant that she made comments that revealed to students the unequal power structures and systems of dominance that pervaded U.S. life.

Mrs. Sánchez's work as a cultural broker helped students understand systems beyond the classroom and school. For example, many students were working to get their residence cards with help from an immigration attorney, and they often brought in correspondence to Mrs. Sánchez to seek help in understanding it. The following example illuminates the nuanced familiarity Mrs. Sánchez had with the students' experiences.

> A student brings paperwork in an envelope to Mrs. Sánchez and takes out the paper, disposing of the envelope in the trashcan next to her desk. Mrs. Sánchez glances at the envelope and tells the student to keep the envelope so that she has the postmark date documented, and the student fishes it out of the trashcan. Mrs. Sánchez points to the corner of the envelope to show her where the date is on the envelope and the student nods in understanding. (Field notes, October 10, 2016)

Mrs. Sánchez knew that keeping the envelope was important in proving dates received, should the need to do that arise. The student learned an important lesson in self-advocacy with a small but powerful teaching moment. Mrs. Sánchez explained to me that she knew that many students were trying to get their residence status, so she tried to add information about the systems and structures in the United States—including privileged knowledge—based on her own experiences that would help them in that process.

Part of Mrs. Sánchez's work in the classroom was to translate from the textbook written in English to Spanish. I observed that she added in subtle details and cues when she translated, such as when Mrs. Durham asked about who George Washington was. When Alejandro asked, "He is on the dollar bill?" Mrs. Sánchez confirmed that and added that they should know that for the citizenship test (Field notes, October 5, 2016). I asked her why she decided to add that information, and she explained, "It just comes to me 'cause I'm working on eventually getting [U.S. residence]. And I think knowing who the first president was is very important" (personal communication, December 15, 2016). She took advantage of the tiny moments in which she could add this important teaching, and the teaching was grounded in her own experience, which afforded her credibility with students.

Mrs. Sánchez often added information to what Mrs. Durham said; in this way, she connected the curriculum to students' lived realities. One example of this was when they were studying women's suffrage. Mrs. Durham noted as she projected the slide, "Now in America, anyone over 18 can vote." Mrs. Sánchez translated that and then added, "as long as they are American citizens" (Field notes, November 16, 2016). Clearly, this was relevant and meaningful information in these students' lives. *Not* everyone over 18 can vote in the United States, and many of these students were among them. Sayra explained that Mrs. Sánchez enriches an otherwise simple curriculum. This allowed them access to information and more "details" about what they were learning:

> There are things that we understand but in a short version and [Mrs. Sánchez] kind of prolongs it and explains it to us better. She gives us more details. We understand Mrs. Durham but there are certain words that when Mrs. Sanchez explains it better we're like, "Ah! Yes, we understand what she's trying to say now." (personal communication, December 14, 2016)

Sayra valued Mrs. Sánchez for the extra information to which she gave them access.

Mrs. Sánchez's care was oriented toward demystifying the systems of power in the United States, as well as helping students see themselves in what they were learning. As they constructed citizen identities in this space, Mrs. Sánchez guided them to learn about the institutions and systems that organize life in the U.S. so that they could navigate them in order to claim space and belonging within it. She noted that what students needed most was "support from somebody. [. . .] Feel that no matter what you're going through that there's somebody that you can go to all the time" (personal communication, December 15, 2016). This care implied that she was there to guide and help students, but she did not do the work for them.

Care Between Mrs. Durham and the Students

Mrs. Durham, on the other hand, demonstrated care that positioned her as a protector of her students. While she took care of her students, whether by helping them get a driver's license or by offering them something to eat when they had not eaten breakfast, she also reminded them often of the extent to which she went to help them. She realized the wide range of needs of her students, and she worked long hours addressing those needs. However, she spent so much time on the problems of their daily lives that she rarely spent as much time disrupting the monolithic and whitewashed curriculum of U.S. history to be more connected to the students in the room.

Mrs. Durham was purposeful in encouraging the students in her classroom to regard one another as a family, and she hoped they viewed her classroom as a safe space. When students expressed trepidation about their lives under a Trump presidency on the morning following his election, she responded, "This room will always be a safe place." She continued, trying to lighten their moods, "I don't have a very large basement . . . but I do have a basement. You can come live with me" (Field notes, November 9, 2016). While some students chuckled, the unrealistic idea that 38 people could go to live in her basement hung in the air as an empty promise. She was trying to express her care for them, but her levity diminished the validity of their very real fears and did little to help assuage them.

Mrs. Durham taught her U.S. history class entirely in English. Even with Mrs. Sánchez's translations in Spanish, the students had only one opportunity to understand the content in Spanish. If they were to reread the text, their notes, or the study guide as review for an exam, it was all in English. This sent a clear message that English was a prerequisite to learning U.S. history. Anyelín acknowledged as much when she explained to me that she did not remember anything from history class because she needed to learn more English first.

Newcomer students clearly need to learn American history (including the evolution of the rights and responsibilities of citizenship) if they are to develop a fuller understanding of their positions and agency in U.S. society. They also need to learn English if they are to navigate the institutional structures that constitute American democracy. However, in the case of Mrs. Durham's classroom in which students were engaged with learning U.S. history through English, the experience was counterproductive; students felt comfortable neither with the content nor with their English language development as a result.

The students in this study described the classroom and their teachers as "helpful" and "caring"—qualities they attributed to "good people." Mrs. Durham and Mrs. Sánchez both mentioned on several occasions how much they cared *about* their students; indeed, they both supported students in different ways. The students manifested care for themselves, their families, their teachers, and one another by helping each other in all kinds of ways and by serving as guides to the frequently arriving new students. As students demonstrated care for one another, they also modeled how to navigate and manipulate the structures of schooling, which gave them practice with societal institutions as well. The differences in these kinds of care suggest different expectations for citizenship within a shared democratic society, ranging from a more individualistic concern for immediate needs to a more collectivist and justice-oriented stance.

Missed Opportunities for Cultivating Inclusive Spaces

The arrival of newcomer students to a school most certainly prompts some adjustments; however, Washington River High School's response to newcomer students was more focused on fitting students into the existing structure of the school than on transforming itself to integrate newcomers' experiences and backgrounds. Throughout my research in WRHS, I noted a number of missed opportunities to integrate newcomers into the classroom, the curriculum, and the daily life of the school. What I viewed as opportunities were regarded by the school as problems or sometimes overlooked altogether.

As noted in the previous section, Mrs. Durham spent a lot of time attending to students' daily survival needs. However, she did not regard their academic needs with as much urgency. There were frequent missed opportunities to integrate newcomers into U.S. history and the national narrative of the United

States through the history curriculum. In some instances, students seemed dumbfounded by the neglect of how the course material related to their lives. For example, as students were learning about the wave of immigration from Northern Europe during the mid-1800s, Mrs. Durham referenced a chart from the textbook that depicted Ireland and Germany as the two main "sources of immigration" between 1820 and 1860 (Duran et al., 2005, p. 132).

> Mrs. Durham, sitting at her desk, finishes the passage in the textbook about U.S. immigration in the 1820s and when Mrs. Sánchez finishes translating it, she asks, "So, who are immigrants?" There is laughter from all the students. She smiles, "I know we have a roomful . . ." and Alejandro suggests, "Nosotros." She nods dubiously, and rephrasing her question, asks, "Which two countries had the most immigrants?" Someone shouts, "Guatemala!" and they all laugh again because clearly, he was right. The room was full of Guatemalan immigrants. Mrs. Durham clarifies, ". . . in 1820?" and someone mumbles, "Ireland and England," and Mrs. Durham praises their answer. (Field notes, November 11, 2016)

The passage in the textbook most certainly resonated with the students in the room, including sentences like, "[Immigrants] came in search of jobs and freedom," and "The immigrants left their home countries to escape huge problems. Some people left because of wars" (Duran et al., 2005, p. 132). However, the connections to current immigrants searching for jobs and an escape from the problems and wars in their home countries and any other reasons for migration were completely neglected. The opportunity to explore current immigration in relation to the broader history of U.S. immigration and to validate their own reasons for im/migrating was lost as the immigrants of the mid-1800s were isolated from their own experiences.

There were also missed opportunities to integrate newcomer students into the school community. While their physical isolation was evident in the location of the English learning classrooms at the back corner of the school, newcomer students were further marginalized when they were not allowed or encouraged to participate in all-school gatherings, such as pep rallies or assemblies. For example, on the occasion of a visit to the school from the District Representative in the U.S. House of Representatives, all junior- and senior-level social studies classes were invited (i.e., required) to go to the school auditorium to hear him address the group, but students in the English learning program's social studies classes did not attend, because, according to Mrs. Durham, "they wouldn't understand what he was saying anyway" (Field notes, October 24, 2016).

Newcomer students could have benefited from the experience of coming face to face with the representative from their community who had a voice in Washington, DC, and English-dominant students would have benefited from sharing the same public space with their newcomer peers. Keeping the newcomer students out of the auditorium during this meeting allowed the U.S. Representative to ignore their presence as well. Unfortunately, the additional logistical considerations of translating the monolingual representative's remarks outweighed the perceived benefits.

Excluding newcomer students from the full realm of public space has problematic implications for who they understand themselves to be as citizens who belong in the public sphere. Relegating them to the margins limited their opportunities to co-construct the rules and norms by which they would live, and instead asked them to accept the status quo that had been constructed by people who were culturally and linguistically different from them. Essentially, excluding students from the full life of the school taught them that they did not have a right to claim space in the wider public sphere. Inclusive schooling policies and practices, on the other hand, have the potential to foster belonging and encourage all students to claim space and belonging in their shared world.

IMAGINING AND REENGINEERING "BETTER"

In imagining and reengineering what better might look like, we can ask whether newcomer students are regarded as citizens of the school and afforded the same rights and responsibilities of all students. Rosaldo (1994) describes "cultural citizenship" as "the right to be different and to belong in a participatory democratic sense" (p. 402). The notion of cultural citizenship offers an honest acknowledgment of the institutionalized forms of oppression that are at play in U.S. schools and in Washington River High School (i.e., racism, classism, sexism, linguicism, nativism, White privilege). Cultural citizenship in a democracy insists upon equity among all citizens, even when societal constructions have privileged certain groups over others.

Returning to the aim of this chapter to imagine more inclusive schooling for newcomer students, a justice-oriented stance and reengineering approach reframes the social problem of the mismatch between WRHS's extant policies and practices and newcomers' realities as an opportunity for transformation: How might newcomers transform this school? Interrogating the assumptions about what school is and how we "do school," and even articulating who "we" is, is an important step in more equitably welcoming newcomer students.

Schools can do better, and the examples in this chapter provide starting points for doing so. The framework I outline below is not intended as a linear progression, but rather a recursive process. First, moving toward more inclusive schooling for all students means simply *noticing* what can and ought to be better. Are newcomer students visible and regarded as full citizens of the school? How are their knowledges and backgrounds honored and leveraged for learning? Second, codifying a vision of better in policy and practice communicates a message of belonging and an expectation of transformation. How do school policies need to change to match newcomer students' realities? And third, enacting better in the quotidian life of school actually constructs better and more inclusive schooling. How are the justice-oriented policies operationalized by staff and students within the school?

Noticing What Can and Ought to Be Better

Noticing what can and ought to be better requires asking who or what transforms in the school. Are students expected to assimilate, or is the school actively reflecting on how its policies and practices can change in light of students' realities and the diverse experiences and knowledge they bring? Noticing what can and ought to be better also requires disrupting fossilized policies and practices that perpetuate and elevate whiteness and white supremacy, especially when the demographic of newcomers is nonwhite and non-English dominant.

Addressing students' dual realities of being both adults and youths prompts questions about school schedules and school rules. Given that many newcomer students in this study held jobs in order to provide for themselves and/or their families, how might school schedules become more flexible to accommodate students' dual responsibilities? Additionally, how might schools acknowledge and honor the valuable knowledge and skills students learn through their work in order to make progress toward graduation?

Grappling with school rules requires an honest look at what the rules are intended to do. Are the rules meant to control students' bodies and minds, or are they intended to remind everyone of our responsibilities to ourselves and others within a learning environment? When rules are consistently broken, do we vilify the perpetrators or interrogate the rules? Operating a peaceful and productive learning environment most certainly requires a set of agreed-upon rules and norms by which teachers, staff, and students abide. However, assuming that the same rules and norms can and should remain in effect amidst changing cultural, linguistic, and religious demographics evades opportunities to integrate newcomers' realities into the practices of school life. The "no cell phone" rule, for example, positioned the teacher and educational support staff to police Mateo's body and property and distracted from opportunities for authentic teaching and learning. If students consistently violate this rule, instead of continuing to punish their behavior, we might instead ask *why* they break the rule. Rather than ask what is wrong with the student, we can ask whether and how the rule might change.

Noticing what can be better requires asking where students spend their time and looking for where they have opportunities to participate in making the rules by which they live in school. Newcomer students at WRHS were segregated from the rest of the school community because they spent the vast majority of their school day in one of two classrooms with other newcomer students. Where are there opportunities for authentic interactions between general education and newcomer students on a regular basis? Do they learn together, especially in social studies classes, where the purpose is to co-construct and reconstruct the world they share? The times that newcomer students spent outside of the English learning classrooms each day were when they attended homerooms that were divided into groups by grade level. This part of the day encouraged interaction about their daily lives, providing academic support to each other, and intercultural communication. Likewise, extracurricular activities like music and athletics provided similar opportunities for authentic interaction, but they still did not learn academic content alongside one another.

Newcomer students arrive with diverse "funds of knowledge" (Moll et al., 1992) that can be leveraged in their learning and enrich the school community both culturally and linguistically. Do newcomer students have equitable opportunities to leverage their dominant languages and emerging multilingualism in their learning? Are students' languages regarded as important knowledge on which to build new understandings, or is the focus on a perceived deficit in English? What is the language of learning in the school? Moreover, Spanish classes for Spanish-dominant Latinx newcomer students from Mexico, Guatemala, El Salvador, and Honduras at WRHS ought to have been a space where their funds of knowledge were privileged. However, these courses instead perpetuated the notion of an elite Spanish that rendered their knowledge of Spanish inferior to the Castilian Spanish found in their textbooks.

Noticing what can be better also requires interrogating how white supremacy is embedded in the policies and practices of the school. Understanding how whiteness is privileged means examining what kinds of behaviors are regarded as desirable, which languages are heard in informal and formal school spaces, and interrogating the stories students explore as they learn about U.S. history and refine their literacy skills. Schools must recognize opportunities to disrupt "majoritarian stories" (Love, 2004) that are perpetuated through curriculum and instruction, as well as the daily life of the school. Love (2004) defines majoritarian stories as "the description of events as told by members of dominant/majority groups, accompanied by values and beliefs that justify the actions taken by dominants to ensure their dominant position" (p. 228). Majoritarian stories are embedded in curriculum as well as in the social life of schools.

Codifying Better

It is important to codify better—to enact policy that reflects a thoughtful and justice-oriented vision for the school. School policies address everything from what students learn to how they act and dress, and they outline professional expectations for teachers and educational support staff as well. McLaughlin's (1987) assertion that teachers are "street-level bureaucrats," actively creating policies as they operationalize them and go about their work, is a useful reminder that policy constructs and is constructed by practice. Therefore, creating a policy is a necessary step, but it is not enough to transform practice on its own.

Curriculum encodes what is considered official knowledge and is therefore of most worth (Apple, 2014). He notes that this is especially problematic given the dominance of conservative ideologies embedded in curriculum and mediated through textbooks that rarely include diverse ranges of perspectives. Curriculum audits can illuminate absences of the representation of marginalized people and groups in the curricula and invite more voices into discussions of standards and materials.

Schools can also consider how guidance around their daily practices can foster more equitable opportunities for students. Policies about language and language use in school can guarantee students' and families' rights to access instruction and communications in their home languages. Operationally, how might attendance hours or cafeteria offerings need to change in response to their students' lives and backgrounds? Further, how might graduation requirements be modified to honor the work students do to acquire English in addition to earning the general education credits, or the knowledge they gain in their jobs?

Representation matters in how students experience belonging in school, as was demonstrated by Mrs. Sánchez's presence in Washington River High School. Given that her life experiences and identities intersected with those of many newcomer students, she was able to leverage her lived experiences and her multilingualism in her work with students. However, she was a paraeducator, which did not come with the rights and privilege of certified teaching or administrative staff. Schools might ask how marginalized groups are represented in positions with institutionalized power in the school (in positions like teachers, counselors, school leaders, etc.). What languages, races, and genders are represented in these positions?

Teacher education and administrator licensure programs also play a role in preparing teachers to work with students in culturally responsive ways and to mediate curriculum in culturally relevant ways. Requirements for educator licensure can prepare them to disrupt white supremacy and foster multilingualism, perhaps through a second language requirement or experience with critical pedagogy. Requiring continuing professional development in these areas for in-service educators can also work to disrupt white supremacy, especially in a field in which the teaching demographics are so grossly mismatched with student demographics.

Enacting Better

As stated above, policies are interpreted by diverse individuals with their own values and ideological beliefs that guide their understanding and enactment of them. Therefore, codified policies are not sufficient on their own to transform practice. As such, there must be diligent enforcement of and continued reflection on policies designed to foster inclusion. Enacting practices oriented toward better in the daily life of the school must also be a part of enacting better.

What languages are encouraged and honored in the daily life of the school, for example in school wide announcements and communications? Schools must interrupt the notion that English is the language of learning so that newcomers' full linguistic repertoire is leveraged in their learning. Certainly, learning English is important, but it should not be a barrier to learning content and earning credit in academic areas. For example, how might professional development in translanguaging practices and pedagogies (García, 2009) in *all classes* (not just EL classes) cultivate multilingual students *and* teachers, administrators, and staff? Centering the language(s) of *learning* instead of the language(s) of *instruction* reframes the problem as an opportunity to cultivate multilingualism, not just for newcomer students learning English, but for other students and educators as well, and positions all stakeholders as learners.

In evaluating instruction, we can look for how the curriculum is mediated to respond to the learners in the room. If the required standards represent a monolithic curricular voice, how are teachers actively disrupting them to include more diverse voices and stories in practice? All teachers are language teachers, and evaluating how they teach and foster language in their classes ensures equitable access to academic vocabulary and discursive strategies.

CONCLUSION

I have intentionally used the term "school" inclusively throughout this chapter to refer broadly to all the stakeholders, influencers, social actors, and the policies and practices they construct, interpret, and enact. However, it is worth pausing to consider who and what school is. Of course, students and their families, teachers, educational support staff, and administrators are integral social actors within the school. However, given that many newcomers come to NLD communities seeking work, the corporations that recruit and employ them have an obligation to help the community and school integrate newcomers as well. The wider community is responsible, too, for providing resources and supports for newcomers and the schools serving them. How might community resources and supports for newcomers (e.g., public health offices, attorneys, housing resources) locate themselves to be more accessible to newcomers and their families? A more expansive understanding of who and what school is distributes responsibility across the community to create more inclusive and equitable schooling for all students.

Who are the "We" in the "We the People" to whom the U.S. Constitution guarantees the rights and responsibilities of citizenship? Flores (2003) argues that as Latinx newcomers "set out to construct their vision of society, as they create space to live it and claim rights and entitlement based on it, they are not only 'imagining' America but re-creating it" (p. 305). Ultimately, two questions can be helpful in assessing progress toward more inclusive schooling for all students. First, are newcomers regarded as a problem or do they present opportunities? How are they positioned as citizens in the life of the school? And second, how is the institution transforming in response to the people in it? As newcomers claim space and belonging in school, those spaces must transform as they do so.

REFERENCES

Apple, M. W. (2014). *Official knowledge: Democratic education in a conservative age* (3rd ed.). Routledge.

Chomsky, A. (2007). *"They take our jobs!" And 20 other myths about immigration.* Beacon Press.

Deschenes, S., Cuban, L., & Tyack, D. (2001). Mismatch: Historical perspectives on schools and students who don't fit them. *Teachers College Record, 103(4)*, 525–547.

Dewey, J. D. (1916/2011). *Democracy and education* (Simon & Brown ed.). Simon & Brown.

Duran, E., Gusman, J., & Shefelbine, J. (2005). *Access American history: Building literacy through learning*. Great Source Education Group.

Flores, W. V. (2003). New citizens, new rights: Undocumented immigrants and Latino cultural citizenship. *Latin American Perspectives, 30(2)*, 295–308.

García, O. (2009). *Bilingual education in the 21st century*. Wiley and Sons.

Gentemann, K. M., & Whitehead, T. L. (1983). The cultural broker concept in bicultural education. *The Journal of Negro Education, 52(2)*, 118–129.

Gutierrez, K., Rymes, B., & Larson, J. (1995). Script, counterscript, and underlife in the classroom: James Brown versus *Brown v. Board of Education*. *Harvard Educational Review, 65(3)*, 445–471.

Hamann, E. T., Wortham, S., & Murillo, E. G., Jr. (2002). Education and policy in the new Latino diaspora. In S. Wortham, E. G. Murillo, Jr., & E. T. Hamann (Eds.), *Education in the new Latino diaspora: Policy and the politics of identity*. Ablex Publishing.

Hamann, E. T., Wortham, S., & Murillo, E. G., Jr. (Eds.). (2015). *Revisiting education in the new Latino diaspora*. Information Age Publishing.

Jackson, P. W. (1990). *Life in classrooms* (Revised ed.). Teachers College Press.

Ladson-Billings, G. (2004). Culture versus citizenship: The challenge of racialized citizenship in the United States. In J. A. Banks (Ed.), *Diversity and citizenship education* (pp. 99–126). Jossey-Bass.

Levinson, M. (2012). *No citizen left behind*. Harvard University Press.

Love, B. J. (2004). *Brown* plus 50 counter-storytelling: A critical race theory analysis of the "majoritarian achievement gap" story. *Equity & Excellence in Education, 37(3)*, 227–246.

McLaughlin, M. W. (1987). Learning from experience: Lessons from policy implementation. *Educational Evaluation and Policy Analysis, 9(2)*, 171–178.

Moll, L. C., Amanti, C., Neff, D., & Gonzalez, N. (1992). Funds of knowledge for teaching: Using a qualitative approach to connect homes and classrooms. *Theory Into Practice, 31(2)*, 132–141.

Rosaldo, R. (1994). Cultural citizenship and educational democracy. *Cultural Anthropology, 9(3)*, 402–411.

Short, D. J. (2002). Newcomer programs: An educational alternative for secondary immigrant students. *Education and Urban Society, 34(2)*, 173–198.

Transactional Records Access Clearinghouse (TRAC). (2021). *Immigration court backlog tool: Pending cases and length of wait by nationality, state, court, and hearing location*. https://trac.syr.edu/phptools/immigration/court_backlog/

Tyack, D., & Cuban, L. (1995). *Tinkering toward utopia: A century of public school reform*. Harvard University Press.

Valdés, G. (1996). *Con respeto: Bridging the distances between culturally diverse families and schools*. Teachers College Press.

Viesca, K., & Gray, T. (2021). Disrupting evasion pedagogies. *Journal of Language, Identity, and Education, 20(3)*, 213–220.

CHAPTER 7

Lessons From the New Latinx Diaspora in Idaho
Negotiating Access to School Success and Well-Being

Eulalia Gallegos Buitron and Vanessa Anthony-Stevens

In this chapter, we take up a repertoire of practice lens (Gutiérrez & Rogoff, 2003) to understand ways Mexican im/migrant families leverage community cultural wealth (Yosso, 2005) to negotiate both constraints and opportunities faced in K–12 settings in the NLD. (We further explain "repertoire of practice" and "community cultural wealth" momentarily; Arzubiaga et al. [2009] uses "im/migrant" to refer to those persons who have been labeled "immigrant, migrant, and refugee, including the undocumented" [p. 246].) Using ethnographic interviews and autoethnographic field notes, we profile "La Familia," a Mexican im/migrant family with roots in Michoacán, Mexico, and Parma, Idaho. La Familia includes two parents and nine siblings. We consider how the family supported all nine children to completion of secondary education and higher education in the United States, examining how family members, individually and collectively, negotiated access to school success and family well-being even as they experienced racial hostilities, navigated economic constraints, and confronted linguistic barriers. Our findings challenge the premise held by many from the dominant culture in schools who assume Latino/a/x im/migrant youth/families will fail to succeed in schools "because they are migrant farm workers or English-language learners" (Gutiérrez & Rogoff, 2003). We use the experience of La Familia to shed light on the varied and diverse ways Latino/a/x im/migrant families utilize community cultural wealth to reframe school engagement through familial networks and the development of new alliances and structures in support of educational opportunity. From a "solution to educational challenges" standpoint, the strategies of La Familia stand as examples of what families may be able to do to support/enable their children's economic success.

IDAHO AS NLD LANDSCAPE: DIVERSITY AND RURALITY IN EDUCATION

As a region, Idaho is commonly characterized as politically conservative, rural, and White, although, as noted in the same 2022 American Community Survey data cited in the first chapter (U.S. Census Bureau, n.d.), almost 20% of Idaho's under-18 population was identified as Hispanic. The state's economy includes a large agricultural sector powered by a robust im/migrant labor force. Mexican im/migrant families are among the largest contributors of labor to Idaho's rural agricultural economy. Idaho's Hispanic and Latinx population rose 30.5% from 2010 to 2019, compared to a 14% increase for the state's overall population (Foy, 2020) and Mexican im/immigrant children account for a 42% increase in the state's K–12 population, representing the largest-growing population in the state for the last 2 decades (Foy, 2020).

Rural areas are often mischaracterized as remote and isolated, and composed of "monocultural white people who are self-sufficient, engaged in agriculture or a related field, and economically advantaged as compared to their metropolitan counterparts" (Parmar, 2017, p. 164). Contrary to perception, rural Idaho is increasingly diverse, with a growing population of Latinx people. In Idaho, Hispanic/Latinx people are 33% more likely than non-Hispanic/non-Latinx people to live in rural counties (Dearien & Salant, 2016). Furthermore, 21.3% of rural students are from a minoritized population, and 5% are considered ELL students (Showalter et al., 2017). Similar to other rural areas, Latinx population growth counteracts population decline and is critical for the recovery of local economies (Biddle & Azano, 2016).

Rural school districts often face many challenges, such as lack of adequate resources, difficulties with teacher recruitment and retention, and a shortage of early childhood services (Biddle & Azano, 2016; Showalter et al., 2017). In 2015–2016, Idaho spent less than any other state on instruction per student, spending an average of $4,336 per student, compared to the national average of $6,067 (Showalter et al., 2017). As noted elsewhere (e.g., Hamann & Harklau, 2022), the state's graduation rates and other indicators used to identify student success frame Latinx students as falling short or lagging behind their White peers in educational achievement. For example, for the year 2019, the Hispanic and Latinx population graduation rate was 73.9%, compared to 82.6% of non-Hispanic non-Latinx students throughout the state (Idaho State Department of Education, 2021).

Although Idaho has a significant Latinx population, there is a lack of research on the educational experience of Latinx students in the state. Among the few studies published, persistent inequities faced by Latinx youth in K–12 is a dominant theme. Hondo et al. (2008) described the experience of nine Latinx students in rural Idaho who did not obtain a high school diploma, characterizing "dropping out" as an act of resistance for the Latinx students in their study.

Call-Cummings (2017) documented the ways Latinx students in dairy production regions of Idaho navigate racist comments and policy from teachers and experience racial battle fatigue as a fact of K–12 education. Both Hondo et al. (2008) and Call-Cummings (2017) called for educational institutions to be culturally responsive and for rural schools to foster critical consciousness and engage in equity-building work with Latinx students/families.

Even as evidence supports a growing need to confront racism in K–12 education, Idaho politics continue a contentious trend of silencing Latinx voices. On April 28, 2021, Idaho Governor Brad Little signed into law Bill H.377, which characterized any teaching about racial inequities as divisive and un-American and "explained" that teaching "critical race theory ... exacerbate[s] and inflame[s] divisions on the basis of sex, race, ethnicity, religion, color, national origin, or other criteria in ways contrary to the unity of the nation and the well-being of the state of Idaho" (Asmelash, 2021).

In a rural landscape marked by political, economic, and educational inequalities, it is crucial for educational researchers, policymakers, and teachers to understand the challenges faced by Latinx youth. However, it is equally important to depict productive family-school navigations, such as the successful strategies employed by Latinx youth and their families.

COMMUNITY CULTURAL WEALTH AS A FRAMEWORK FOR CENTERING LATINX WELL-BEING IN THE NLD

If patterned inequalities (and prohibitions against teaching about them) characterize educational problems Latinx learners have to navigate in Idaho, family strategies that imbue characteristics of community cultural wealth (Yosso, 2005) and repertoires of practice (Gutiérrez & Rogoff, 2003) lenses constitute prospective responses. Yosso's six-part notion of community cultural wealth builds on earlier notions of cultural capital to consider that im/migrant, BIPOC, and other minoritized populations can draw on aspirational capital, familial capital, social capital, linguistic capital, resistance capital, and navigational capital as resources, or assets, as they attempt to be successful. Initially Yosso was particularly concerned with success at college, but this framing has been used to consider student resources in other educational spaces. Gutiérrez and Rogoff's notion of repertoires of practice pays similar attention to the skills and familiarities that children and others from various backgrounds develop and draw from to navigate the world. Repertoires focus on what children/students *do* have, which is dramatically different from a deficit frame that begins with a focus on what target individuals *do not* have. These lenses/theories help describe the rich and nuanced ways many Latinx students and families participate and experience educational spaces. Drawing on these theories, we analyze La Familia's educational journeys as testaments to ways Latinx people can experience education and successfully respond to opportunities and challenges inside and beyond educational spaces in the NLD.

Yosso's (2005) theory of community cultural wealth (CCW)—which Monisha Bajaj and colleagues (2023) recently identified as central to their 20 strategies for *Humanizing Education for Immigrant and Refugee Youth*—counters dominant cultural capital frameworks (Bourdieu, 1986) that assume students of color lack the social and cultural capital for social mobility or arrange culture on a hierarchical scale. Yosso draws attention to the many ways youth and communities of color "survive and resist macro and micro-forms of oppression" in educational institutions designed without their consideration (Yosso, 2005, p. 121).

Looking at Yosso's six forms of capital that intertwine in CCW,

> *Aspirational capital* is a "strength of spirit combined with a critical awareness regarding how society functions" (DeNicolo et al., 2015, p. 234).
> *Navigational capital* is the ability and resilience to navigate through educational institutions and other dominant structures not created in the interest of communities of color, or with them in mind (DeNicolo et al., 2015; Yosso, 2005).
> *Social capital* "refers to the networks of people and community resources that provide instrumental and emotional support" (Yosso, 2005, p. 79).
> *Linguistic capital* is "intellectual and social skills attained through communication experiences in more than one language and/or style" (Yosso, 2005, p. 78).
> *Familial capital* is the "cultural knowledge nurtured among *familia* (kin) that carry a sense of community history, memory, and cultural intuition" (Yosso, 2005, p. 79). Familial capital was informed by funds of knowledge (Moll et al., 1992) and pedagogies of the home (Delgado Bernal, 2001).
> *Resistance capital* references experiences with securing equal rights and freedom.

Gutiérrez and Rogoff (2003) help us understand the significance of *pedagogies of home* in ways that account for nuance and combat cultural stereotypes and acknowledges linguistic and cultural-historical repertoires developed and reflected in the everyday activities they engage in. Through a cultural-historical lens, diversity in cultural communities is attributed to variations in people's participation, which evolves, overlaps, and is relational. Attention to repertoires of practice allows educators to counteract ideologies that group people into bounded and monolithic groups and helps teachers move toward seeing cultural repertoires within family practices as intergenerational and context based.

Research demonstrates that among nondominant groups, repertoires of home practices are often distinct from that of schools and these practices often go unrecognized by teachers and school leaders (Hurtig & Dyrness, 2011; Villenas & Moreno, 2001). Within many academic spaces, familial expertise and students' cultural practices are perceived as unrelated or irrelevant to students' disciplinary learning (Ishimaru et al., 2015). Examination of the situated knowledge and skills Latinx families possess as they navigate schools with youth allows for more nuanced conversations of familial engagement and involvement. In the NLD, decentering Eurocentric, monolingual approaches to measure students' cultural and linguistic aptitudes for learning is critical. Further, we are interested here in understanding how families navigate school together to support community-based models of familial engagement that are more relational, collective, and reciprocal (Ishimaru et al., 2015).

LA FAMILIA

The undergirding study from which this chapter was derived features La Familia, a family of two parents and nine siblings. Members of La Familia were between the ages of 20 and 60 at the time of the study. Parents Amá and Apá were both born in rural Michoacán, Mexico, where their families practiced subsistence farming. After marrying, the family immigrated to Oregon in the late 1980s. Their subsequent migration to Idaho followed relatives and other Latinx people who had taken up jobs in the forestry and meat-packing industries there. Initially, Amá, Apá, and the three older children lacked documentation. Apá and Amá obtained their residency status because of the Immigration Reform and Control Act of 1986, which concurrently promised tighter immigration control and an amnesty to those who had been in the United States without papers prior to 1982. The legislation also prioritized family reunification. La Familia has been living in Idaho for 30 years. La Familia has also lived in Michoacán, Mexico, for up to a year and nine months.

All nine children in La Familia attended K–12 schools in Idaho and obtained a high school diploma from the same rural high school. Eight of the nine children subsequently graduated with postsecondary degrees from institutions in Idaho, pursuing a variety of educational and professional trajectories. Three children earned master's degrees, three earned bachelor's degrees, and two earned associate's degrees as the highest postsecondary degree attained. Institutions in Idaho conferred all but one degree. Among the nine siblings, there are engineers, a business professional, a teacher, a family liaison, a steel fabricator, a grant writer, a maintenance technician, and a PhD student in the field of education. Table 7.1 introduces key information about members of La Familia, including age range, highest degree attained, and region of college or university.

We know Latinx im/migrant and transnational families are not monolithic and do not present La Familia as a model Mexican im/migrant family (Wortham et al., 2009). Still, we believe that zooming in to study the nuanced educational experiences of one NLD family helps to shed light on how teachers and school leaders can conceptualize effective, inclusive, responsive praxis for NLD youth.

Table 7.1. Participant Information

Pseudonym	Age range	Highest degree attained	Type of institution and location
Amá	Early 50s	Third grade	Rural public school, Michoacán, MX
Apá	Late 50s	Third grade	Rural public school, Michoacán, MX
Gabriel	Mid-30s	Associate degree in welding	Community college/ Idaho
Rosalva	Mid-30s	3 years of university; degree not completed	Christian university/ Idaho
Susana	Early 30s	Master's degree, education policy	Public university, California
Carlos	Early 30s	Associate's degree, electronics technician	Community college, Idaho
Miriam	Late 20s	Bachelor's degree, elementary education	Private liberal arts college, Idaho
Eulalia	Late 20s	Master's degree in education	Public university, Idaho
Alvaro	Mid-20s	Master's degree in mechanical engineering	Public university, Idaho
Clarissa	Mid-20s	Bachelor's degree in chemical engineering	Public university, Idaho
Joaquin	Mid-20s	Bachelor's degree in business	Public university, Idaho

Methods of Data Collection

Data for this study were collected between February 2020 and August 2020 (just as the COVID-19 pandemic first massively disrupted life in the United States, including Idaho). Nine interviews were conducted by either Eulalia or Vanessa, with seven conducted via Zoom, as Eulalia was living in Michoacán, Mexico, at the time of data collection. Audio was recorded for each interview. All interviews were transcribed in the language in which they were spoken (Spanish/ English/both). Other forms of data, including field notes and documents, were analyzed as verbal discussions between the authors or written communications. Based on close bonds with all the participants, Eulalia discussed research topics with them, taking field notes on conversations, and confirmed findings. She coded interviews using the Quirkos software during two of her doctoral research courses (one taught by Vanessa). Using Quirkos to support a grounded theory inquiry, Eulalia uncovered the five themes regarding how members of La

Familia navigated new landscapes to build networks that supported educational success.

FIVE THEMES

In a larger rural Idaho milieu where Latinx students often struggled, the siblings of La Familia stand as a solid success story, and it is worth considering why to see if dimensions of their experience could be emulated by others. The La Familia siblings leveraged CCW to survive and thrive as they faced micro/macroaggressions and racism in K–12 settings. Members of La Familia experienced the NLD in complex and nuanced ways. Their lived experiences were impacted by macro- and micro-social policies as well as changes in the familial dynamics.

The family moved to Idaho and enrolled the older six children in the local school district in the mid-1990s. Apá signed a mortgage for a plot of land in collaboration with his brother, with the intent of breaking up the land between the two brothers when the mortgage was paid off. The rural landscape appealed to Amá and Apá because the family would be able to keep animals and be away from noise found in urban areas.

Celebrating Their Children's Success as Aspirational Capital

Participation and engagement by Amá and Apá in their children's K–12 processes changed throughout the years and varied for each sibling. For example, while the older children were starting school, Amá was caring for four young children, all below the age of five. Apá was primarily responsible for sustaining the family financially. His jobs included planting pine trees across the Northwest, pruning and picking fruit, and fighting wildland fires. Apá was gone for weeks at a time, leaving Amá to be the primary caregiver who attended most mandatory parent events, including school enrollment and parent–teacher conferences. However, parent participation roles were fluid. For example, Apá was available to participate in school functions during afternoons, days off, or off-season. As the children reached working age, Amá and the older children often worked alongside Apá in the orchards and fields. When the youngest was born, Amá joined Apá as a seasonal wildland firefighter, leaving the children under the care of close family and the older siblings during the summers.

Amá and Apá prioritized celebrating their children's success, nurturing their aspirational capital. In an interview, Apá told a story of celebrating his daughter's success by inviting his paternal uncle to an elementary award ceremony for his third child, daughter Susana, who was then a 2nd-grade student. The award ceremony took place during school hours on a weekday. Of the ceremony, Apá stated,

> [Susana] wanted us to go with her because they [her teachers and school principal] were going to give her [an award], something was going to be recognized. And

I invited your uncle Toño. And when they called her and gave her an acknowledgment, they called her and gave her *another* recognition, and they called her *again* and gave her *another* recognition. When she came back, she brought three [awards], sat down and stood up and she was given *another*. And when she came, she went straight to your uncle and said, "Why do you cry, *tío*?" He was excited to see that they recognized her because she was a very good student [. . .]. "I have so many recognitions [from you children] that one day I want to decorate a house. I want to decorate the living room, a dining room, the room, because I have, I don't know, hundreds of awards. I have them all in a suitcase."

In the interview, Apá highlighted how he celebrated the success of each of his children, wanting to display their accomplishments through the house, demonstrating the value he placed on his children's academic success and resiliency in educational settings. Part of aspirational capital, "these stories nurture a culture of possibility" (Yosso, 2005, p. 78). Furthermore, the story was repeated by Amá during an interview with her, demonstrating the significance of the story.

Building Familial Capital in the Huertas

As the older siblings became of working age, they contributed to household support by paying bills for utilities, school supplies, school clothes, and other essentials. During the summers, weekends, and other school breaks, siblings worked alongside their parents pruning trees, picking fruit, or weeding vegetables. While working at a young age came with many physical and emotional hardships and sacrifices, the children of La Familia nurtured their familial capital, a sense of community, history, memory, and cultural intuition by working alongside their parents, community members, and peers (Yosso, 2005). Working in the fields allowed members of La Familia to maintain a connection to their community while observing Amá, Apá, and extended family's "model lessons of caring, coping and providing (*educación*)" (Yosso, 2005, p. 79).

As an undergraduate college student, Clarissa was invited to give a speech during a virtual Farm Worker Awareness Week. In her speech, she narrated the impact the orchards had on her identity:

> By 7:00 a.m., it's fully awake. The roar of tractors, people hollering from the top of the trees. Their jokes and stories traveling thorough branches and across rows. And the horn of the *lonchera*, there to feed anyone with a craving for a *torta* and a thirst for an ice cold *Jarrito de Tamarindo*. Everyone is hustling. If you think about it, these orchards raised me [. . .]. I carry these experiences and memories of being in the orchards with me all the time. They are in my thoughts and in my heart as I struggle with my homework, trying to determine the best way to arrange and size reactors to obtain the highest conversion from a chemical reaction. And they are with me through my worst episodes of anxiety when it reminds me of the resilience and strength that lies within me. (Clarissa, May 2020, Transcript of Farm Worker Awareness Speech)

For Clarissa, working in the orchards meant hearing jokes and stories while observing others' "hustle." The statement, "these orchards raised me" evokes Yosso's (2005) definition of familial capital, as the "cultural knowledges nurtured among *familia* (kin) that carry a sense of community history, memory and cultural intuition" and captures family as a "broad understanding of kinship" (p. 79). Laborious fieldwork has been described as a motivator for keeping students focused on attaining college degrees while teaching hard work, perseverance, and responsibility (Bejarano & Valverde, 2012, p. 26). Clarissa described working in the orchards as an integral part of her identity and helpful for her perseverance as an undergraduate student performing chemical engineering work. Through the lens of familial capital, Clarissa captured how memories of working in the orchards conjured resilience and strength for members of La Familia as they faced challenges. She converted that orientation into a tool for academic success.

"We Just Saw Our Older Siblings"

Younger members of La Familia described relying on and being supported by older siblings as they completed their secondary and postsecondary journeys. Family members provided financial, academic, and emotional support to navigate academic institutions, nurturing one another's social capital. Statements such as "I'm the next one," "He went to college, now we're going to go to college," and "just having them as examples" demonstrated the significant influence members of La Familia had on one another's drive to obtain high grades and complete secondary and postsecondary studies.

Additionally, Amá and Apá's emotional support was instrumental to the children's academic success, sharing words of praise for individual accomplishments and motivation such as *"échale ganas"* [Do your best] and *"tu puedes"* [You can do it]. While they did not speak fluent English and were not familiar with the college preparation process, they supported their children by being available for parent meetings; providing relevant paperwork to complete the college application process, including federal income tax information; and speaking to their children about the value of obtaining an education. Furthermore, Amá and Apá linked more particular comments to a broader narrative about moving to the United States from Mexico to allow their children the opportunity to obtain a higher education.

The experience of Gabriel, as the oldest, had an impact on the academic trajectory of younger siblings. For example, Eulalia stated in an interview with Vanessa, "It was after [Gabriel] enrolled in college ... that's when it really set things up. Now it's not going to be a choice. He went to college, now *we're* going to go to college" (Eulalia, Interview, April 2020). Following Gabriel's academic trajectory, seven of the younger siblings completed a postsecondary degree. For Gabriel and other members of La Familia, the college preparation process was possible because of collaboration between school leaders, community resources, parents, and siblings. For example, Gabriel described how a college recruiter helped him, Amá, and Apá understand the college enrollment process by meeting with them at a local restaurant. Gabriel completed the Free Application for Federal Student Aid (FAFSA) during a class at school where he received step-by-step instructions. He described the process:

> I got accepted to those two schools and then I remember [the college recruiter] telling me, "Okay, we have to do your FAFSA." There was a class in school. Like it was . . . they helped us fill out our FAFSA and I remember taking my mom and dad's papers and then [teachers and the school counselors] would help me with that. They helped me with all that paperwork. They would be like, "This is how you do it." They would tell me step by step, but I would do it. (Gabriel, Interview, March 2020)

Gabriel enrolled in a community college after high school to pursue an associate's degree in welding. The college recruiter, teachers, and counselors who supported Gabriel in applying for college, choosing a school, and completing the FAFSA provided Gabriel, Amá, and Apá with informational capital, or the "knowledge derived from school adults that can be processed, stored, and transmitted into a set of actions that support and empower students toward academic and social success" (Liou et al., 2016, p. 121). The informational capital gained by Gabriel, Amá, and Apá served to support the eight younger siblings as they pursued a postsecondary education and navigated similar institutional processes.

"He Was So Encouraging": Leveraging Institutional Resources

Members of the community and teachers were at times anchors for children in La Familia. While not all interactions were positive, siblings were able to leverage social capital embedded in institutionalized organizations and the support of individual teachers during their academic journey. Connections to organizations and individual teachers helped the siblings access higher education by sharing words of praise, writing letters of recommendation, extending invitations for funding and learning opportunities, and encouraging students to pursue higher education. Among the influential figures were Latinx community leaders who strategically networked to introduce members of La Familia to other Latinx students and mentors. For example, all members of La Familia, except for Gabriel, participated in an organization, Latinx Youth (pseudonym), that was led by Hispanic high school students in southwestern Idaho whose mission was to ensure Latinx youth completed high school and to promote Latinx cultural pride and civic engagement. As high school students, Eulalia, Clarissa, Alvaro, Miriam, Susana, and Rosalva filled leadership roles in Latinx Youth by organizing fundraisers, educational programs, and community service projects, such as voter registration. Membership in Latinx Youth facilitated members of La Familia in augmenting their social capital and networking with Latinx high school students, Latinx leaders, and college recruiters.

Some teachers at the siblings' high school also encouraged members of La Familia to pursue higher education. For example, Carlos recalled his experience with two high school teachers, a history teacher who was a White man, and a special education teacher who was a White woman. Both teachers expressed caring for Carlos and his success in school, sports, and college readiness with statements such as "You are going to do great. You *need* to do great." Carlos explained:

> I had a teacher that would just tell me, ". . . you could actually take higher classes, better classes if you want to." Or . . . "Have you applied for college yet? You need to try to do a little bit more." But one of them was teaching history. The other one . . . she was a special education teacher. She told me that I didn't even need to be [in special education]. She said, "but if you want to, I'm going to keep you here just so that you can do your homework." And she told me that from the very first week that I was a freshman in high school. And I was like, "Man, you're the first teacher that ever told me that." All the other teachers didn't even care. They just wanted to have more students in their classroom so that they could keep their programs open. And I was like, "Okay." (Carlos, Interview, August 2020)

Carlos discussed how teachers were invested in his academic trajectory, expressing their expectations for him, and providing words of encouragement. These teachers contributed to Carlos's social capital by mentoring him in applying for college and setting high expectations for his academic performance in high school. When a teacher expressed that he might be able to exit the special education program, Carlos enacted his resistance capital by not following this suggestion. Instead, he continued to take advantage of the courses that he had been enrolled in to complete all his homework. This is especially significant given the wider discourse around the misrepresentation and misplacement of minoritized students in special education programs.

Educational Resiliency: "She Was Just So Oblivious" and Other Microaggressions

Members of La Familia demonstrated resilience as they worked through challenging and stressful educational processes, manifesting new possibilities beyond their circumstances, and enacting their aspirational capital (Yosso, 2005). Racism manifested in both micro- and macroaggressions experienced in everyday interactions. In the examples that follow, we describe how Joaquin, Clarissa, and Amá navigated racism.

As a high school student, Joaquin, the youngest sibling, was enrolled in an advanced physics course. Joaquin maintained high grades, was enrolled in the highest math courses, and was preceded in the "good student" reputation of his older siblings. Joaquin described being singled out by the teacher in an advanced science course. Mrs. Rhodes, a white, middle-aged woman, taught college-track science courses for high school students. Joaquin was enrolled in the two advanced science courses and interacted with her daily. Joaquin stated,

I had like the second highest grade in the class. You know, I was almost

> there at the award and she still treated me like I didn't know anything. Mrs. Rhodes made me repeat equations in front of the class like three times so I would remember it. And I was just like, "Okay." And even my buddy, even Kevin was like . . . you know, I have always been a standout student. He was like, "Dude, why is she doing that to you? I think she thinks you're dumb." (Joaquin, Interview, July 2020)

In a course with few Latinx students, Joaquin was singled out to repeat questions. Kevin's interaction implies that other classmates sensed a disconnect between the teacher's treatment of Joaquin's peers and her treatment of Joaquin and felt it was overt racism. Despite being singled out, Joaquin achieved high academics outcomes in the physics courses and was pronounced valedictorian at graduation.

Amá perceived that her children experienced racism at school and made choices about her children's school lunch to mitigate negative or traumatic interactions. During an interview with us, Amá told the story of packing Joaquin's lunch for a field trip in elementary school. She recalled,

> And then for Joaquin, I made some sandwiches with cookies, with cheese and ham. And I said, "Here are your tacos." And then when he arrived, he was embarrassed to take them out because he thought they were tacos. And they were cookies [and] sandwiches. [Laughs]

Having had eight older children and regularly participating as a chaperone on field trips, Amá knew the type of food that would be acceptable for her children to take to school field trips and programs. Engaging her resistant capital and considering which norms to contest and which to accede to, Amá drew on her knowledge of the structures of racism to make Joaquin's educational experience tolerable.

For siblings Miriam and Clarissa, racism manifested in different forms throughout their K–12 journey. Race was a factor in which classes siblings were assigned to and in their everyday sense of belonging in school. Miriam described feeling out of place as an elementary student. When asked about her experience as a student, Miriam stated

> I always loved school. I loved learning. So, but I do remember being . . . I knew that I was not in the right spot a lot of the times. I knew like "Oh, I probably shouldn't" . . . Why am I with all the "bad" kids? You know?" (Miriam, Interview, March 2020)

As an elementary student, Miriam recognized the existence of structures that separated her from peers who took grade-level courses. These separations had the impact of organizing students into groups that received greater perceived privileges or lesser privileges. In elementary school, Clarissa saw racism manifested in white classmates' renaming of the World-Class Instructional Design and Assessment (WIDA) placement test as the "Mexican test." Through middle school and high school, Clarissa described being placed in rigorous courses while some of her Latinx peers were pushed to take less rigorous classes. While members of La Familia were encouraged by some teachers and counselors to pursue higher education, Clarissa captured how other Latinx students experienced academic segregation in the statement that follows:

> But what makes me sad is, I guess is that I was one of the, I was just *one* of the Latina students who was pushed in that direction. It just makes me sad that there wasn't more. Not, like all students were pushed to think in creative ways, you know. (Clarissa, Interview, March 2020)

Clarissa identified how Latinx students at the high school experienced stratifying racialized patterns of enrollment, just like those experienced by Latinx students in other parts of the NLD (like Nebraska, as recounted in the previous chapter [Gray, Chapter 6]). This was also the case for other members of La Familia. For example, Alvaro, who now holds a master's in mechanical engineering, was denied access to a college-credit-bearing high school English course based on an essay application that was required for enrollment. Despite having maintained high marks in previous English courses, his essay supposedly was inadequate.

For members of La Familia, these excerpts highlighted varied forms of racism manifested through interactions with peers, curriculum, teachers, structures, and process. Members of La Familia drew on their CCW to navigate the racially hostile situations and to obtain access to resources that prepared them for postsecondary studies. As Acevedo and Solorzano (2021) write, "Having a reservoir of community cultural wealth allows students to persist in pursuing their higher education goals even when told it was not possible because of their background" (p. 7).

WHAT DO WE LEARN FROM LA FAMILIA?

As a case study, we see that members of La Familia had expert knowledge of the ways Mexican im/migrant families could navigate new cultural, linguistic, economic, and geographic landscapes to build networks that support educational success. Through an embedded analysis of La Familia's stories, documents, and pictures, we gain nuanced insight into the experience of Latinx students in this part of the NLD.

La Familia's stories and experiences are captured as actions and dispositions that are a result of histories of engagements with specific cultural activities (Gutiérrez & Rogoff, 2003). It is not our intention to portray La Familia as figures to be idealized or idolized, nor to ignore the structures that produced racialized disparities and racialized class hierarchy (Gonzalez, 2017).

IMPLICATIONS

For members of La Familia, teachers variously served as motivators and gatekeepers for resources, such as Carlos's history and special education teacher (who affirmed his capability and helped assure space for homework completion), versus Alvaro's English teacher (who ignored his solid GPA in language arts and denied him access to a college preparatory writing class, claiming Alvaro's application essay was inadequate). While it is important for us to praise the former and decry the latter, as advice to NLD parents about teachers, we point out that some teachers help and are allies, while others aren't. In turn, to teachers we note how parents (like Amá and Apá) and siblings can be sources of encouragement, persistence, comfort, and ultimately success for Latinx students even when their English is halting and their formal educational attainment is modest. Poza et al. (2014) and Auerbach (2007) note that parents' involvement in support of their children can be unrecognized by and/or invisible to school personnel, but that does not mean it is lacking or inconsequential. If too often NLD parents' favorable contributions to their children's academic and broader well-being are ignored or left invisible, we propose engineering systems where those efforts and the student and youth repertoires that they help build are recognized.

REFERENCES

Acevedo, N., & Solorzano, D. G. (2021). An overview of community cultural wealth: Toward a protective factor against racism. *Urban Education*. Advance online publication. https://doi.org/10.1177/00420859211016531

Arzubiaga, A. E., Noguerón, S. C., & Sullivan, A. L. (2009). The education of children in im/migrant families. *Review of Research in Education, 33*, 246–271.

Asmelash, L. (2021, May 6). *Idaho moves to ban critical race theory instruction in all public schools, including universities.* CNN. https://www.cnn.com/2021/04/27/us/critical-race-theory-idaho-bill-trnd/index.html

Auerbach, S. (2007). From moral supporters to struggling advocates: Reconceptualizing parent roles in education through the experience of working-class families of color. *Urban Education, 42*(3), 250–283. https://doi.org/10.1177/0042085907300433

Bajaj, M., Walsh, D., Bartlett, L., & Martínez, G. (Eds.). (2023). *Humanizing education for immigrant & refugee youth: 20 strategies for the classroom and beyond.* Teachers College Press.

Bejarano, C., & Valverde, M. (2012). From the fields to the university: Charting educational access and success for farmworker students using a Community Cultural Wealth framework. *Association of Mexican American Educators Journal, 6*(2), 22–29.

Biddle, C., & Azano, A. P. (2016). Constructing and reconstructing the "rural school problem": A century of rural education research. *Review of Research in Education, 40*(1), 298–325. https://doi.org/10.3102/0091732X16667700

Bourdieu, P. (1986). The forms of capital. In J. Richardson (Ed.), *Handbook of theory and research for the sociology of education* (pp. 241–58). Greenwood Press.

Call-Cummings, M. (2017). "It's too political": The overt and covert silencing of critical Latino/a voices. *Latino Studies, 15*(4), 532–540. https://doi.org/10.1057/s41276-017-0086-7

Dearien, C., & Salant, P. (2016). *Hispanics: An overview*. University of Idaho. https://www.uidaho.edu/-/media/UIdaho-Responsive/Files/president/direct-reports/mcclure-center/Idaho-at-a-Glance/IAG-hispanics-an-overview.pdf

Delgado Bernal, D. (2001). Learning and living pedagogies of the home: The mestiza consciousness of Chicana students. *International Journal of Qualitative Studies in Education, 14*, 623–639.

DeNicolo, C., González, M., Morales, S., & Romaní, L. (2015). Teaching through *testimonio*: Accessing community cultural wealth in school. *Journal of Latinos and Education, 14*(4), 228–243. https://doi.org/10.1080/15348431.2014.1000541

Foy, N. (2020, July 18). Report: Idaho's Latino population grew faster than rest of the state's last year. *Idaho Statesman*. https://www.idahostatesman.com/news/northwest/idaho/article244305002.html

Gonzalez, L. D. (2017). Revising the grounds for the study of grit. In P. A. Pasque & V. M. Lechuga (Eds.), *Qualitative inquiry in higher education organization and policy research* (pp. 113–128). Taylor & Francis.

Gutiérrez, K. D., & Rogoff, B. (2003). Cultural ways of learning: Individual traits or repertoires of practice. *Educational Researcher, 32*(5), 19–25. https://doi.org/10.3102/0013189X032005019

Hamann, E. T., & Harklau, L. (2022). Changing faces and persistent patterns for education in the new Latinx diaspora. In E. G. Murillo, Jr. (Ed.), *Handbook of Latinos and education: Theory, research, and practice* (2nd ed., pp. 81–92). Routledge.

Hondo, C., Gardiner, M. E., & Sapien, Y. (2008). *Latino dropouts in rural America*. SUNY Press.

Hurtig, J., & Dyrness, A. (2011). Parents as critical educators and ethnographers of schooling. In B. A. U. Levinson, & M. Pollock (Eds.), *Companion to the anthropology of education* (pp. 530–546). Blackwell Publishing Ltd.

Idaho State Department of Education. (2021). *Graduation rate*. State of Idaho. https://idahoschools.org/state/ID/graduation

Ishimaru, A. M., Barajas-López, F., & Bang, M. (2015). Centering family knowledge to develop children's empowered mathematics identities. *Journal of Family Diversity in Education, 1*(4), 1–21.

Liou, D. D., Nieves-Martinez, A., & Rotheram-Fuller, E. (2016). "Don't give up on me": Critical mentoring pedagogy for the classroom building students' community cultural wealth. *International Journal of Qualitative Studies in Education, 29*(1), 104–129.

Moll, L., Amanti, C., Neff, D., & Gonzalez, N. (1992). Funds of knowledge for teaching: Using a qualitative approach to connect homes and classrooms. *Theory Into Practice, 31*(2), 132–141.

Parmar, P. (2017). Who am I? Cultural identity in rural schools. In W. E. Reynolds (Ed.), *Forgotten places: Critical studies in rural education* (pp. 157–168). Peter Lang. https://www.jstor.org/stable/45177659?seq=1#metadata_info_tab_contents

Poza, L., Brooks, M. D., & Valdés, G. (2014). *Entre familia*: Immigrant parents' strategies for involvement in children's schooling. *Schools Community Journal, 24*(1), 119–148. https://files.eric.ed.gov/fulltext/EJ1032245.pdf

Showalter, D., Klein, R., Johnson, J., & Hartman, S. L. (2017). *Why rural matters 2015–2016: Understanding the changing landscape. A report of the rural school and community trust.* Rural School and Community Trust. https://files.eric.ed.gov/fulltext/ED590169.pdf

U.S. Census Bureau. (n.d.). *American Community Survey 2022: Annual State Resident Population Estimates for 6 Race Groups by Age, Sex, and Hispanic Origin.* U.S. Department of Commerce. Retrieved Aug. 1, 2024, from https://www.census.gov/data/datasets/time-series/demo/popest/2020s-state-detail.html

Villenas, S., & Moreno, M. (2001). To *valerse por si misma* between race, capitalism, and patriarchy: Latina mother-daughter pedagogies in North Carolina. *International Journal of Qualitative Studies in Education, 14*(5), 671–687.

Wortham, S., Mortimer, K., & Allard, E. (2009). Mexicans as model minorities in the new Latino diaspora. *Anthropology & Education Quarterly, 40*(4), 388–404.

Yosso, T. J. (2005). Whose culture has capital? A critical race theory discussion of community cultural wealth. *Race Ethnicity and Education, 8*(1), 69–91. https://doi.org/10.1080/1361332052000341006

CHAPTER 8

Intersectional Potentialities in Non-Urban K–12 Education
Envisioning the Future for
New Latinx Diaspora Nebraska

Jessica Sierk

About 30 years ago, lawyer, civil rights advocate, and scholar Kimberlé Crenshaw coined the term "intersectionality." Intersectionality aims to "disrupt the tendencies to see race and gender as exclusive or separable ... [T]he concept can and should be expanded by factoring in issues such as class, sexual orientation, age, and color" (1991, pp. 1244–1245). Over the past 3 decades, this concept has been applied to many aspects of education, including higher education (e.g., Byrd et al., 2019; Mitchell et al., 2014), teacher education (e.g., Carter & Vavrus, 2018), urban education (e.g., Grant & Zwier, 2014), and research methods (e.g., Olive et al., 2015). But how might it apply to education in the New Latinx Diaspora (NLD), specifically in non-urban K–12 settings? And how might that application allow us to envision a better way of educating students in NLD schools? This chapter starts by sharing ethnographic data and then begins charting potentialities for how recognizing intersectionality can shape policies and practices that lead to a better future.

In this chapter, I recommend a two-way, intersectional model of education—advocating, promoting, and facilitating solidarity through critical social justice interventions. While there are many such interventions that could be examined, here I illustrate how the following approaches overlap: racial literacy, critical Latinx Indigeneity, geopolitics and border studies, dual language immersion, and intergroup dialogue. Any of these approaches could be used alone. However, looking at them through an intersectional lens shows how they reinforce each other. As Bettina Love (2019) says:

> Intersectionality is not just about listing and naming your identities—it is a necessary analytic tool to explain the complexities and the realities of discrimination and of power or the lack thereof, and how they intersect with identities ... "Intersectionality" is more than counting representation in a room or within a

group; it is understanding community power, or its lack, and ensuring inclusivity in social justice movements. (p. 3)

Based on this understanding, an intersectional approach to education in the post-Trump NLD must go beyond simply acknowledging that Latinx students are in our classrooms. That status quo lacks an accounting of the power dynamics present in NLD schools. The approach I advocate for in this chapter looks at how race, ethnicity, Indigeneity, citizenship, language, and intergroup relations all contribute to students' experiences with discrimination. Together, these interventions form a five-tier support for Latinx students that accounts for their multiplex identities.

This chapter stems from a larger ethnographic study (Sierk, 2016) completed just before Trump's presidency gave new license to some of America's longest-standing nativist voices. That study described the "coming of age" experiences of youth from two non-urban NLD communities (referred to here as Springvale and Stockbridge) on the Great Plains. In this chapter, I will share data from that research as an illustration for why the interventions I propose are necessary in NLD schools, namely, that Latinx students felt misunderstood by their white peers and school personnel. This misunderstanding is of concern because these students' identities are more complex than educators recognize. Identity intertwines with academic success, well-being, and sense of belonging. Data from these students show that they were acutely aware of the stereotyping and microaggressions that they experienced at school and in their communities. As a result, the education system did not serve them as carefully and comprehensively as their White peers, whose identities more closely reflected those of educators in these two schools in particular, and of the national teaching force more broadly.

More than a decade before the research presented in this chapter was conducted, Hamann et al. (2002) wrote of the fast-changing and improvisational interethnic interactions associated with the often rapid demographic change happening in NLD communities. But now that the dust has settled, those improvised decisions have been solidified into inadequate policies and procedures (Hamann & Harklau, 2015). These policies and procedures mirror Bettina Love's (2019) critique of schools approaching race with "slogans (e.g., No Excuses), gimmicks (e.g., grit), best practices (e.g., benchmarking), and professional developments (e.g., Understanding Poverty)," some of which have, in fact, been implemented in one or both of my research sites (p. 13). These types of interventions background race in favor of deficit views related to poverty, language barriers, and trauma. Focusing on students' supposed deficiencies leaves racism, settler colonialism, linguicism, and other forms of oppression ignored and unaddressed.

SITES AND PARTICIPANTS

Springvale, once a predominantly Swedish and German town, is now the site of a food-processing plant that attracts many Hispanic workers. The rural community's school, a K–12 building, graduates about 30 students each year, about half of whom are Hispanic. Stockbridge, a micropolitan community, is about 10 times the size of Springvale and is further along in its process of demographic change. Stockbridge began seeing Hispanic newcomers in the 1990s, and by 2005 was a "majority-minority" school district. Now it is about two-thirds Hispanic and a quarter White, with a small but growing African refugee population.

Participants in my study included fourteen 12th-grade students (class of 2015) from Springvale and seven 12th-grade students from Stockbridge, as well as 31 school personnel, including 24 teachers (nine from Springvale, 15 from Stockbridge), five guidance counselors (one from Springvale, four from Stockbridge), and two administrators (one from each school). Forty-three percent of the participating students from Springvale identified as Hispanic/Mexican/Guatemalan, and 57% identified as White/Caucasian. This sample of students was reasonably representative of the demographics of the schools (i.e., 46% Hispanic, 51% White) at the time, although it did not represent the school's small populations of American Indian and Black/African American students. Springvale is now (in 2021) majority Latinx.

Seventy-one percent of the participating students from Stockbridge identified as Hispanic/Mexican, 29% identified as White, and 14% identified as Asian.[1] This sample too was fairly representative of the demographics of the school, with the exception of not representing the school's small American Indian, Black/African American, and Pacific Islander populations (i.e., 63% Hispanic, 24% White, 3% Asian). All of the school personnel self-identified as White. This is fairly representative of all school personnel at the two schools (i.e., 100% White at Springvale, 93% White at Stockbridge). Three school personnel (all from Stockbridge) indicated that they were second-language Spanish speakers.

Data Collection and Analysis

Data were collected between February and December 2015, including 27 nonconsecutive days of participant observations (Spradley, 1980) on various days of the week and in different settings (e.g., assemblies, school hallways, homeroom periods, and classrooms). I also conducted ethnographic interviews (Spradley, 1979) with 31 school personnel and 21 students in spring 2015, and follow-up interviews with 13 students in fall 2015. I utilized Fasching-Varner's (2014) twofold approach to data analysis when analyzing field notes, interview transcripts, and other artifacts by first coding individual participant datasets, then refining codes based on cross-case comparisons. This approach allowed me to see the interconnectivity of my participants' narratives.

FINDINGS

Findings from that larger study indicated that the social environments of both schools were composed of status hierarchies based on race, ethnicity, nationality, and language, among other identities. As such, data were analyzed according to a variety of constructs, paying careful attention to the nuanced dimensions of students' asserted and ascribed identities. While diversity was predominantly viewed in a positive light, it was generally viewed in terms of its derived benefits, which were almost exclusively available to White students. This current one-way, exposure model of multicultural education flattened students' identities, reducing them to discrete categories of difference, more consistent with essentialism than with intersectionality. White students gained because it was presumed their "exposure" to nonwhite peers made them more cosmopolitan and welcoming (in place of rural or small-town heartland stereotypes that might otherwise have been ascribed to them).

With almost a decade now to reflect on this initial study, it is my core belief that complex problems require complex solutions. The social hierarchies within the two high schools from this study were more complex than students' racial and ethnic demographics alone. For example, a male Guatemalan whose local longevity matched many Mexican-background peers (instead of more recently arriving Indigenous Guatemalans) was often welcome in multiple peer groups and learning spaces, affordances not available to all Latinx students. As such, educators must think through the other social identities these students and their peers embody and how learning environments of the NLD can best attend to these nuances. In the following sections, starting with a vignette from my field notes, I will describe how racial literacy, critical Latinx Indigeneity, geopolitics and border studies, dual language immersion, and intergroup dialogue can be used together to more fully ensure equal educational outcomes and affirming educational experiences for all students. (All names are pseudonyms.)

RATIONALE AND DEFINITIONS

Someone in the class brings up a Native American senior from last year who got mad when people assumed she was Hispanic just because she was Brown and went to Springvale. Another student in the class says that the same thing used to happen to him. Mrs. Ferguson asks why people thought he was Hispanic. He replies that it was because he is Brown. Mrs. Ferguson tells him that he isn't Brown, he's White. Someone else says that he can't be Hispanic because he has dimples. Mrs. Ferguson corrects the student, saying that dimples are not a racial feature.

Another student makes the claim that people don't like him because he's Brown. Alexis [a White student, referred to several times in the coming pages] responds that she hates it when people say that. The student proceeds to accuse the principal of being racist because Javier always gets detention. Another student says that Javier is never in first period, suggesting that that's why he gets detention. The student who accused the principal of being racist asks me if there were Brown people in my high school. I reply that there were. He mentions that Springvale doesn't have any Black people and asserts that if they did have Black people, they would have won the state basketball tournament. Other students in the class offer counterexamples to disprove his point, listing Black students from other schools who play basketball but aren't very good. Someone mentions that there are a couple of Black students in the 7th grade at Springvale, to which someone replies, asserting that they're not Black because their mom is a "ginger." The initial student changes his original claim stating that Springvale doesn't have any "real Black people." He then proceeds to contrast Springvale with neighboring communities, which he says are full of White people, adding that Springvale has Brown people because of the food-processing plant. (Springvale High, field notes, April 22, 2015)

Due to Springvale's large Hispanic population, "Brown" students who were Native American were sometimes misidentified as Hispanic, as the school's Native American population was comparatively small, although with three American Indian reservations within an hour's drive of Springvale, the perpetuation of these mistakes also reflected the low consequences for those who misidentified others. The student who Mrs. Ferguson (a White teacher) contends is "White" after he identified himself as "Brown" is actually half Native American. However, this identity, even though it was overtly asserted, was ignored/rejected by Mrs. Ferguson, suggesting a not-so-subtle understanding of which identity might be preferable.

In the middle of the vignette, the student's accusations of racism and discrimination are dismissed, specifically by Alexis (a White student) who contends that she does not like it when people say that they are treated differently "because they're Brown." Although frequently, like for the U.S. Census, Hispanic is considered an ethnic label, students in both communities treated it as a racial category. This is consistent with the state's education report card, which categorizes students into the following options for race/ethnicity: American Indian/Alaskan Native, Asian, Black or African American, Hispanic, Native Hawaiian or Other Pacific Islander, White, Two or More Races. Students all fit in only one category (noting that "Two or More Races" is a single category).

Alexis's denial of racism is symptomatic of colorblindness. However, the student who complained about his own experiences with discrimination uses this conversation to stereotype Black students, blaming Springvale High's lack of "real" Black students for their losses in basketball. Thus, as suggested by Leonardo (2007), "Whiteness is a skin collective that cannot be reduced to its members. Blacks, Latinos and Asians participate in whiteness, although it benefits whites in absolute terms" (p. 272). In reducing Black students to a stereotype and categorizing them as "real" or "not real," this particular student participates in the same system that he simultaneously criticizes.

In a later interview with Mrs. Ferguson, she addressed occurrences like those featured in this vignette, stating:

I think that it speaks volumes that the kids get along. Every once in a while . . . you've been in here when we had the one student who always goes off about being Brown and that's just part of who he is. I just let it go because that's just the way he is. There might be some resentments or racism that goes on that we don't know about, but I think for the most part the kids truly do get along and accept each other for the way they are. (Interview, May 14, 2015)

She ascribes the students' comments about "being Brown" to a personal trait ("that's just part of who he is") rather than an institutional bias and implies that if kids "truly get along" then there must be an absence of racism. Mrs. Ferguson also rids herself and fellow teachers of any responsibility to act by asserting that they are unaware of any racism occurring in the school, even though the vignette clearly shows that students bring up discrimination in her classroom.

This is but one example of how race came up in my observations and interviews, and a clear illustration of why racial literacy and intergroup dialogue are needed. Rogers and Mosley (2008) provide the following definition: "Racial literacy involves a set of tools (psychological, conceptual, discursive, material) which individuals (both people of color and White people) use to describe, interpret, explain and act on the constellation of practices (e.g., historical, economic, psychological, interactional) that comprise racism and anti-racism" (p. 125). It becomes apparent throughout incidents like the one shared here that students and teachers of all racial groups could benefit from a more robust toolset when race is brought up.

Nagda and Gurin (2007) state, "The communicative possibility embedded in intergroup dialogue provides an understanding of societal divisions and inequalities but also demonstrates that we are neither confined nor destined to remain static in social estrangement" (p. 39). Students' assertions of racism need to be addressed if school is to become a place where they feel validated, seen, and welcomed. On the flip side, White students and teachers need tools to confront their emotions about these assertions of racism and overall colorblindness. Intergroup dialogue would be beneficial in helping students and school personnel truly hear and learn from one another's lived experiences.

In these schools, being Mexican was less stigmatized than being Guatemalan, presumably due in large part to the Indigenous backgrounds of many of the Guatemalan newcomers. For example, Eddie alluded to anti-Guatemalan sentiment as he identified himself racially/ethnically, stating, "I am Hispanic. I am Guatemalan and for some reason at school it's kind of like they see us lower and joke around so I'd rather be called a Hispanic. It's more of an equal thing" (interview, April 7, 2015). In my interviews with Mexican students like Javier, it became apparent that the dialects and Indigenous languages of Guatemalan students were seen as inferior. Neither school understood the Spanish language spoken by many (but not all) of the Latinx students as an academic resource worth further developing (with the minor exception of Spanish-as-a-world language classes), nor did I find any attempt to acknowledge the linguistic skills of some of the Central American newcomers who spoke Indigenous languages (e.g., Eddie, who spoke Q'anjob'al).

Urrieta and Calderón (2019) state that

> [Critical Latinx Indigeneity] encourages the examination, for example, of the transnational movement of anti-Indian hatred that allows us to delve into a deeper exploration of multiple colonialities, including of how the Latinx category erases Indigenous difference even as it enacts violence against Indigenous migrants, refugees, and youth. (pp. 166–167)

This type of internalized anti-Indian hatred was present in how Eddie chose to hide his Mayan roots and how Javier stereotyped Guatemalans as "short and really brown and ugly" (interview, May 5, 2015). This was compounded by White girls like Chloe who also invoked anti-Guatemalan sentiment: "I just feel like the White people . . . at least the White girls feel like they really have to be careful with them because they're kind of creeps" (interview, May 5, 2015).

Educators in both schools tended to lump all Latinx students together into the monolithic category of "Hispanic." However, from my interviews, it was clear that this was neither condoned nor agreed upon by the students themselves. This homogenous categorization ignored the underlying self-differentiation, animosity, and racial tensions that were prevalent among students. These tensions could and should be addressed using the aforementioned racial literacy and intergroup dialogue interventions, while also keeping a critical Latinx Indigeneity (CLI) lens at the forefront.

Casanova (2019) has noted,

> [Yucatec-Maya students] described being Maya beyond the borders of nation states, which includes understanding their positions within their Indigenous immigrant families in the context of the U.S., but also having an awareness of their own Indigenous worldviews that transcend regional and hemispheric post-colonial borders. (pp. 53–54)

As such, schools are sites of tricultural adaptation for some students who are negotiating Latinx (e.g., Mexican, Guatemalan), Indigenous (e.g., Yucatec, Maya), *and* American identities. Therefore, schools should be mindful of how these three identities intersect for students and how each can be positively reflected in the curriculum so that these students see themselves reflected, while non-Latinx or non-Indigenous peers can come to understand them better.

Borders and migration are also something to which NLD schools need to attend. During my interview with Grace, a White student, she expressed, "I feel like if you're going to ask someone like, 'Did you immigrate here?' you'd have to really word it carefully to not seem like you're breaking them down for coming here" (interview, November 24, 2015). Grace's statement mirrors a colorblind approach to race, as it erroneously equates acknowledging migration with xenophobia, just as colorblindness mistakenly correlates seeing race as being racist. Out of fear of participating in a charged conversation, White students and school personnel avoided talking about immigration. What this silence ends up communicating is that immigration is something taboo. However, García (2003) asserts that migration is something we all have in common:

> All groups inside the U.S. have a history of migration. African-Americans suffered forced migration for slave labor to the United States. Native Americans suffered forced migration from their homelands to reservations in the name of greed. Asian and Latinas/os are forced from their home countries by the hegemonic political and economic forces that pull them into the United States. (p. 534)

Moreover, migration patterns and discourse about it may have affected the various hierarchies among Latinx populations. Although my research predated the further vilification of migrants that characterized the Trump administration (and much Republican rhetoric since), at the time of my research, net migration between the United States and Mexico was flowing more from the U.S. to Mexico than vice versa, whereas migration from Northern Triangle countries (El Salvador, Guatemala, and Honduras) continued to rise and political rhetoric described migrant caravans originating in Central America as scary hordes rather than migrants moving in groups for the relative safety that moving en masse provided. This all stands to contextualize the existence of social hierarchies between groups of Latinx students (e.g., Guatemalan newcomers had lower social status than the school's extant Mexican student population).

Given all this, migration is something that should absolutely be taught, and taught as both a contemporary and age-old human process. Van Houtum (2005) poses several thought-provoking questions that schools can, and perhaps should, help students grapple with:

> If indeed we accept the view that borders are human made, it would be needed to not only ask the question why humans are producing and reproducing borders, but also what moral consequences do the (re)produced borders have, are they justified, and are there socio-spatial alternatives that could be produced? In what way does the maintenance of borders help or not help to create a more equal world? What reality are we making when b/ordering ourselves and others? And at what price? (p. 678)

Putting the socially constructed nature of borders at the forefront and questioning the purposes and intentions behind borders has the potential to address xenophobia and teach students that migration is not a taboo topic to avoid. Rather, migration is a constant throughout the history of the world.

Lastly, while I continue to advocate for dual language education (see Sierk & Catalano, 2019), the limitation of just two languages in such programs is problematic for reasons both clarified below about valuing some languages but not others and additional ones that are too tangential to this chapter's focus on intersectionality (see, for example, Sierk, 2021). Morales and colleagues (2019, p. 117) described three Zapotec students from Mexico in a dual language program where their Spanish skills were valued but their Zapotec skills were ignored and left to whither/be less valued.

Thus, it would be most beneficial to combine the strengths of dual language education with a CLI lens that also includes Indigenous languages spoken by students and their families. In my interview with Javier, he asserted that the Guatemalan newcomers should be able to communicate with students like him in Spanish. However, the Spanish spoken by the Mexican-American students at Springvale was often very different from the Spanish the Guatemalan newcomers spoke, if they spoke Spanish at all. Alexis shared:

> [The ESL teacher] got a student who was from Guatemala, but was from a specific tribe in Guatemala that had its own dialect . . . so it wasn't Spanish, but he could understand Spanish, but it was another specific dialect like super, super rare type thing. (Interview, October 23, 2015)

Alexis frames Indigenous languages as rare. Eddie is one of about 87,000–148,000 Q'anjob'al speakers in the world. While that number doesn't rival Spanish (572 million) or English (1.5 billion), that shouldn't dismiss a key element of Eddie's linguistic identity. Yet its dismissal does illuminate part of how student-to-student hierarchies are performed.

While dual language typically falls short when it comes to Indigenous languages (see Heath, 1972), with some exceptions (see McCarty, 2002), it does represent a better linguistic norm than the transitional bilingual programming that these two schools utilized for English learners, which only value non-English linguistic skills temporarily. I would, however, suggest that when schools do implement dual language programming, they also heed Leeman's (2005) call to critically examine the language-power nexus:

> The discussion of the language-power nexus needs to be explicit not only in addressing the social and political reasons why certain language varieties and practices have been systemically subordinated, but also in examining how such subordination has been carried out. (p. 41)

This relates back to Bettina Love's (2019) clarification that intersectionality is about more than representation; it's about addressing power dynamics. Examining the language-power nexus in the NLD needs to happen on two levels. First, the dominance of English needs to be questioned. Second, the systematic devaluing of Indigenous languages must be challenged. They haven't always been "super, super rare," to use Alexis's words.

The language-power nexus bridges the dual language, CLI, and geopolitics interventions. The Americas, writ large, have a long history of colonization, be it British, French, Portuguese, or Spanish. While initial colonizing may have occurred long ago, I join others (e.g., Macedo, 2000; Shin & Kubota, 2008;

Shohat, 1992) in viewing colonization as an ongoing process that still occurs to this day), borders of nation-states have evolved and changed. But it is to a core premise of colonization that I want to direct attention—the colonizer's presumption that what they bring (language, knowledge, customs) has value and what they encounter does not. So colonization includes acts of linguistic violence, which have contributed to language shift and loss. Ironically, given Spanish's historic role in displacing Indigenous languages in Latin America, the colonial premises of schooling in my two NLD research sites subordinated Spanish to English (i.e., viewing it has having little value) and then further subordinated, even ignored, students' prospective and existing skills and capacities in various Indigenous languages. This two-tiered subordination intertwines language hierarchy with views of race and Indigeneity (hence the intersectionality) and leaves unnamed and unaddressed the United States' role in creating the Central American dislocations (García, 2003) that brought students of Guatemalan heritages to this country and these schools in the first place. Decolonizing education, then, requires dramatically rethinking who those students are and what they and we together agree they need and deserve from both schooling and, more holistically, coming of age more generally.

IMAGINEERING

I, myself, am a product of an NLD school (which has had a majority Latinx enrollment now for almost 2 decades). During my undergraduate studies, I took the opportunity to engage in research about my hometown. This sparked a curiosity and ultimately a critical perspective about my previous educational experiences and those of my peers. Since that project concluded in 2009, I've committed myself to further examination of NLD schools. Now I am ready to make some recommendations—an imagineering, if you will—for how to improve NLD schools specifically for students of marginalized groups.

As I have grown in my advocacy and activism, I have wished that I had had an earlier start in my understanding of inequity and oppression. Accordingly, I think it's also important for these interventions to target White students (like I was) in NLD schools. In this section, I will share concrete action steps that I think NLD schools should implement to radically change the educational environment and experience they offer their students.

First, recognizing that the teaching forces in NLD schools in Nebraska are overwhelmingly White (see Chapter 2 this volume), teachers must interrogate their White racial identities and related privilege. We cannot expect students to be able to do this until their teachers are ready to guide them and facilitate hard (and oftentimes uncomfortable) conversations. As previously stated, almost all of the school personnel from Springvale and Stockbridge were White. This mirrors a trend nationwide. Teacher education's response to a predominantly White teaching force teaching an increasingly diverse student population in the United

States has been to add diversity requirements to their certification programs. According to Akiba et al. (2010), "Almost all states had, at least at a minimum level, a diversity related requirement in their teacher certification or program accreditation standards" (p. 455). However, these required courses and program components often focus more on cultural differences and deficit perspectives of diversity, thereby leaving teacher candidates' racial identities unexamined and untroubled.

Ultimately, any social justice professional development program must begin with getting school personnel (of any background) to recognize how they have been socialized into white supremacy, settler colonialism, xenophobia, and linguicism. This explicitly ties together all five interventions. Racial literacy relies heavily on people seeing themselves as racial beings, something that is unfamiliar to most White individuals. CLI necessitates unveiling settler colonialism to see how colonization is not just a thing of the past, but an ongoing presence in schools and other institutions. Geopolitics requires an honest look at the xenophobic beliefs we hold and how education perpetuates nationalist agendas. Dual language immersion demands the use of a critical lens toward English-only policies and the overwhelming adherence to monolingualism in the United States. It requires questioning how even the limited valuing of other languages almost always focuses just on a handful of world languages (e.g., Spanish, French, Mandarin) and justifies their inclusion in the curriculum as expedient for international commerce and cosmopolitanism rather than as resources for identity development and leveraging existing knowledge for new learning. Ultimately, intergroup dialogue presents a methodology for having all of these conversations.

Zúñiga et al. (2007) outline four stages of intergroup dialogue: (a) forming and building relationships, (b) exploring differences and commonalities of experience, (c) exploring and dialoging about hot topics, and (d) action planning and alliance building. As someone trained in intergroup dialogue, I can attest to the importance of experiencing intergroup dialogue as a participant before learning to facilitate intergroup dialogue. Intergroup dialogue is not a quick fix in education; rather, it requires and embodies a paradigm shift in how education is done and how conflict is handled.

The first phase of intergroup dialogue addresses the importance of discussing issues of identity. It also differentiates between dialogue and debate (Zúñiga et al., 2007). This relates to what Ijeoma Oluo asks in her book *So You Want to Talk About Race*: "Am I trying to be right, or am I trying to do better?" (2019, p. 48). The former, being right, is the goal of debate, whereas the latter, trying to do better, is the goal of dialogue. The humility associated with this question, and with dialogue more broadly, highlights that challenging racism, settler colonialism, xenophobia, and linguicism are lifelong growth opportunities. This requires a paradigm shift from teachers being the all-knowing experts in the room, to teachers being what Freire (2006) calls teacher-students. Teachers, especially White teachers, need to take on the role of learner in their classrooms. They must remain open to learning from and about their students' funds of knowledge (Moll et al., 2001), as well as taking on the task of educating themselves about the various systems of oppression impacting their students and communities.

The second phase of intergroup dialogue is when participants begin to examine their own identities through speaking and listening. It also aims to build a common understanding of terminology, including how we are all impacted by oppression (Zúñiga et al., 2007). Jamila Lyiscott (2019) addresses this type of skill-building, giving the following example:

> Within any given space with say, 12 teachers, there may exist 12 different understandings of white privilege. . . . The moment that we can acknowledge our roles in constructing, reinforcing, and misunderstanding the definitions of social locations such as racial identity, we understand our complicity in social reproduction and our capacity to engage in social disruption. (p. 30)

Understanding key concepts surrounding identity and oppression is crucial to understanding how we embody both privilege and marginalization. This phase relies heavily on phase 1. Intergroup dialogue is, at its core, an exercise in vulnerability. As such, trusting relationships are of the utmost importance for intergroup dialogue to be successful.

In the third phase, participants begin discussing topics that are often construed as polarizing or controversial. This is something that is generally avoided in school settings, as shown in Sierk (2019). Zúñiga et al. (2007) suggest utilizing activities like "shocking statement" or "recall a critical incident or experience" to initiate these discussions. The latter activity presents an opportunity for school personnel to reflect on things that have happened in their classrooms; for example, Mrs. Ferguson could bring up students' discussion from the vignette shared earlier in this chapter. This could initiate a collaborative conversation about how to engage with students around issues of race and allow school personnel to be more prepared to facilitate critical conversations with students in the future. This phase also involves metacognitive activities wherein participants reflect on the dialogue process. It is important to note (as the Mrs. Ferguson example shows) that versions of these kinds of conversation are happening in NLD classrooms, but in classrooms where teachers are neither expected nor prepared to productively facilitate them.

In the final phase, participants begin to plan for action. Merely learning about oppression is not enough to dismantle complex systems like white supremacy, settler colonialism, xenophobia, and linguicism. However, without the education to back up the action, the potential for harm is great. Nagda and Gurin (2007) discuss how students engaged with this phase through an intergroup collaboration project:

> For the Intergroup Collaboration Project, teams of three or four students work together on an action project supporting diversity and justice on the campus or in the

community—brainstorming ideas, selecting an action, and planning, implementing, and debriefing their learning. Students report several lessons from these intergroup collaborations: a deeper understanding of inequality; an acute awareness of how issues of dominance, privilege, and oppression get enacted in their own teams; and a heightened confidence in using their learning to educate and inform others, challenge oppressive remarks and actions, and build alliances for social justice. (p. 41)

Similarly, groups of school personnel, be it by subject area, grade level, or in mixed groups, could engage in their own action projects. This contrasts with Mrs. Ferguson's shirking of responsibility for a more engaged and active role in dismantling oppressive forces that negatively impact students.

With these suggestions in mind, I assert that schools ought to be more thoughtful about how they are spending both time and money when it comes to professional development and innovation. What is the intended outcome and how is it going to serve students, specifically those from historically marginalized communities? How is your school's professional development helping educators and staff members adjust their classroom and school practices to (relatively) new populations? Intergroup dialogue is not a "one-and-done" type of professional development; instead, it is an ongoing process that can be engaged on several levels. I have outlined here what this looks like at the level of school personnel; however, I strongly recommend that once school personnel have become proficient in intergroup dialogue, the focus be expanded to include students. I also contend that for these to become parts of teacher conversations and teacher praxis, there needs to be a valuing of this kind of activity "up the food chain" (e.g., at the school administration and school district levels).

It was quite apparent in my interviews and observations that students were not as interpersonally and interculturally adept as their teachers made them out to be. I would characterize the students I studied as "tolerant" or "accepting," when we need to be aiming for affirmation, solidarity, and critique (Nieto, 2010). This is something that intergroup dialogue can and must be used for. I envision a group of students and school personnel, some of whom identify as Indigenous, engaged in intergroup dialogue to unpack and challenge the anti-Guatemalan sentiments reflected in my data. I can imagine a group of students and school personnel, some immigrants and some natural-born citizens, utilizing intergroup dialogue to combat xenophobia and critique the obsession with borders our society holds. The NLD allows us to imagine and propose different and better worlds. Readying and exciting teachers to support intergroup dialogue makes the possible more probable.

NOTE

1. Jenny is counted in both the Hispanic and White percentages due to her self-identification as White Hispanic.

REFERENCES

Akiba, M., Cockrell, K. S., Simmons, J. C., Han, S., & Agarwal, G. (2010). Preparing teachers for diversity: Examination of teacher certification and program accreditation standards in the 50 states and Washington, DC. *Equity & Excellence in Education, 43*(4), 446–462.

Byrd, W. C., Brunn-Bevel, R. J., & Ovink, S. M. (2019), *Intersectionality and higher education: Identity and inequality on college campuses.* Rutgers University Press.

Carter, N. P., & Vavrus, M. (2018). *Intersectionality of race, ethnicity, class, and gender in teaching and teacher education.* Brill.

Casanova, S. (2019). *Aprendiendo y sobresaliendo*: Resilient Indigeneity & Yucatec-Maya youth. *Association of Mexican American Educators Journal, 13*(2), 42–65.

Crenshaw, K. (1991). Mapping the margins: Intersectionality, identity politics, and violence against women of color. *Stanford Law Review, 43*(6), 1241–1299.

Fasching-Varner, K. J. (2014). (Re)searching whiteness: New considerations in studying and researching whiteness. In A. D. Dixson (Ed.), *Researching race in education: Policy, practice, and qualitative research* (pp. 153–168). Information Age Publishing.

Freire, P. (2006). *Pedagogy of the oppressed* (30th anniversary ed.). Continuum.

García, R. J. (2003). Across the borders: Immigrant status and identity in law and LatCrit theory. *Florida Law Review, 55*, 512–537.

Grant, C. A., & Zwier, E. (2014). *Intersectionality and urban education.* Information Age Publishing.

Hamann, E. T., & Harklau, L. (2015). Revisiting education in the new Latino diaspora. In E. T. Hamann, S. Wortham, & E. G. Murillo, Jr. (Eds.), *Revisiting education in the new Latino diaspora* (pp. 3–25). Information Age Publishing.

Hamann, E. T., Wortham, S., & Murillo Jr., E. G. (2002). Education and policy in the new Latino diaspora. In S. Wortham, E. G. Murillo, Jr., & E. T. Hamann (Eds.), *Education in the new Latino diaspora: Policy and the politics of identity* (pp. 1–16). Ablex Publishing.

Heath, S. B. (1972). *Telling tongues: Language policy in Mexico, colony to nation.* Teachers College Press.

Leeman, J. (2005). Engaging critical pedagogy: Spanish for native speakers. *Foreign Language Annals, 38*(1), 35–45.

Leonardo, Z. (2007). The war on schools: NCLB, nation creation and the educational construction of whiteness. *Race Ethnicity and Education, 10*(3), 261–278.

Love, B. L. (2019). *We want to do more than survive: Abolitionist teaching and the pursuit of educational freedom.* Beacon Press.

Lyiscott, J. (2019). *Black appetite. White food. Issues of race, voice, and justice within and beyond the classroom.* Routledge.

Macedo, D. (2000). The colonialism of the English only movement. *Educational Researcher, 29*(3), 15–24.

McCarty, T. L. (2002). *A place to be Navajo: Rough Rock and the struggle for self-determination in Indigenous schooling.* Routledge.

Mitchell, D., Simmons, C. Y., & Greyerbiehl, L. A. (2014). *Intersectionality & higher education.* Peter Lang.

Moll, L. C., Amanti, C., Neff, D., & Gonzalez, N. (2001). Funds of knowledge for teaching: Using a qualitative approach to connect homes and classrooms. *Theory Into Practice, 31*(2), 132–141.

Morales, P. Z., Saravia, L. A., & Pérez-Iribe, M. F. (2019). Multilingual Mexican-origin students' perspectives on their Indigenous heritage language. *Association of Mexican American Educators Journal, 13*(2), 91–121.

Nagda, B. A., & Gurin, P. (2007). Intergroup dialogue: A critical-dialogic approach to learning about difference, inequality, and social justice. *New Directions for Teaching and Learning, 111*, 35–45.

Nieto, S. (2010). Affirmation, solidarity, and critique: Moving beyond tolerance in multicultural education. In *Language, culture, and teaching: Critical perspectives* (2nd ed.) (pp. 247–263). Routledge.

Olive, D. J., Brunn-Bevel, R. J., & Olive, J. L. (2015). *Intersectionality in educational research*. Stylus.

Oluo, I. (2019). *So you want to talk about race*. Seal Press.

Rogers, R., & Mosley, M. (2008). A critical discourse analysis of racial literacy in teacher education. *Linguistics and Education, 19*, 107–131.

Shin, H., & Kubota, R. (2008). Post-colonialism and globalization in language education. In B. Spolsky & F. M. Hult (Eds.), *The handbook of educational linguistics* (pp. 206–219). Blackwell Publishing.

Shohat, E. (1992). Notes on the 'post-colonial.' *Social Text, 31/32*, 99–113.

Sierk, J. L. (2016). *Coming of age in the new Latino diaspora: An ethnographic study of high school seniors in Nebraska* (doctoral dissertation). University of Nebraska, Lincoln, NE.

Sierk, J. (2019). Being nice to the elephant in the (class)room: Whiteness in new Latino diaspora Nebraska. In A. E. Castagno (Ed.), *The price of nice: How good intentions maintain educational inequity* (pp. 37–53). University of Minnesota Press.

Sierk, J. (2021). Language 'barriers' or barriers to translanguaging? Language as a 'problem' in the new Latinx diaspora. In P. Juvonen & M. Källkvist (Eds.), *Pedagogical translanguaging: Theoretical, methodological, and empirical perspectives* (pp. 167–185). Multilingual Matters.

Sierk, J., & Catalano, T. (2019). The downfall: Listening to non-urban communities and their language ideologies. *Critical Inquiry in Language Studies, 17*(2), 121–142.

Spradley, J. P. (1979). *The ethnographic interview*. Wadsworth.

Spradley, J. P. (1980). *Participant observation*. Holt, Rinehart and Winston.

Urrieta, L., Jr., & Calderón, D. (2019). Critical Latinx Indigeneities: Unpacking Indigeneity from within and outside of Latinized entanglements. *Association of Mexican American Educators Journal, 13*(2), 145–174.

Van Houtum, H. (2005). The geopolitics of borders and boundaries. *Geopolitics, 10*(4), 672–679.

Zúñiga, X., Nagda, B. A., Chesler, M., & Cytron-Walker, A. (2007). Intergroup dialogue in higher education: Meaningful learning about social justice. *ASHE Higher Education Report, 32*(4), 1–128.

CHAPTER 9

Leveraging Existing Educator Expertise
Serving Latinx Students in the Rural Southeast

Julie Yammine and Rebecca Lowenhaupt

INTRODUCTION

Over the last few decades, the pseudonymous Cotter Public School District (CPSD) has had to adapt to meet the changing needs of their student population, which has diversified since many migrant families from Latin America settled in this area to work in the food-processing industry. In this nontraditional immigrant destination in the U.S. South, the rural school district's Latinx population consists primarily of second-generation immigrant students of Central America heritage who make up a third of the student body, alongside White and African American students. Serving a high percentage of low-income students across these groups, the district prides itself on creatively using its limited resources to support all students.

This chapter draws on a qualitative case study of CPSD to explore how educators in the district approach their work with Latinx students. It comes from a larger study (Lowenhaupt, Bradley et al., 2020; Lowenhaupt, Dabach et al., 2021) that focuses on how districts support immigrant-origin youth (broadly defined) to include immigrant youth as well as immigrant-origin youth from various countries and of different races, ethnicities, and immigration statuses. In the case of CPSD, the immigrant-origin youth served in the area were Latinx students whose families immigrated from Central America and Mexico. In addition to unpacking the ways in which they approach supporting students given the particularities of this district context, we also consider how these efforts might be reengineered in context-sensitive ways to more effectively address the nuanced, complex experiences of students in this district.

Isolated from more established bilingual networks and educator resources, the district employs a few key staff members who focus primarily on supporting Latinx students, many of whom are children of immigrants and identified as English learners. These educators, who identify as Latinx and bilingual themselves, have been invaluable resources for students, families, and fellow staff members. In many ways, they have contributed to informal leadership in the district where formal leaders rely heavily on the expertise of these few individuals with knowledge about Latinx families and specialized training about teaching Spanish-speaking immigrant students.

Our work examines how educators in the district have approached working with the Latinx community—that is, Latinx students, parents, caregivers, and/or other family members. We discuss how educators in the district viewed Latinx students as similar to all students and relied on particular educators' expertise when students had specific needs such as language learning that needed to be addressed. We consider the implications of their approach and explore how the district might further expand its efforts to more effectively serve their Latinx students. More specifically, we envision ways district leadership might embrace a more nuanced approach to serving Latinx students and expand the reach of knowledgeable educators by including their voices in strategic planning and identifying ways to use their knowledge to develop expertise in others, as well as eventually moving these educators into formal leadership roles. In addition to delving into ways to leverage existing educator expertise, we explore how the district could attract more Latinx educators. Before examining the district's approach to serving Latinx students, we present further details about the district's context and describe the research methods we used to explore these topics.

DISTRICT CONTEXT

Since the early 2000s, CPSD's Latinx population has grown to over 30% of the total enrollment as migrant workers from Central America settled in Cotter due to the availability of jobs in nearby food-processing plants. Although we use the term "Latinx," which is more common in academia, in Cotter this particular group is formally identified as "Hispanic," a term that includes both longer-term and more recent arrivals with a range of linguistic and cultural repertoires.

As a small PK–12 district serving approximately 2,000 students, CPSD prides itself on its ability to respond to the needs of individual students and groups of students. There are only four schools in the district—an elementary school, a middle school, a high school, and an alternative school. About a third of the student body identifies as White, a third as Black or African American, and a third as Hispanic or Latinx. While most Latinx parents/caregivers were born outside of the United States, most CPSD Latinx students were born in the U.S. The district does, however, still receive a few newcomers each year and identifies about 10% of its population as English learners (ELs) eligible for English to Speakers of Other Languages (ESOL). Given that some students are eligible for federal Migrant Education Title 1 Part C support, the district also has identified a small group of migrant education students and operates extra programs for them. While it was not openly discussed during the visit, some interviews suggest that the district recognizes that several students are themselves or have family members who are undocumented and face the possibility of deportation.

Due to the high percentage of low-income families across all racial groups, the district qualifies as a Title I school and receives many federal and state funds related to student poverty. At the time of the study, only about 25% of CPSD students scored at or above proficient levels on Georgia's standardized assessments in language arts and mathematics, approximately 10% below statewide averages.

Given that the majority of students in the district qualify as low-income, administrators have focused efforts on providing additional support, such as academic enrichment, guidance on college access, and facilitating connections with community organizations that offer a variety of social services. Although these supports are anchored in the needs of all students, the district has sought to develop practices aimed at the particular needs of some Hispanic students, such as their ESOL program.

Many of the Latinx families live in trailers and temporary housing that can easily flood and lose power during major rainstorms. In the face of these hazards, the Latinx families, along with families from all racial groups, rely on the churches to provide social and economic support. Due to its location and lack of public transportation, CPSD struggles to access resources, such as bilingual networks, advocacy groups, and social service organizations, that could help immigrant-origin students and families (Bright, 2018). Conversely, its relatively small size allows the Georgia district to build strong relationships among staff, students, and families.

METHODS

We collected the data to be analyzed for this study as part of a larger project involving research-practice partnerships with six immigrant-serving districts around the country (Lowenhaupt et al., 2021). After conducting all-staff surveys across districts in the spring of 2018, our team conducted a series of site visits to gather qualitative data about how districts were serving immigrant-origin youth in the face of anti-immigrant discourse and policy at the federal level (Crawford & Dorner, 2020; Gándara & Ee, 2021). In autumn 2019, one coauthor spent one week in CPSD to conduct interviews and observations. In collaboration with a district leader, we selected 10 interview participants from each district who were heavily involved in practices to support Latinx students, a form of purposive sampling. Table 9.1 shows the participant pseudonyms and roles.

One-on-one interviews were conducted with all participants using a semi-structured interview protocol. The protocol was created in collaboration with other project researchers and piloted with practitioners. It was designed to highlight and expand on findings from the spring 2018 survey about practices to support immigrant-origin students in the sociopolitical context at that time. Field notes were written based on jottings taken throughout the visit (Emerson et al., 2011) to capture the context of the interviews. Field notes provided a running

Table 9.1. Description of Interview Participants

Name	Role
Lucas	District Superintendent
Meredith	District Assistant Superintendent
Cristina	District Migrant Coordinator
Eric	Elementary School Principal
Bailey	Elementary School Instructional Coach
Isabella	Elementary School EL Teacher
Margaret	Elementary School Counselor
Clara	Middle School Counselor
Helen	High School Graduation Coach
Kayla	High School Counselor

log of the observations and thoughts that arose through each day spent at the district. They were used to triangulate views, perceptions, and reflections made during the interviews.

Findings and Implications

We found that the district approached their support for Latinx students with an emphasis on minimizing difference, while relying on a few educators who either self-identified as Latinx or who had specialized expertise to relate to and support Latinx students.

Perspective 1: Viewing Latinx Students as Not Significantly Different

As a visitor to the district, one coauthor soon realized that the Georgia educators did not use the terms "Latinx," "immigrant," or "immigrant-origin" to refer to their students who had at least one foreign-born parent. They referred to these students as Hispanic students or ESOL students. Some of the students whose parents were migrant workers were also referred to as migrant students. Bailey, an elementary school instructional coach, pointed out that the ESOL population is almost entirely Hispanic. So sometimes these terms are used interchangeably by the district's educators: "We have such a huge immigrant population, but we don't use that term here. We just use ESOL, and I guess we just use it interchangeably. Y'all say immigrant, we say ESOL."

Not all Latinx students are in the ESOL program because they have graduated out of the program or have grown up speaking English at home, especially those who are second- or third-generation immigrants. According to Meredith, the assistant superintendent, the ESOL population was about 230 students, or

12% of the total population. The migrant program included 30 students. Even when we used the terms Hispanic and ESOL to prompt the educators to speak about their Latinx students, many chose to instead speak generally about how they serve all students, rather than a certain subset of students. They acknowledged that language may be an issue for some first-generation Latinx students, but mostly they viewed their Latinx students as simply part of the district, facing similar challenges as their non-immigrant peers.

Margaret, an elementary school counselor, stated that she and other educators work with Latinx students "just in the same way that we work with all of our students." She noted, "There's not a big distinction, I don't think, in our role. We work with them as often as we do everyone else." In a similar vein, Bailey stated, "We treat our Hispanic children just like everybody else. . . . In the 20 years I've been here, it has always felt like this is where they belong. . . . I mean, they're just part of us. We don't look at them as any different." Throughout almost all interviews, there was an emphasis on treating everyone the same, no matter their identity.

This view of Latinx students as not significantly different from non-Latinx students is connected to the fact that many of them start attending the district from pre-kindergarten and stay in the district throughout their school experience. Because many Latinx students are not newcomers (although their parents are), Margaret believed that the Latinx students are "very acclimated to our school and our community." She further explained, "Their parents work here. They're a part of us." This quote demonstrates how both the students and their families were seen as part of the community, not just socially at school, but economically in the town as well.

Due to poverty and finite access to resources, the majority of students in this rural Georgia district were viewed by many educators as having socioeconomic barriers to educational success. In this way, Latinx students were not seen as a significantly more marginalized than non-Latinx students. Lucas, the superintendent, explained:

> The common factor for us is poverty. And because of that, I think you don't see as much divisiveness within cultures and within the community. Events like the Hispanic Reading Festival are meant to be an opportunity to engage the Hispanic community, but it is all-encompassing.

Efforts to engage the Latinx community were viewed ultimately as efforts to engage the whole community, not just a particular subset.

However, the participants who worked at the high school identified some differences in the Latinx students that were not mentioned by educators who worked at the other grade levels or at the district level. Helen, the high school graduation coach, noticed that more Latinx students dropped out of school to "earn a living and help contribute to the family." She did not see that as much in her "Caucasian and African American populations."

Kayla, the high school counselor, mentioned, "I do find a lot of the Hispanics don't reach out as much as our other kids would reach out for help." It seems that even though educators perceive Latinx students as seamlessly fitting into the school environment at the elementary and middle school levels, their status as a Latinx student correlates with some more noticeable differences later. As they transition into post–high school life, their status as an immigrant or child of immigrants may have a larger impact on their daily lives. But even as the high school educators spoke to these differences, they minimized them by stating a strong conviction that their role is to serve all children and that too much attention to heterogeneity would lead away from that responsibility.

Only two of the 10 interviewees viewed their roles as primarily focused on Latinx students and families. They were also the only two participants who identified as Spanish-speaking immigrants from Central America. Their viewpoints did not align with this approach of "viewing Latinx students as not significantly different from non-Latinx students," and the district relied on them for more targeted programming. We will discuss these two educators' perspectives later.

Most of the participating educators in the Georgia district did not describe their Latinx student population as different from their non-Latinx population and worked to support them in just the same ways they supported their other students. Other scholars have critiqued this perspective as a form of colorblind racism (Bell & Hartmann, 2007; Bonilla-Silva, 2014; Pollock, 2009) that perpetuates the systemic marginalization of Latinx students because it allows privileged groups to dismiss differences and specific challenges faced by these students. This perspective allows non-Latinx educators to justify their practices of supporting Latinx students as equitable and adequate without deeply examining their own biases or unintentional ways of marginalizing students' experiences.

Initially, our research team shared this critique, but then we began questioning the affordances of this approach. There could be potential positive implications of such an approach in CPSD. First, it might have felt dangerous in the anti-immigrant sociopolitical context at the time to bring attention to the obvious differences between Latinx students and non-Latinx students, such as citizenship status (Dabach, 2015; Gonzales, 2015).

Second, we considered the importance of religion as an organizing frame in the region. Most of the students and families, regardless of racial background, shared a Christian faith, which educators also shared. Participants often identified religion as a rationale for their own perspectives and referred to all students as similar in the eyes of God. By drawing on faith and emphasizing a shared commitment to supporting all children, educators emphasized the common experiences shared by all in the community, despite clear cultural, racial, and linguistic differences. Thus, while minimizing difference may inhibit specific responsiveness, it also inhibits specific exclusion.

The predominant CPSD perspective went hand in hand with inclusive approaches to services. Students were served in integrated classrooms, even those who qualified for additional language supports. It is also worth noting here that the assistant superintendent shared that, according to academic data, Latinx students in this district, on average, achieved on par with or slightly higher than their non-Latinx peers. Because their achievement data were similar to other student groups, the strategy of minimizing difference and supporting students via push-in models that emphasized integration and inclusion can be viewed as a strength. This approach protects the district from creating substantially separate classes or marginalizing experiences for students, which can happen particularly for students identified as English learners (Hopkins et al., 2016; Lowenhaupt, Bradley et al., 2020). By approaching distinctions among students as minimal, educators pursue more inclusive strategies for supporting all students and promote a sense of shared responsibility for the success of all students, including their Latinx students.

Perspective 2: Developing More Nuanced Understandings

Although we have identified some of the opportunities for inclusive practice that educators promote based on their perspectives of shared responsibility for all students, CPSD could preserve the affordances of its inclusive approach while also enacting a more widespread commitment to understanding the particular needs and experiences of Latinx students. While still focusing on equitable treatment of all CPSD students, the district could involve more educators in a learning process about the unique experiences and backgrounds that the Latinx students bring to the district. Drawing on these assets, educators might seek to develop instruction that builds on and highlights Latinx student experiences through culturally responsive approaches (Ladson-Billings, 2014; Paris, 2012).

As we discuss below, the district has tended to lean heavily on a few teachers with particular expertise. However, in order to truly serve all students, all educators would need to build the capacity to support their Latinx students (Miramontes, et al., 2011). Professional development opportunities for all educators, as well as structures to support co-planning and collaborative teaching, can help foster a sense of shared responsibility and capability to address particular experiences that Latinx students bring to their education (Hopkins et al., 2015; Lowenhaupt et al., 2021). District leaders would need to orchestrate this collective and collaborative work. Below, we show how acknowledging and getting to know specific experiences of Latinx students leads to deeper connections and insights that can inform more specified forms of reengineered support for Latinx students.

Though all participants spoke positively about their Latinx students and families, most lacked deeper knowledge about how Latinx students and families experience being part of the district. Margaret, the counselor, admitted that she does not "always know what happens outside of school, culturally or with the families [of immigrant-origin students]." But she has a sense that most immigrant-origin students have a "good experience" in the schools and that the parents are "very respectful of school and their children being educated."

She conceded, however, that she was "not as in touch with those families are as our ESOL teachers probably are." So there was an element of hope without evidence to her assumption that Latinx students were getting a good experience in the schools.

In contrast to more distant perspectives like Margaret's, many of our interviewees mentioned two key Latinx educators—Cristina, the migrant coordinator, and Isabella, an elementary school ESOL teacher—as important sources of information when asked about their Latinx students. CPSD relies on them to communicate with Spanish-speaking parents and to reach out to families. The interviews with Cristina and Isabella were noticeably different from the other interviews as both freely shared their biographies of moving to the United States from different countries. They also shared more specific stories of Latinx students and families they have worked with through their career in the district, in comparison to other educators who tended to relay more general ideas about Latinx students.

Over the last 20 years, Cristina has gotten to know the Latinx families in the district. She has earned the community's trust and thus has been privy to many of their personal challenges. She recalled a story of a student who had immigrated to the United States by crossing the U.S.-Mexico border:

> This student wrote me a note and told me that seeing me go through illness taught her that she can do anything in this world because she said that my strength helped her to see that she could do more for herself.

Cristina became emotional when thinking of her students and the struggles they have endured just to get to where they are. Having gone through a difficult event, she connected further with the students and modeled for them strength in the face of extreme difficulties. She shared that the students call her "Tia Cristina" (Aunt Cristina in Spanish) and "Grandma Cristina." In return, she calls the students her "grandbabies," even though they are not her actual grandchildren.

She also shared that during the Obama administration, immigration officers showed up one summer in the areas of Cotter where the immigrant families lived. The families were so scared that summer school was canceled that year and students recalled hiding in the grass when the immigration officers came around. Cristina was aware that she is the frontline for many immigrant families, whether or not they are in the Migrant program. She made herself available to all immigrant families, and her reputation preceded herself. She knew that she was an important resource to the district not only because of her ability to speak Spanish, but because she has been in the district for some time and has a deep sense of what the immigrant families had been going through for the last 20 years.

Latinx families were not the only ones reaching out to Cristina as a resource. Other educators in the district reach out to Cristina when they are not sure how to help a student, especially in regard to post–high school transition planning.

Helen shared why she reaches out to Cristina: "I don't understand, legally, everything either. So I reach out to my Migrant teacher. She's very helpful. I don't know most of the time what to say and how to advise these students." Kayla also mentioned turning often to Cristina when Latinx students without Social Security numbers start asking questions about going to college. She shared, "Cristina helps a lot because she's been in the system helping them for many years. She is a big asset and knows a lot of things." Clara, the middle school counselor, explained, "[Cristina] is great about working with our families and helping make sure all the documents are there and that—meaning if they need shots or anything like that, just to communicate and just get a plan for extra support." Cristina is trusted by both educators and families to help them with important life transitions, which she does readily with warm assurance and hard-earned competence.

Isabella is another educator that many families and teachers rely on to connect with immigrant-origin students and their families. Isabella attended CPSD as a student and came back to work as an ESOL teacher. When Isabella started attending school in this district, there were only a handful of Latinx students in the school. She described the culture shock she experienced then, feeling mostly alone because the other Latinx students had been born here and spoke English. Even though she was supposed to be in first grade, the school placed her in kindergarten because she could not speak English yet. She shared the difficult emotions she felt as a young student: "I was terrified. I didn't want to be here. I hated it and I would cry every day when I came to school. . . . I still have vivid pictures. It was in this wing, the first classroom to the left." She recalled the environment being unwelcoming and the years it took for her to get acclimated to the school. Looking back, she sees that the curriculum tried to "Americanize" her right away and "forced [her] to forget about [her] culture, [her] language." These negative experiences have fueled her desire to help change the district environment for Latinx students.

Isabella credited good high school mentorship and changes in her documentation status as crucial elements to her being able to continue her education upon graduation, which she has pursued to the postgraduate level. At CPSD, she has orchestrated districtwide cultural celebrations for the Hispanic community and made important changes to the ESOL program. Since she grew up in the area, she has a lot of connections that have helped her to pull off big events and also spread the word about available programs. In the classroom, she has been able to connect with her students by telling them her story and encouraging them to set high expectations for themselves.

Echoing Colomer and Harklau (2009), Isabella has sometimes found herself being pulled from her teaching responsibilities in order to act as a translator for a Latinx family. Having personally experienced the struggle of feeling like an outsider to the school, she was very invested in engaging immigrant families and helping them to advocate for their children. Like Cristina, Isabella was sought after by families not only because of her ability to speak Spanish, but because of the trust she has built by being part of this community for most of her life.

Participants who work as administrators—Lucas, Meredith, Bailey, and Eric—mentioned Isabella in their interviews. They all highlighted her individual "grow-your-own" story as a Latinx student who grew up in this district and came back to work there. They acknowledged that she knew firsthand what it is like to be from an immigrant background, and they were eager to empower her to help the district improve its practices to support immigrant families. In fact, the district relied on these two educators as key liaisons for our larger, ongoing research project, illustrating that the district views them as informal leaders when it comes to their Latinx population. While district administrators support leadership from Cristina and Isabella, this also hints at an unstated calculation that Cristina and Isabella have more responsibility for the success of Cotter's Latinx and immigrant students than some of their colleagues.

Research shows that students of color benefit academically and socially from having educators who share their racial backgrounds (Billingsley et al., 2019; Gist & Bristol, 2021; Meier & Stewart, 1991). In CPSD, Latinx students benefit from having educators who can build cultural bridges for learning (Villegas & Irvine, 2010), but it is clear that that benefit for Latinx students and families in CPSD relied heavily on these two key Latinx educators.

Latinx students would benefit further from having critical educators (Lac, 2019) like Isabella help them make sense of their place in society and empower themselves to change situations that lead to marginalization of Latinx people. Per her own assertions, Isabella has been thinking critically about her own experiences as a CPSD student and trying to change the ways that the district's curriculum tries to "Americanize," a limitation not seen by other CPSD interviewees. Isabella sought to have students see their own cultural backgrounds reflected in the curriculum, although she did not further specify how she pursues this and thinks others should too.

Thus, CPSD could improve the ways it supports its Latinx students by committing to hire more Latinx staff. Of course, simply hiring more Latinx staff is not enough. The district needs to pay attention to the contexts that these Latinx staff were being acculturated into and make space for culture changes. Achinstein and Ogawa (2011) have found that well-meaning teachers of color often become change(d) agents as they find themselves unable to realize their aspirations because they work in marginalizing systems and conditions. Hiring more Latinx staff would not be sufficient or sustainable on its own to improve supports for Latinx students. The district would need to examine any local problems or issues Latinx staff experience as affecting their ability to serve students.

REENGINEERING PRACTICES TO SUPPORT LATINX STUDENTS

Above, we have discussed how two approaches (the dominant difference minimization approach and the much less common affirmative support approach) to supporting Latinx students have played out in the particular context of CPSD and the implications of these approaches for existing and potential practices. While one is clearly more directly responsive than the other, the stance of minimizing difference pushes against accepting lesser conditions for Latinx students and provides an important larger context for schooling (a larger context that could be hostile instead). Based on how the district has worked to minimize difference and relied on a few key educators for outreach to the Latinx community, we considered how practices have been shaped and might be expanded to align with these approaches. Specifically, we have surfaced the need to reengineer new strategies to provide specific support for Latinx students while maintaining a commitment to inclusion and sense of shared responsibility among all educators in the district. Below, we discuss three key recommendations that have emerged from our study.

Identify Specific Supports and Resources for Latinx Students

Districts like CPSD can work to identify specific supports and resources for Latinx students. For example, in the case of CPSD, there is a need to acknowledge citizenship status and how it might affect student experiences and planning for their future. Identifying ways to draw on the "funds of knowledge" students bring to school is also an important next step for educators to fully embrace an asset-based approach to their students (Moll et al., 1992). Although minimizing difference has allowed educators in CPSD to ensure access to general education opportunities, exploring how distinct experiences impact Latinx students is an important step to fostering a community of difference that can both include and acknowledge students (Shields, 2000). Bridging the experiences of home and school can be an important role for educators to play (Valdés, 1997) and can facilitate the kind of deepening understanding that educators may need to identify support. Providing all educators with opportunities to learn about Latinx student experiences both within and outside of school would be a complementary strategy the district may try.

In addition to the specified supports and approaches for all educators, CPSD can build a long-term pipeline for Latinx staff so that Latinx students and families can see themselves reflected in the staff. Isabella was an exciting, but so far singular "homegrown" educator because she attended CPSD as a student before becoming a teacher. She understood the experiences of Latinx students in this district because she went through that experience herself.

High school graduation coaches like Helen could counsel current Latinx students about future careers in education so that the district can build a long-term pipeline for Latinx staff. Promising students could be encouraged to pursue education majors and district funds could be used to pay such students to apprentice as educators by working with younger students in the district during the summer or after school hours.

Engage Teachers in Learning Opportunities

We also envision the opportunity to creatively configure roles so that all CPSD teachers have the opportunity to learn from their Latinx peers. At the time of our study, most of the expertise (and expectation) was concentrated on a few staff members, which made the district vulnerable to losing institutional knowledge about their Latinx students if and when these Latinx staff members retired/left. Districts serving Latinx students need to create a stronger web of relationships instead of concentrating expertise to a few people. They need to create more opportunities for expert educators to develop their craft and connect with other educators doing similar work in other districts. Migrant coordinators already have regional meetings. Thus, leaders of these meetings can capitalize on these existing connections and build in more opportunities for cross-district learning. Districts can also find university partnerships such as the ones established in our larger project where networks of immigrant-serving districts can connect over similar problems of practice and identify solutions (Lowenhaupt, Yammine, et al., 2020).

Conceptualize Leadership in New Ways

In order to build more widespread commitment, the district could take a more explicit distributed leadership approach (Spillane, 2005). This leadership theory focuses attention on interactions among people and their situations in a school system. If a leadership goal is to have more educators understand the diverse cultures and backgrounds of their Latinx students, a distributed leadership approach would bring educators together in collaborative and collective ways to achieve this goal. Instead of having the work of understanding Latinx students fall only upon the shoulders of ESOL teachers and administrators, district leaders could shift practices and systems so that the responsibility of understanding Latinx students is shared with a wider array of educators.

Latinx-serving districts could create new cabinet-level positions that allow knowledgeable educators who have already built trusting relationships with Latinx students and families to engage in formal leadership opportunities. We have observed another district in our project partnership create a director of Family and Community Engagement as a way to better engage immigrant families. Instead of hiring a person from outside of the district, that district was able to build this position with a candidate already in mind. This candidate had worked in the district for many years as a director of a parent center. Thus, she had already built strong relationships with immigrant families over a long period of time.

Ultimately, our work has taught us how important it is to consider the role of context in both crafting and evaluating practices to support Latinx students. In some contexts, the approaches embraced by CPSD might be viewed as limiting. In other contexts, these approaches may provide the best protection against marginalization and lack of access. Bringing a perspective of understanding to our engagement with CPSD helped us challenge ourselves to identify context-sensitive strategies that might enhance the support for Latinx students while remaining true to the district's approach and culture.

ACKNOWLEDGMENTS

We wish to acknowledge the generous support of the W. T. Grant and Spencer Foundations, which made the research presented here possible. We also wish to acknowledge the contributions of Dafney Blanca Dabach, Ariana Mangual Figueroa, and Roberto Gonzales, who serve as co-principal investigators on the larger study, as well as the research assistance of Paulette Andrade-Gonzalez, Jennifer Queenan, Edom Tesfa, and Brian Tauzel. Finally, we wish to thank our district partners whose insights about the innovations and limitations in their own context shaped this study and the reflections presented here. We hope our work conveys our admiration and appreciation for the complexity of serving immigrant-origin students during these uncertain times.

REFERENCES

Achinstein, B., & Ogawa, R. (2011). *Change(d) agents: New teachers of color in urban schools*. Teachers College Press.

Bell, J. M., & Hartmann, D. (2007). Diversity in everyday discourse: The cultural ambiguities and consequences of "happy talk." *American Sociological Review*, 72(6), 895–914. https://doi.org/10.1177/000312240707200603

Billingsley, B. S., Bettini, E. A., & Williams, T. O. (2019). Teacher racial/ethnic diversity: Distribution of special and general educators of color across schools. *Remedial and Special Education*, 40(4), 199–212. https://doi.org/10.1177/0741932517733047

Bonilla-Silva, E. (2014). *Racism without racists: Color-blind racism and the persistence of racial inequality in America* (4th ed.). Rowman & Littlefield.

Bright, D. J. (2018). The rural gap: The need for exploration and intervention. *Journal of School Counseling*, 16(21), 1–27.

Colomer, S. E., & Harklau, L. (2009). Spanish teachers as impromptu translators and liaisons in new Latino communities. *Foreign Language Annals*, 42, 658–672.

Crawford, E., & Dorner, L. (Eds.). (2020). *Educational leadership of immigrants: Case studies in times of change*. Routledge.

Dabach, D. B. (2015). "My student was apprehended by immigration": A civics teacher's breach of silence in a mixed-citizenship classroom. *Harvard Educational Review*, 85(3), 383–412.

Emerson, R. M., Fretz, R. I., & Shaw, L. L. (2011). *Writing ethnographic fieldnotes*. University of Chicago Press.

Gándara, P., & Ee, J. (Eds.). (2021). *Schools under siege: The impact of immigration enforcement on educational equity*. Harvard Education Press.

Gist, D., & Bristol, T. (2021). Building a more ethnoracially diverse teaching force: New directions in research, policy, and practice. *Phi Delta Kappan*, 103(2), 1–77.

Gonzales, R. G. (2015). *Lives in limbo*. University of California Press.

Hopkins, M., Lowenhaupt, R., & Sweet, T. (2015). Organizing English learner instruction in new immigrant destinations: District infrastructure and subject-specific school practice. *American Educational Research Journal, 52*(3), 408–439.

Hopkins, M., Malsbary, C. B., & Morales, P. Z. (2016). Responsive federal policy for bi/multilingual students. *Educational Policy, 30*(4), 573–605.

Lac, V. T. (2019). The critical educators of color pipeline: Leveraging youth research to nurture future critical educators of color. *The Urban Review, 51*(5), 845–867. https://doi.org/10.1007/s11256-019-00507-4

Ladson-Billings, G. (2014). Culturally relevant pedagogy 2.0: A. K. A. the remix. *Harvard Educational Review, 84*(1), 74–84.

Lowenhaupt, R., Bradley, S., & Dallas, J. (2020). The (re)classification of English learners: A district case study of identification, integration, and the design of services. *Leadership and Policy in Schools, 19*(1), 60–80.

Lowenhaupt, R., Yammine, J., Morales, M., Andrade, P., Mangual Figueroa, A., Queenan, J. Dabach, D., Gonzales, R., & Tesfa, E. (2020, August). *Connectivity and creativity in the time of COVID-19: Immigrant serving districts respond to the pandemic.* Policy brief for the Immigration Initiative at Harvard. https://immigrationinitiative.harvard.edu/wp-content/uploads/2020/08/brief_4_english.pdf

Lowenhaupt, R., Dabach, D. B., & Mangual Figueroa, A. (2021). Safety and belonging in immigrant-serving districts: Domains of educator practice in a charged political landscape. *AERA Open, 7*, 233285842110400. https://doi.org/10.1177/23328584211040084

Meier, K., & Stewart, J. (1991). *The politics of Hispanic education: Un paso pa'lante y dos pa'tras*. State University of New York Press.

Miramontes, O., Nadeau, A., & Commins, N. L. (2011). *Restructuring schools for linguistic diversity: Linking decision making to effective programs* (2nd ed.). Teachers College Press.

Moll, L., Amanti, C., Neff, D., & Gonzalez, N. (1992). Funds of knowledge for teaching: Using a qualitative approach to connect homes and classrooms. *Theory Into Practice, 31*(2), 132–141.

Paris, D. (2012). Culturally sustaining pedagogy: A needed change in stance, terminology, and practice. *Educational Researcher, 41*(3), 93–97.

Pollock, M. (2009). *Colormute: Race talk dilemmas in an American school*. Princeton University Press.

Shields, C. (2000). Learning from difference: Considerations for schools as communities. *Curriculum Inquiry, 30*(3), 275–294.

Spillane, J. P. (2005). Distributed leadership. *The Educational Forum, 69*(2), 143–150.

Valdés, G. (1997). *Con Respeto*. Teachers College Press.

Villegas, A. M., & Irvine, J. J. (2010). Diversifying the teaching force: An examination of major arguments. *The Urban Review, 42*(3), 175–192. https://doi.org/10.1007/s11256-010-0150-1

CHAPTER 10

Luchando Contra La Corriente (Fighting Against the Current)
Historicizing Our Latinx Identities

Socorro G. Herrera, Lisa Lynn Porter, and Katherine Barko-Alva

INTRODUCTION

Most salient to this chapter and the book it is part of, it seems important to understand the undergirding tropes and experiences that inform continued pressures for cultural and linguistic assimilation, as well as resistance to the same. In turn, we need to consider the institution of schooling as a major conduit for such assimilation, but also as the prospective sight for cultural affirmation and the building of skills that allow autonomy and self-governance. In other words, we want to distinguish between *what has been* and *what could be*.

Latine/o/x communities in the American Southwest predate Mexico gaining independence from Spain and thus substantially predate the U.S. annexation of previously Mexican land as a result of the war-ending Treaty of Guadalupe Hidalgo in 1848. These communities were proximate to portions of what scholars more recently have called the New Latino Diaspora. Kansas, for example, has been referenced as part of the NLD—that is, part of the region where interaction between dominant (i.e., White) and significant Latinx populations is relatively new (mainly postdating the 1965 Immigration and Nationality Act)—yet its Southwest corner where present-day majority Latine/o/x populations live in Dodge City, Garden City, and Liberal was claimed by Mexico as part of Mexico, then Texas as part of the short-lived Lone Star Republic (1836–1845), before the Treaty of Guadalupe Hidalgo settled any significant further contestation that it was and would be part of the United States.

Since that treaty was signed, as numerous Chicano historians and political scientists have documented, Latine/o/x citizens have suffered a legacy of frustration and dehumanization in the U.S. Southwest (e.g., Acuña, 2021; San Miguel & Valencia, 1998) and it seems apt to wonder: How much of that legacy informs more contemporary patterns in Southwest Kansas? Framed another way, is part of the Latine/o/x experience in the NLD shaped by the discourses (of both domination and resistance) that originate in parts of the United States (like the Southwest) with a very long-standing Latine/o/x presence?

While moments of resistance to assimilation and exploitation have persisted throughout history, members of the dominant White culture have often demonized these reactions through a process of labeling and false characterization, such as *Latine/x/o people are lazy and lack ambition*, *Latine/x/o families do not care about their child's education*, and *Latine/x/o individuals are all criminals who cannot be trusted*. Perhaps of greatest concern is that these and other pejorative characterizations persist to the present (Chavez, 2013; Santa Ana, 2002). Nearly 175 years after the Treaty of Guadalupe Hidalgo was ratified, deficit perspectives remain destructive tools of systemic racism intended to limit the trajectories of Latine/x/o students by truncating their possibilities for success in all facets.

In this chapter, informed particularly by our decades of work in Southwest Kansas, we first frame past and present policies, programs, and practices that have served to dehumanize Latine/x/o families and communities. The historicizing of society's dominant narrative since the annexation has become the script for deficit-based orientations of community and schooling for Latine/x/o populations. This has resulted in generational dissonance, the prevention of upward mobility of families, and limitations to the academic success of students who inherit and internalize this narrative. The chapter concludes by offering recommendations for how educators at all levels must take action if Latine/o/x folks living in Kansas, elsewhere in the NLD, or in parts of the United States with century-plus Latine/o/x roots are to heal, regenerate, and flourish.

TO BE OR NOT TO BE: *LA BATALLA* (THE BATTLE)

Dismissive and/or malicious notions of Latine/o/x identity have been imposed by the dominant White majority since the Mexican cession and the Treaty of Guadalupe Hidalgo, often as a process forced assimilation otherwise known as *Americanization* (Gonzales, 2020; San Miguel & Valencia, 1998). Yet, ironically, the full assimilation purportedly on offer (which is problematic for its violent erasure of Latine/x/o identity) has actually never been available, with the dominant culture continuing to mark Latine/x/os as different and thus ineligible for what they (we!) supposedly needed. For centuries, the idea of America as a monolithic, favored, "civilized," primarily White, and European American culture has fueled processes of assimilation, erroneous classification, and the othering of all Latine/x/o as one population, usually as "just Mexican" (Martin, 2015, p. 97), irrespective of actual origin(s) (e.g., Puerto Rican, Honduran, Colombian). Elsewhere, Alcoff (2006, 2015) and others (Herrera et al., 2022) further this argument, asserting that these race-visible identities (e.g., person of color) remain the most indicative predictors of social status, power, and hegemony in Western societies. These socially imposed, race-based valuation hierarchies tend to be systematically reinforced via social institutions.

Schools have long been a battleground for reinforcing pervasive hegemonic notions and practices. Systemic characterizations of Latine/x/o families and students seldom account for long-standing patterns of dismissal and mistreatment. In the 175 years since the Treaty of Guadalupe Hidalgo, this system has thrust hardships upon generations of Latine/x/o citizens who had been displaced from their homes, lost their property and wealth, and have not been allowed to speak or teach their native language (Ontiveros, 2014). The battle cry heard from Latine/x/o activists for decades was *we didn't cross the border, the border crossed us* (e.g., Castañeda et al., 1972). Characterizations of Latine/x/o families and students in Southwest Kansas that separate them from this Chicano history, labeling them as newcomers or immigrants, blur and obscure how contemporary treatment echoes older patterns and discourages solidarity including solidarity that would have newer generations learn from the resistance and survival strategies of those who have preceded them.

This subjugation has been replicated in the schools through ongoing classification and reclassification based on arbitrary perceptions, hegemonic norms, and academic capital (Zwiers, 2007). To date, members of the dominant (i.e., white) social group, including educators who are guided by their own biographies, values, and perspectives, have characterized members of the Latine/x/o population as uneducated, unambitious, unimportant, criminal, foreign, without a past, and so on. Each of these are archetypal examples of *blaming the victim*. In *esta batalla*, historicizing the impact of politics and propaganda informs and reminds us that counterstories, reflecting agency and advocacy especially among community members, voters, and educators, are essential to expose that which is often suppressed. This lens further allows us to appreciate and comprehend contemporary viewpoints and reactions of Latine/x/o communities. So we look back partially to claim a history to be heirs to, but also to clarify the deep, hegemonic roots of unequal educational practices that are concurrently ordinary and invisible to many in the dominant culture and thus perpetuated.

Forced Displacement and the Claiming of Language and a Culture, 1930s–1960s

Just as it had for Latine/x/o families dispossessed by the Mexican Annexation, the phrase, *we didn't cross the border, the border has crossed us,* once again served as the call to battle for Mexicanos and Chicanos who began to organize and champion Latine/x/o causes beginning in the 1930s and cresting in the 1960s Civil Rights Movement. Activists began to openly challenge a historical era of intense efforts to Americanize Latine/x/o or any individual whose race, language, or culture differed from that of the dominant group (Acuña, 2021). Many of these efforts centered on linguistic justice and the preservation of cultural integrity.

As early as the 1930s, positivists (under the pretense of science and empiricism) began to discriminate against students of color and eventually leveraged the results of so-called "standardized" national examinations (e.g., the Stanford Binet) to assert that the intelligence of Mexican American students was inferior to that of Anglo children (Gonzales, 2020). These arguments began to receive strong criticism by both academics and Latine/o/x advocacy groups for their foundations in research designs that failed to account for Mexican American students whose first language was not English (Ford, 2004). Compounding this issue, neither the heritage culture of Latine/x/o students (e.g., Mexican) nor their home socialization (linguistic, economic, and otherwise) aligned with the population to which such examinations were often normed (Kim & Zabelina, 2015).

Around this time, both theoretical and philosophical arguments indicated that Latine/x/o children, especially newcomers, suffered from forced assimilation to English-only policies (Pac, 2012; Phillipson, 1992; San Miguel & Valencia, 1998), and that the prohibition of their native language deprived them of critical linkages to their home culture, families, and communities (Gonzales, 2020). Beginning with legal cases in the 1960s that continued into the 1970s, including *Serna v. Portales* (ruling issued in 1974) and *Lau v. Nichols* (ruling issued in 1974), advocates and Latine/x/o families elevated their claims regarding the widespread miseducation to a more nationally visible level (Herrera & Murry, 2016).

Beyond language acquisition, Latine/x/o students and their families were the focus of debates on pre- and post-instructional assessments, curricula and programming, family involvement, and college readiness throughout the 1960s (Gonzales, 2020). In fact, multiple school districts throughout the country explicitly determined Latine/x/o students to be unworthy of preparation for higher education by surmising that the appropriate schooling objectives should be to prepare Latine/x/o (Mexican) students to "lead happy lives" by contributing to the community and learning a trade (Gonzales, 2020; Schneider et al., 2006). On our own campuses, Latine/o/x students remain substantially under-represented (when compared to the Latino proportion of the K–12 population in Kansas) despite 2 decades plus of our efforts and efforts by our allies.

The long predominant deficit view of purportedly appropriate schooling for Latine/x/o students was (and among many educational systems, continues to be) grounded in a technocratic perspective on the management and leadership of educational systems (Murry et al., 2021). This business-based model emphasizes efficiencies, economies of scale, standardization, and regimented (if not scripted) teaching and learning (Getz, 1997; Mehta, 2013; Murry et al., 2020). According to Murry and colleagues (2020),

> Deficit perceptions are fundamentally grounded in a technocratic perspective on schooling and teaching.... its function [the function of the public education system] is to efficiently graduate the highest percentage of candidates, who also happen to be those who are best prepared (i.e., bring the lowest compensatory cost) for

current system design. Accordingly, those students who arrive with biographies that don't match the expectations of the technocratic system are not unlike suppliers who bring inadequate or nonstandard materials to the job of building readiness for graduation.... the technocratic perspective argues that students with deficits (and/or nonstandard challenges) should be remediated (or prepared in auxiliary programs/locations) prior to full entry into the efficient, educational system. (p. 104)

In terms of system outputs or outcomes, the technocratic view holds that it is not the educational system, but rather the Latine/x/o students and families who are accountable for high dropout rates and/or failure to graduate from high school prepared for college.

Although the technocratic perspective also prompted greater attention to educational outcomes for Latine/x/o students, inordinate emphasis on the results of associated (and often linguistically challenging) assessments frequently resulted in *teaching to the test* instead of attending to the assets and needs of Latine/x/o and other students of color. So the technocratic perspective has frequently undergirded deficit views of Latine/x/o students, families, nondominant cultures, and instructional differentiation in exchange for a more efficient, business-like model of schooling, system management, and target outputs rooted in historical patterns of assimilation (Getz, 1997; Mehta, 2013).

While much of what we have just discussed originates outside the NLD, particularly in the American Southwest, but also in the longtime Latine/x/o-hosting northern cities of New York and Chicago, it pertains to contemporary NLD experiences in at least two important ways. These long-standing patterns and tropes remain available to educators and others shaping school systems and thus inform how they make sense of who Latine/x/o students and families are. Because it was common, for example, for hegemonic (i.e., mainly White) educators to view Latine/x/o students in Arizona or Texas in deficit terms, then it's not so surprising that this presumption has been substantially reproduced in Kansas. Similarly, as the complaint of those who note their descent from those who "had the border changed on them" highlights, there is a longtime rejection of seeing of Latine/x/o populations as *of* and deserving to be *of* where they live.

False Hope, 1960s-1990s

The Supreme Court decision of *Brown v. Board of Education* in 1954, the Elementary and Secondary Education Act of 1965 (and its 1968 extension with the Bilingual Education Act), and the civil rights movement that extended into the 1970s symbolized hope for a new era in schooling that would dismantle segregation, English-only agendas, and racist ideologies. In fact, a report of the U.S. Commission on Civil Rights clearly laid out the history of the "The Excluded Student" and "The Unfinished Education" of Mexican-American/Latine/x/o populations (U.S. Commission on Civil Rights, 1972). Unfortunately, these progressive initiatives came with very few tangible ways of achieving equity for families and students through programming and becoming responsive to culture and language within systems already deeply entrenched in viewing Latine/x/o families and students through a deficit lens under the dogma of "science."

The challenges and discourse surrounding border patrol and immigration in the United States heightened during this time frame (Hernandez, 2010), which found families and students embattled in a search for identity while finding safe spaces where their agency could be recognized and affirmed. Legal efforts toward the end of the time frame, like 1986's Immigration Reform and Control Act, paradoxically welcomed (and amnestied) millions while concurrently constructing other prospective newcomers as needing to be "controlled" or "kept out." The struggle and the searching led to a new generation of scholars, educators, and community members who began to question what was happening within the Latine/x/o communities as new immigrants from Mexico and Central America continued to arrive, massively growing and diversifying what has become America's largest nonwhite population. Scholars and activists (e.g., Rodolfo "Corky" Gonzales, Gloria Anzaldúa, Cherrie Moraga, Berta Cáceres) conveyed a sense of urgency in renewing Latine/x/o agency in pushing back against racist and xenophobic rhetoric while prioritizing cultural identity. This growing momentum for identity and agency led to the emergence of countless heritage and ethnic studies programs as well as K–12 bilingual education programs throughout the country (García & Baetens, 2009).

Although conversations across the nation began to indicate an intent to do better (just as Latine/o/x populations began to dramatically grow in the NLD), the impact of new programming and "heritage" agendas fell short of achieving lasting change. Instead, reactionary groups who upheld assimilation rhetoric while supporting punitive immigration policies that increased during the recession of the 1970s continued to challenge and even block progress and any ensuing hope (Crawford, 1992; García & Baetens, 2009). It was not long until English-only movements resurfaced and diminished the prospects for bilingual and heritage programs across the country by way of budget cuts, board reversals, and closures. Underlying causes included the limited role that Spanish-speaking families and other advocates were afforded in decision-making processes at the legislative, local, and school leadership levels. Furthermore, opponents of bilingual and heritage programs spread unsubstantiated arguments that claimed bilingual education was unpatriotic, a disruption to English language acquisition, and/or an unnecessary expense for state taxpayers (Gándara & Contreras, 2009). Hamann (2003) described a Georgia program that began with Title VII funding for "systemwide bilingual education" but rapidly got reimagined as needing to "teach English" as local leaders internalized increasingly common anti-bilingual education sentiments extant in the national discourse.

Generations of Marginalization and Exclusion at the Crossroads, 1990s to Present

From Risk to Opportunity: Fulfilling the Educational Needs of Hispanic Americans in the 21st Century was the title of a report commissioned by President George W. Bush's Advisory Commission on Educational Excellence for Hispanic Americans in 2001. Based on an 18-month study, the report highlighted lower reading levels among Hispanic students compared to those of their non-Hispanic counterparts and further demonstrated higher dropout rates and lower college attendance rates among the Hispanic population. The report found that parents could not attain the dreams and aspirations they had worked so hard to fulfill for their children. The report addressed the fact that educational systems and society in general continued to reflect low expectations for this population *From Risk to Opportunity* (President's Advisory Commission on Educational Excellence for Hispanic Americans, 2003). It also included a proposed action plan on how to address this crisis to close the educational achievement gap. The six-point plan included preparing teachers more adequately, setting higher standards, engaging parents, and of course using scientific research to drive this agenda. The mantra for the plan was to "leave no (Hispanic) child behind."

As the rhetoric of meeting the needs of Hispanic families and students occurred at the federal level, the sociocultural and sociopolitical threats continued at the state and local levels. Proposition 227 took hold in California and revived an English-only movement that once again spread across the nation, disrupting programs, instituting English-only policies in schools, dismantling state certification programs, and providing a new opportunity for educators to pull out and dust off their "only English spoken here" signs from years past.

Proposition 227 reminded activists and educators of a hazardous neo-assimilationsist agenda. Although assimilation (or Americanization) purports to unite the population, it instead is a divisive and racist platform that divides the United States by labeling those who are not White or who speak another language as "other" or even "intruder." More recently, this same narrative has been used by Donald Trump to rally supporters threatened by cultural and racial diversity who refuse to view the nation's diverse demographics as a strength (McCaughan, 2020).

Current political agendas targeting low reading achievement, testing, and/or teacher preparation and instruction have changed little since No Child Left Behind (NCLB) legislation, or even the policies discussed in the 1930s, in that they are framed using a deficit perspective. Latine/o/x families and students continue to be denied programming based on a "science that is not limiting" and suffer from generational dissonance as a result of language loss and pressures to suppress cultural ties and identities (Ward et al., 2019). The ongoing and relentless agenda to whitewash the nation under the guise of Americanization has far-reaching impacts on present and future generations, as evidenced by the voices of our communities, families, and students.

These systemic patterns of racism, anti-culturalism, and linguicism toward Latine/o/x families and students, especially those who have recently immigrated to the United States, are and will continue to prove self-defeating for schools. In part, this is true because the number of Latine/o/x students attending public schools is on the rise across the country. In fact, the Latine/o/x student population in K–12 schools is the fastest-growing student population the United States and this trend is projected to continue (National Center for Education Statistics, 2022). As the historical pattern persists, so too will the failure of schools and school systems that have yet to assess how society has neglected to learn from the past to inform the future.

Twenty-plus years ago, originators of the idea of an NLD broached the prospect that the NLD could be different, with interethnic interaction there sufficiently new and improvisational, that it was not inevitable that the mistakes and racism of places that have long been home to Latine/o/x populations would be repeated. However, the borrowing of deficit and technocratic frames that dismiss Latine/o/x knowledges, cosmologies, and belonging means that the prospect of Latine/o/x finding more favorable processes and outcomes in the NLD has largely not been realized.

DIMMING OF THE DREAM: IMPACT OF POLITICS ON THE NEW LATINE/X/O DIASPORA

The premise of an "American Dream" for and with Latine/x/o populations remains elusive as the years pass. The concept itself has negated the narratives of Latine/x/o families while serving as the anchor for immigration politics that reify pervasive and even violent assimilation, particularly surrounding formal notions of schooling. Much like a crowd responds to "Fire, fire!" in a public setting, policies surrounding immigration and education are often reactive and chaotic, attempting to create order among the masses without understanding the blueprint of the structure aflame. Policies crafted to diffuse a particular "fire" or issue are usually created in isolation from the very same community they attempt to serve; that is, they provide a "solution" (i.e., policy/legislation) without including Latine/x/o communities in the process.

National discourse surrounding education and immigration often claim that educational programs will increase accessibility, productivity, and advancement for those who historically have been marginalized. Yet, such programs typically fail to center the communities they are intended to serve. Rather, they are often a quick fix that distracts the public, if only temporarily, from recognizing the instability of the system. Fueled by hegemonic norms that thwart inclusivity, equity, and substantive change, these policies endorse a stagnant definition of productivity and advancement while contradicting the very meaning of accessibility. Further, they place Latine/x/o students at the margins without involving families in the educational planning or decision-making processes for their children. These types of realities are illustrated through three vignettes that follow. We are intentionally not geographically stamping these vignettes. While we assert that each of them could transpire in Kansas, we also know that they just as easily could be describing Latine/o/x family experiences with U.S. schooling in other NLD states as well.

Vignette 1: Reaching From the Margins

The following vignette illustrates how reactive policies surrounding education and immigration can lead to the creation of programs that operate reactively, assigning a plan without knowing the narratives of families served. Instead of recognizing the assets of Latine/o/x students and families, these programs often operate from a deficit perspective. This pseudonymous vignette additionally illustrates how Latine/o/x students are often racialized and categorized.

> Mario Santos (6 years old) and his family arrived in the United States when he was only two years old. His parents, Rosa and Luis—both from Guatemala—decided to move because they were seeking a different/safer path for Mario. Upon arriving, Mario and his parents lived in a resourceful Afro-Latine/x/o & Latine/x/o community and their network of support comprised family and friends who were multilingual. While Mario grew up learning both Spanish and English simultaneously, his parents made the conscious decision to speak only Spanish at home so that Mario would be close to his *raíces* (roots) and keep his family connections in Guatemala. As a result, Mario developed during his early childhood in a rich multilingual environment.
>
> Prior to the start of first grade, his parents relocated the family to a nearby city for an employment opportunity. As Rosa and Luis were completing the school registration forms, they indicated that "a language other than English" was spoken at home in the home language survey. Given this and his Spanish-sounding last name, Mario was automatically placed in the ESL program as he waited to be tested. Unfortunately, his new school was short-staffed, so it took the ESL specialist three months to administer the intake test. Without this assessment, they could not determine whether Mario qualified for ESL services. Because this was a new community and school for them, Rosa and Luis were just beginning to create their networks of support. During that time, Mario was placed in a self-contained/sheltered ESL classroom.
>
> Four months into the school year, it was determined that Mario was a simultaneous multilingual student and did not require ESL services. Unfortunately, when he transitioned to his new classroom, Mario found it difficult to adjust to his new learning community and learn the routines already established. Rosa and Luis saw Mario's love for learning dwindle and became frustrated by the lack of responsiveness of the system.

In this vignette, assumptions were made that had lasting effects on Mario's educational outcomes. Programs, such as ESL programming, are intended to address educational equity for linguistically diverse communities, yet they often operate with a shortage of staff coupled with a "one size fits all" approach to decision making. Specifically, assumptions are often made regarding English proficiency and presumed knowledge base of parents (based on stereotypes) without knowing the biographies of families. Such assumptions are rooted in systemic racism that tie back to perceptions of Latine/x/o communities that have existed for centuries in this nation.

Vignette 2: Irreplaceable Loss

The following story demonstrates the generational dissonance that can happen when Latine/x/o students are continually pushed into an Americana narrative that is void of the language, stories, culture, and assets of Latine/x/o communities. As a result, younger generations feel compelled to choose between cultures (Bickham-Mendez & Barko-Alva, 2022; Huq et al., 2016), as seen with Celeste.

> Luisa (mother) and Celeste (daughter) are having issues communicating due to their drastically different language practices. Although Luisa attempted to raise Celeste speaking Spanish, her efforts have not been fully successful. Between working two shifts, a lack of dual language programming in the school district, and not having close access to Spanish-speaking community members, her efforts toward language maintenance have not resulted in the bilingual identity for her daughter that she had desired. Celeste now refuses to speak Spanish and uses a translation app to communicate with her mother and the rest of her family at home. Luisa is growing increasingly frustrated and believes Celeste is not even trying to use her family's home language. The ongoing confrontation is causing Celeste pain and frustration. She is questioning her identity and her roots on multiple levels.

The sociological and psychological impact for countless Latine/x/o adolescents like Celeste depicts one of the deepest levels of loss. Students are facing an internal struggle in finding a sense of belonging. Despite their rich cultural history, they are receiving messages that some of their prospective practices (like speaking Spanish) would inhibit their fitting into the larger society. Youth feel the undercurrent of the anti-immigrant movement that has been perpetuated for centuries, sending the message to reject aspects of the self that do not fit the norm. This undercurrent often leads to a growing disconnect between generations within the family.

Despite discrimination, cultural backlash from the dominant White society, pressures to assimilate, and policies that strip away the rich cultural and linguistic assets of Latine/x/o culture, many immigrant families continue to hold tight to the American Dream as a way out of turmoil or into a life of economic security and educational advancement, even if this means letting go of cultural traditions in order to "make it" in this country.

Vignette 3: First Do No Harm

This final vignette demonstrates the tensions or dissonance between generations within the Latine/x/o community as well as the ongoing trauma of having to justify one's being and positionality. It provides an opportunity to reflect on school and societal messages of upward mobility—and at what cost. As Shashi Tharoor (2016), international diplomat and scholar of imperial history, once observed, "If you don't know where you come from, how will you know where you are going?"

> Julissa Rodriguez is an elementary teacher in a predominantly Latine/x/o community. Although her parents spoke a mixture of Spanish and English with her in the home, they insisted she speak English in other settings partly because they grew up being reprimanded if they spoke Spanish at school or in the community at large. As a second-generation Latina, Julissa was raised to think that English equated to success. Now, because of her last name and skin tone, families within her school district assume she speaks fluent Spanish. She feels embarrassed that she cannot communicate fluently in Spanish but also frustrated that everyone assumes she speaks Spanish because or her surname and complexion.

Julissa's parents were a product of the English-only initiatives of the 1980s–1990s. To them, the ability to master the English language signified success in this country. Yet, 2 decades later, their daughter is expected by her community and society at large to know Spanish in order to be seen as authentically Latine/x/o. Like many, Julissa is searching within to find what it truly means to be Latina in today's world.

CONCLUSION

The vignettes show how societal constructions of Latine/x/o identities compounded by "one size fits all" approaches to schooling can negatively impact the lives of Latine/x/o families and perceptions of self. Pressures of "measuring up" to White mainstream notions of what it means to be "educated," "successful," and "American" have been a moving target for generations of Latine/o/x families. From Mexico ceding its land to the United States in 1848 to the presidential promises of Donald Trump in 2016 (to supposedly secure the U.S./Mexican border from "criminals and rapists"), a pervasive narrative that depicts Mexicans and the greater Latine/x/o community as "less than" has prevailed.

Over the decades, this deficit perception of Latine/o/x people has led to politics and programs within public schooling ostensibly intended to serve and enhance the progress of Latine/x/o families that in practice actually reproduce exclusive notions of what it means to be American. Beginning with nativist curricula and enforced language policies in the early 20th century and continuing with a push for increased standardization and testing fueled by NCLB, as well as continued language initiatives in the late 20th century, a "do unto" approach (that fully identifies what "they" need) fuels the script for the daily practices of public schooling. Although purportedly intended to enhance learning and success, this ongoing script has had lasting negative impacts resulting in generational dissonance, the prevention of upward mobility of families, and limited academic advancement for students who inherit and internalize it.

The "Fire, fire!" analogy used to illustrate the reactive and uninformed educational policies intended to protect those "in distress" (i.e., Latine/x/o families and students) also involves warning messages to families such as, "Your child doesn't speak English . . ." "Your child will never go to college." The system quickly responds with an "exit plan" without even knowing the families it serves, thereby usurping the families' agency. This technocratic approach to public schooling has never equitably served Latine/o/x families, whether recent immigrants or U.S. citizens born and raised in this country. The root cause is a racialized system that fails to recognize the cultural wealth of Latine/o/x communities and the contributions and assets they bring. We call bullshit on the rhetoric that continues to be presented to families. Until there is a commitment to culturally responsive and sustaining practices rooted in a radical connection/ kinship between Latine/x/o community members and public school representatives, the historical narrative that racializes and marginalizes the Latine/x/o population within the walls of schools and beyond will continue. Drawing on longer-standing U.S. framings of Latine/o/x populations in the NLD will never lead to inclusive, respectful, affirming, and broadly successful school experiences because these framings are exclusive, deficit-oriented, and discriminatory.

Although history is a narrative often told by the victors, it is also unending, with moments and movements that can change its trajectory. Such has been the case with the many Latine/o/xs who have persisted in maintaining their rich cultural practices and language traditions. In order for U.S. society to thrive, educators must *listen* and then lift and leverage the voices and lived experiences of those within Kansas, the NLD, and ultimately the country as a whole. *Persistence* is the tie that connects a history of struggle to the possibilities of today, and *unity* brings the momentum needed for systemic shifts that lead to lasting change.

REFERENCES

Acuña, R. (2021). *Occupied America: A history of Chicanos* (9th ed.) Pearson.
Alcoff, L. M. (2006). *Visible identities: Race, gender, and the self.* Oxford University Press.
Alcoff, L. M. (2015). *The future of whiteness.* John Wiley & Sons.
Bickham-Mendez, J., & Barko-Alva, K. (2022). "Yo era la única rara": Recently arrived immigrant high school students and belonging in Eastern Virginia (ELs) sense of

belonging within a high school-context. *Journal of Latinos and Education*, 22(5), 1969–1983. https://doi.org/10.1080/15348431.2022.2077335

Castañeda Shular, A., Ybarra-Frausto, T., & Sommers, J. (1972). *Literatura chicana; Texto y contexto. (Chicano literature; text and context)*. Prentice-Hall.

Chavez, L. (2013). *The Latino threat: Constructing immigrants, citizens, and the nation* (2nd ed). Stanford University Press.

Crawford, J. (1992). *Language loyalties: A source book on the official English controversy*. University of Chicago Press.

Ford, D. Y. (2004). *Intelligence testing and cultural diversity: Concerns, cautions, and considerations*. National Research Center on the Gifted and Talented.

Gándara, P., & Contreras, F. (2009). *The Latino education crisis: The consequences of failed social policies*. Harvard University Press.

García, O., & Baetens, B. H. (2009). *Bilingual education in the 21st century: A global perspective*. Wiley-Blackwell.

Getz, L. M. (1997). *Schools of their own: The education of Hispanos in New Mexico, 1850–1940*. University of New Mexico Press.

Gonzales, P. B. (2020). Promise and frustration: The history of Spanish-language bilingual education in New Mexico, 1849–1970. In R. B. Martínez & M. J. H. López (Eds.), *The shoulders we stand on: A history of bilingual education in New Mexico* (pp. 77–106). University of New Mexico Press.

Hamann, E. T. (2003). *The educational welcome of Latinos in the new South*. Praeger.

Hernandez, K. L. (2010). *Migra! A history of the U.S. border patrol*. University of California Press.

Herrera, S., & Murry, K. (2016). *Mastering ESL/EFL methods: Differentiate instruction for culturally and linguistically diverse students* (3rd ed.). Pearson.

Herrera, S., Murry, K., & Holmes, M. (2022). The trajectory of the invisible teacher: Latinx teachers in search of professional belonging. In C. D. Gist & T. J. Bristol (Eds.), *Handbook of research on teachers of color and indigenous teachers* (pp. 867–887). American Educational Research Association.

Huq, N., Stein, G. L., & Gonzalez, L. M. (2016). Acculturation conflict among Latino youth: Discrimination, ethnic identity, and depressive symptoms. *Cultural Diversity and Ethnic Minority Psychology*, 22(3), 377–385. https://doi.org/10.1037/cdp0000070

Kim, K. H., & Zabelina, D.L. (2015). Cultural bias in assessment: Can creativity assessment help? *The International Journal of Critical Pedagogy*, 6(2), 129–148.

Martin, K. (2015). *Comparative representations of Vermont migrant Latino farmworkers* [Honors thesis, University of Vermont]. UVM Patrick Leahy Honors College Senior Theses. https://scholarworks.uvm.edu/hcoltheses/75

McCaughan, E. J. (2020). "We didn't cross the border, the border crossed us": Artists' images of the US-Mexico border and immigration. *Latin American and Latinx Visual Culture*, 2(1), 6–31.

Mehta, J. (2013). The penetration of technocratic logic into the educational field: Rationalizing schooling from the progressives to the present. *Teachers College Record*, 115(5), 1–36.

Murry, K. G., Holmes, M., & Kavimandan, S. (2020). Approximating cultural responsiveness: Teacher readiness for accommodative, biography-driven instruction. *FIRE: Forum for International Research in Education*, 6(2), 103–124. https://eric.ed.gov/?id=EJ1248095

Murry, K., Kavimandan, S., Herrera, S. G., & Holmes, M. (2021). Phenomenological research on biography-driven instruction use in highly diverse classrooms. *Teacher Education Quarterly, 48*(2), 7–23.

National Center for Education Statistics. (2022). *Racial/ethnic enrollment in public schools*. U.S. Department of Education, Institute of Education Sciences. https://nces.ed.gov/programs/coe/indicator/cge

Ontiveros, R. J. (2014). *In the spirit of a new people: the cultural politics of the Chicano movement*. NYU Press.

Pac, T. (2012). The English-only movement in the US and the world in the twenty-first century. *Perspectives on Global Development & Technology, 11*, 192–210.

Phillipson, R. (1992). *Linguistic imperialism*. Oxford University Press.

President's Advisory Commission on Educational Excellence for Hispanic Americans. (2003). *From risk to opportunity: Fulfilling the educational needs of Hispanic Americans in the 21st century. The final report of the President's Advisory Commission on Educational Excellence for Hispanic Americans*. https://govinfo.library.unt.edu/eeha/paceea/finalreport.pdf

San Miguel, G., Jr., & Valencia, R. (1998). From the treaty of Guadalupe Hidalgo to Hopwood: The educational plight and struggle of Mexican Americans in the southwest. *Harvard Educational Review, 68*(3), 353–413.

Santa Ana, O. (2002). *Brown tide rising: Metaphors of Latinos in contemporary American public discourse*. University of Texas Press.

Schneider, B., Martinez, S., & Owens, A. (2006). Barriers to educational opportunities for Hispanics in the United States. In M. Tienda & F. Mitchell (Eds.), *Hispanics and the future of America* (pp. 179–227). The National Academies Press.

Tharoor, S. (2016). *An era of darkness: The British empire in India*. Aleph Book Company.

U.S. Commission on Civil Rights. (1972). *The excluded student: Educational practices affecting Mexican Americans in the Southwest*. U.S. Government Printing Office.

Ward, J. B., Vines, A. I., Haan, M. N., Fernández-Rhodes, L., Miller, E., & Aiello, A. E. (2019). Spanish language use across generations and depressive symptoms among US Latinos. *Child Psychiatry & Human Development, 50*(1), 61–71. https://doi.org/10.1007/s10578-018-0820-x

Zwiers, J. (2007). Teacher practices and perspectives for developing academic language. *International Journal of Applied Linguistics, 17*(1), 93–116.

CHAPTER 11

Transforming K–12 School District Structures to Center Latinx Newcomers

Megan Hopkins and Hayley Weddle

INTRODUCTION

Nativist sentiment and policy have long shaped the experiences of immigrants to the United States (Quinn et al., 2017). Latinx immigrants are often perceived by White Americans as threats to societal cohesion and stability, especially in recent decades as the size of the Latinx population has increased in communities across the country (Estep, 2017). Frequent are depictions of Latinx immigrants as "freeloaders" or "criminals" who do not contribute to U.S. society, especially those who have recently arrived to the United States (who we refer to as newcomers) and those who are undocumented (Newton, 2005). These nativist beliefs contribute to societal constructions of Latinx newcomers as undeserving of policy benefits, often legitimating the conferral of punitive policies onto this group (Ingram & Schneider, 2005; Schneider & Ingram, 1993).

These societal constructions can permeate K–12 school district policy and practice for Latinx newcomer students. For instance, as the national context became fervently anti-immigrant following the Trump administration, resulting increases in immigration enforcement at the local level negatively affected teachers' and students' everyday experiences in immigrant-serving schools (Ee & Gándara, 2020). Further, when broader perceptions of Latinx immigrants as criminals are unchallenged by district leadership, school personnel may respond to a rapid influx of Latinx newcomers by installing metal detectors and/or by requiring multiple forms of identification that effectively precludes undocumented families' enrollment in particular district services (Brezicha & Hopkins, 2016). Overall, much recent research describes the inequitable conditions and deficit-based approaches that newcomer students experience in U.S. schools (e.g., He et al., 2017; Kirksey et al., 2020).

Amidst these often-exclusionary political contexts, school districts are important mediating institutions that can either exacerbate or combat broader inequities (Oakes et al., 2005). More often than not, school districts serve as microcosms of the local community such that district-level policies and practices for newcomers tend to reflect long-standing community beliefs and norms (Hopkins et al., 2021). Yet district leaders can play an important role in shifting these beliefs and norms (Brezicha & Hopkins, 2016). By creating intentional structures that prioritize and integrate Latinx newcomers into the fabric of district policies and practices, leaders can promote positive constructions of newcomers that foreground their many cultural, linguistic, and experiential assets.

In this chapter, we describe what we have learned from engaging with community members and school personnel from several K–12 districts across the New Latinx Diaspora (NLD) that are experiencing rapid increases in their newcomer populations. Newcomers are a highly diverse group, encompassing subgroups such as English learners (ELs), refugees and asylees, unaccompanied minors, and students with limited or interrupted formal education (Umansky et al., 2018; U.S. Department of Education, 2017). Although not all newcomers are identified as ELs, we focused on districts serving newcomers who required assistance with language acquisition due to their score on an initial assessment of English proficiency.

The districts in our study tended to have well-articulated structures for serving two subgroups of newcomer ELs: refugees and students with limited or interrupted formal education (SLIFE). However, few explicit structures were in place for Latinx newcomers who did not fall into one of these groups, and they tended to be grouped either with other Latinx students or with other EL-identified students (Hopkins et al., 2021). Acknowledging these inequities, we build on our findings and present four dimensions that could serve to transform K–12 school district structures for *all* Latinx EL newcomers: (a) community partnerships, (b) welcoming processes, (c) innovate staffing models, and (d) instructional programs.

After providing more detail about our qualitative comparative study, we describe each of the four dimensions. For each dimension, we offer evidence-based scenarios and corresponding reflection questions to support educators with collaboratively navigating structural transformation around their Latinx newcomer populations. Although our study took place before the COVID-19 pandemic, the scenarios and reflection questions have applications across remote and in-person learning environments. To the greatest extent possible, the scenarios and questions also attend to the many inequities faced by Latinx newcomers amidst the pandemic, including limited access to technology and school personnel who speak their home languages, challenges to their well-being exacerbated by a hostile political context, and long periods of time waiting in transit at the U.S. border as Migrant Protection Program hearings were suspended.

THE RESEARCH STUDY

The information we present in this chapter draws on findings from a multiple-case study of six K–12 school districts serving large or growing newcomer EL populations (see Umansky et al., 2018). We focus on data collected in four of these six districts, as these four districts were situated in NLD states, two in the Northwestern United States and two in the Midwestern United States. All four districts were small to midsized (ranging from 3,000 to 40,000 students) and served racially, socioeconomically, and linguistically diverse populations. Across districts, between 5 and 40 percent of students were Latinx, between 40 and 75 percent were economically disadvantaged, and between 4 and 35 percent were formally identified as ELs. While each of the four districts served newcomers from Latin American countries, they also served newcomers from Africa, the Middle East, and the Pacific Islands.

In each district, we spoke to community partners, district leaders, and school staff from one elementary, one middle, and one high school. In total, data included 94 semi-structured interviews: 19 with district leaders, 26 with school leaders, 6 with counselors, 36 with classroom teachers, and 7 with community partners. The range of stakeholders represented helped to deepen our understanding of each district's approaches to serving newcomers across K–12, including how district-level supports unfolded at the school level. During interviews, we asked participants to reflect on their roles, their perceptions of newcomers' strengths and needs, the presence or absence of various supports (e.g., intake processes, instructional supports, family services), and partnerships with community-based organizations.

STRUCTURAL DIMENSIONS SUPPORTING TRANSFORMATION

In the following subsections, we describe four structural dimensions around which leaders can transform their systems: (a) community partnerships, (b) welcoming processes, (c) innovate staffing models, and (d) instructional programs.

Community Partnerships

Community partnerships played a critical role in transforming programming for newcomer students across the four NLD districts we studied. Such partnerships included collaborations with community- and faith-based organizations as well as government organizations and nonprofits focused specifically on providing refugee resettlement services. These community partners provided a range of services in collaboration with school districts, including after-school tutoring, educational summer camps, adult English classes, basic needs services (e.g., food and housing resources), and crisis intervention. In some cases, community organizations also worked with district and school staff to provide opportunities for trauma-informed professional learning for educators. One district leader emphasized the importance of the community in their work: "A welcoming environment [for newcomers] is not created by one person; it's created by the community."

The most effective partnerships demonstrated coherence across community- and district-provided services. One community partner described regularly connecting with district staff to avoid "duplication of their programs" with the goal of "making sure we are serving as many people as possible and meeting those needs." In two districts, advocates facilitated information and resource sharing across community-based organizations and included school district leaders and newcomer families in community network meetings. These networks helped align district and community services and promoted positive perceptions of newcomers. In one district, families signed an agreement so that staff from the district and community-based organizations could exchange information and develop streamlined, individualized services. One district leader described these exchanges: "We talk about what the needs are, and we set up a communitywide action plan to wrap around that family." Importantly, such collaboration was grounded in a shared belief in students' and families' assets. Reflecting this shared belief, a community partner described collaborative efforts across organizations as grounded in "viewing all [newcomers] as valued and contributing members of society."

Although some of the community-based services we heard about centered on refugee resettlement, there is much to be learned from the organizational approaches they took. District leaders in the NLD could begin by identifying community organizations, and collaborating with their staff to either identify opportunities to align their programs or to ensure the organization's services are extended to all newcomer students and families. Dedicating district staff to help foster these partnerships would also be beneficial, especially if these staff are from the community. In the following scenario, we describe the role that family liaisons can play in connecting school and community services, especially during periods of remote instruction.

LEVERAGING COMMUNITY PARTNERSHIPS AMIDST REMOTE LEARNING

Scenario: When taking attendance, a 10th-grade science teacher noted that two newcomer students on his roster had not logged in to any synchronous remote learning sessions since the quarter started two weeks ago. The school's family liaison informed him that these students' families may be worried about their immigration status, which might be contributing to the students' hesitation to check out computers from the school. The teacher sought advice from the principal, who asked the liaison to reassure the family that the school would protect their privacy and to encourage their children's attendance. The liaison also reached out to the director of a local immigrant advocacy organization to learn more about the families' concerns. The advocacy organization's director explained that, although she wasn't aware of specific cases, it was certainly possible that online interactions could be monitored. She suggested that the principal explore the Know Your Rights workshop for educators that was being offered by the national branch of their organization.

Reflection Questions:

1. What information or resources might organizations in your community have that could bolster district services for Latinx newcomers?

> 2. What approaches could district or school leaders take to create and/or maintain meaningful relationships with these organizations?
> 3. What district or school staff would need to be involved in community partnership efforts? What support would need to be in place to facilitate their involvement?

Welcoming Processes

In addition to connecting and aligning community and district programs and resources, we found that clearly articulated processes for welcoming newcomers into the school district were a central feature of transformative systems. Extending beyond brief intake interviews, the district staff we spoke with described extensive enrollment and integration processes, including linguistic, academic, and mental health assessments as well as school tours and introductory visits with teachers. One district staff member outlined the importance of attending to all aspects of newcomers' transitions into the school, including transportation: "If [newcomers] need to use transportation, we will have one of our liaisons ride with them on the bus so they have someone as a guide." When asked to reflect on the impact of these supports, the staff member shared, "The response from families is amazing [. . .] We are very excited about what we are doing."

Within districts with strong welcoming processes, staff described a shared value of promoting newcomers' integration into the community. One leader explained, "we really want [newcomers] to feel comfortable coming to our district, comfortable in our schools, and to feel like they are part of the community." In two districts, supporting newcomers as they transitioned into the district meant having a dedicated physical space, or "welcome center." These centers served as hubs to facilitate intake processes such as language proficiency testing, transcript review, and trauma assessments. In one district, educators collaborated with community partners who used the welcome center as a space for family orientations and adult language classes. Beyond having a dedicated space, district leaders described adapting the layout of these spaces over time to facilitate more "personal interaction" with newcomer students and their families. In the scenario below, district leaders are asked to expand their intake processes to promote Latinx newcomers' integration.

Innovative Staffing Models

As may already be evident, developing strong community partnerships and robust welcoming processes depends on the presence of qualified staff who recognize and appreciate newcomers' diverse needs and assets. Indeed, across all four NLD districts we studied, staffing was cited as foundational to developing coherent systems of support for newcomers. Each district employed innovative staffing models to transform their services for newcomer students and families.

> **EXPANDING WELCOMING PROCESS FOR LATINX NEWCOMERS THROUGH COLLABORATION**
>
> **Scenario:** As schools work to recover from the pandemic, the district EL coordinator has been receiving feedback from several teachers that they do not feel they have sufficient information to support their newcomer students. During remote learning, school staff relied on standard intake processes for newcomers that focused primarily on administering an initial language proficiency screener (i.e., the same process used for all ELs). Yet teachers are asking for more information about newcomers' backgrounds and experiences as they are struggling to develop effective instructional and socioemotional supports. The EL coordinator is eager to improve the district process and decides to convene a working group who will collaborate to develop a more robust newcomer welcoming process.
>
> **Reflection Questions:**
>
> 1. Who should be invited to participate in the working group to ensure the redesigned welcoming process better supports newcomer students and families?
> 2. How might partnerships with local organizations be leveraged to strengthen the process?
> 3. How will the process be adapted for both in-person and online environments?
> 4. How will the district know if the new process is effective?

Distinguishing themselves from districts in which newcomers were "sent off to the [English Language Development] teacher and forgotten," several leaders described the importance of centering newcomers in staffing decisions, even amidst scarce resources. In one high school, for instance, a leader created a hybrid teacher-counselor role to ensure that newcomers did not get "lost in the system" among other ELs. This teacher-counselor both provided guidance counseling and taught several newcomer-specific courses, helping to bridge instructional support with course placement processes.

Further illustrating intentional staffing approaches, three districts reported hiring bilingual assistants and/or cultural brokers to build and sustain relationships with newcomer students and families. One district employed cultural brokers to support a program called "Cross-Cultural Learning with Parents," during which brokers acted as interpreters for families who shared their experiences and insights with district leaders. Beyond family engagement, these specialized staff roles helped to ensure that other educators remained attuned to newcomer students. One school leader described these staff members as important for "protecting" newcomers, stating, "They protect [newcomers] from being neglected." The leader went on to explain that the presence of specialized staff helped to ensure that general education teachers prioritized newcomers, explaining "There's an understanding that we have created a system, and somebody would know [if newcomers were being ignored]." In this sense, newcomer-specific staff roles not only bolstered newcomer programming, but also promoted a broader culture of inclusion. In the scenario below, a bilingual assistant supports the classroom teacher in ensuring that her newcomer students are engaged in instructional activities in the remote learning environment.

Instructional Programs

Moving closer to classroom practice, district and school leaders described two priorities in developing instructional programs to support newcomer students: (a)

CONNECTING HOME AND SCHOOL THROUGH INNOVATIVE STAFFING

Scenario: Corina, a 3rd-grade teacher, was concerned when Esme, her new student from Honduras, did not sign in for her online small-group reading sessions on Tuesday and Wednesday. During her weekly check-in on Thursday with Betsabel, her bilingual assistant, Corina mentioned her concern. Betsabel said she was in regular contact with Esme's mother via WhatsApp, texting multiple times a week to make sure she had what they needed to sign into the online learning platform. On Friday morning, Betsabel emailed Corina to let her know that Esme had spent the week with her grandmother, who did not have Internet access, and would complete her school work by Monday. Corina made a note to follow up with Esme and her mother on Monday to address any questions they might have about the classwork.

Reflection Questions:

1. What structures and/or routines could be established to facilitate collaboration between bilingual assistants and teachers serving newcomers?
2. If the bilingual assistant or similar role does not already exist, what resources could be used to support this role? (For example: Could Title III funds be used? Could responsibilities for current instructional aides be shifted to take on this role? Could family members be hired to serve in this role?)
3. If these positions already exist, how can their assignments be adapted to provide the best "match" in terms of language and cultural understandings?

providing instruction specifically designed to support newcomers' educational needs and build upon their assets, and (b) creating opportunities for newcomers to engage with non-newcomer peers while learning academic content. As opposed to a one-size-fits-all approach, instructional programs were tailored to newcomers' backgrounds, strengths, and needs while also considering available staff and resources. Reflecting the value of newcomer-specific programs (like the International High School at Prospect Heights and Wellstone International High School, both profiled in Bajaj et al., 2023, pp. 26–30, 80–84), many secondary schools provided targeted instruction in "cluster models." An educator explained, "I'm a very firm believer that newcomers need to have a place where they know that's *their* place, the families know that's their place, and the liaisons are at that place." Aligning with this perspective, three districts intentionally placed newcomers in schools that offered specialized newcomer programs. One superintendent explained that this approach enabled newcomer students to feel "safe" and "supported," promoting a sense of belonging. While such programs can be structured in a variety of ways, the districts we studied tended to offer opportunities for newcomers to participate in some classes with other newcomers as well as in courses with the broader student body.

Complementing newcomer-specific programming, school staff also shared a desire to foster newcomers' integration across instructional settings and provide opportunities to develop relationships with non-newcomer peers. However, district and school leaders noted the importance of ensuring the preparedness of *all* teachers to provide effective linguistically and culturally responsive instruction. One school leader explained, "We need to make sure that 100% of our staff—not only the EL teachers—is highly qualified to serve newcomers." Another leader described "complications" stemming from teachers' lack of experience working with newcomers and cited the need for more robust teacher learning opportunities. As noted previously, one way to bolster access to newcomer expertise and strengthen teacher capacity is to partner with relevant community organizations.

SUPPORTING TEACHER PROFESSIONAL LEARNING

Scenario: A district's Latinx newcomer population continues to grow, and there is a shortage of EL-endorsed teachers across schools. To support COVID-19 recovery, the state provided the district with additional funds to support teacher professional learning. District leaders have decided to use those funds to develop all teachers' capacity to serve newcomers.

Reflective questions to consider:

1. How could district leaders assess teachers' professional learning needs as they pertain to newcomer students and families?
2. What partners could be engaged to help design and deliver the professional learning?

3. How can leaders motivate teachers' engagement with the professional learning opportunities and subsequent implementation in their classrooms?
4. How might collaboration between language and content educators support and extend teachers' professional learning opportunities?

CONCLUSION

As the Latinx population continues to grow in communities across the United States, transforming school district structures to effectively support Latinx newcomers is a pressing equity issue. In this chapter, we outlined four structural dimensions that, when attended to, can help to center Latinx newcomers in district transformation: community partnerships, welcoming processes, innovative staffing models, and instructional programs. As leaders attend to these dimensions, it is important to center students' and families' assets in ways that counter any deficit orientations or negative constructions of Latinx immigrants that may exist. Such constructions can stymie systems change efforts if not addressed explicitly, and often require leaders to actively engage stakeholders across the district and local community. As opposed to conceptualizing the four dimensions as independent, we encourage reflecting on opportunities for integration and alignment. For example, how might community partnerships be leveraged to bolster teacher professional learning opportunities? What kind of staff positions would facilitate welcoming processes for Latinx newcomer students and families? Fostering coherence across these structural dimensions represents a meaningful pathway to promote a culture of shared responsibility for Latinx newcomers across schools, districts, and communities.

REFERENCES

Bajaj, M., Walsh, D., Bartlett, L., & Martínez, G. (Eds.) (2023). *Humanizing education for immigrant and refugee youth: 20 strategies for the classroom and beyond*. Teachers College Press.

Brezicha, K., & Hopkins, M. (2016). Shifting the zone of mediation in a suburban new immigrant destination: Community boundary spanners and school district policymaking. *Peabody Journal of Education, 91*(3), 366–382. https://doi.org/10.1080/0161956X.2016.1184945

Ee, J., & Gándara, P. (2020). The impact of immigration enforcement on the nation's schools. *American Educational Research Journal, 57*(2), 840–871. https://doi.org/10.3102/0002831219862998

Estep, K. (2017). Constructing a language problem: Status-based power devaluation and the threat of immigrant inclusion. *Sociological Perspectives, 60*(3), 437–458.

He, Y., Bettez, S. C., & Levin, B. B (2017). Imagined community of education: Voices from refugees and immigrants. *Urban Education, 52*(8), 957–985. https://doi.org/10.1177/0042085915575579

Hopkins, M., Weddle, H., Bjorklund, P., Jr., Umansky, I. M., & Blanca Dabach, D. (2021). "It's created by a community": Local context mediating districts' approaches to serving immigrant and refugee newcomers. *AERA Open, 7.* https://doi.org/10.1177/23328584211032234

Ingram, H. M., & Schneider, A. L. (2005). Introduction: Public policy and the social construction of deservingness. In A. L. Schneider & H. M. Ingram (Eds.), *Deserving and entitled: Social constructions and public policy* (pp. 1–28). SUNY Press.

Kirksey, J. J., Sattin-Bajaj, C., Gottfried, M. A., Freeman, J., & Ozuna, C. S. (2020). Deportations near the schoolyard: Examining immigration enforcement and racial/ethnic gaps in educational outcomes. *AERA Open, 6*(1), 1–18.

Newton, L. (2005). It is not a question of being anti-immigration: Categories of deservedness in immigration policy making. In A. L. Schneider & H. M. Ingram (Eds.), *Deserving and entitled: Social constructions and public policy* (pp. 139–167). SUNY Press.

Oakes, J., Welner, K., Yonezawa, S., & Allen, R. L. (2005). Norms and politics of equity-minded change: Researching the "zone of mediation." In M. Fullan (Ed.), *Fundamental Change* (pp. 282–305). Springer.

Quinn, R., Hopkins, M., & García Bedolla, L. (2017). The politics of immigration and education. *Educational Policy, 31*(6), 707–715. https://doi.org/10.1177/0895904817725729

Schneider, A., & Ingram, H. (1993). Social construction of target populations: Implications for politics and policy. *American Political Science Review, 87*(2), 334–347.

Umansky, I. M., Hopkins, M., Dabach, D. B., Porter, L., Thompson, K., & Pompa, D. (2018). *Understanding and supporting the educational needs of recently arrived immigrant English learner students: Lessons for state and local education agencies.* Council of Chief State School Officers.

U.S. Department of Education. (2017). *Newcomer toolkit.* https://www2.ed.gov/about/offices/list/oela/new-comer-toolkit/ncomertoolkit.pdf

CHAPTER 12

Studying Up to Reimagine and Reframe the Dual Language Bilingual Education Agenda in the New Latino Diaspora

Jessica Mitchell-McCollough

If we are truthful, perhaps we will admit that supporters and proponents of dual-language immersion programs face a dilemma. They want to find ways to support language study among majority group members, and they want to provide minority children with access to the curriculum in a language they can understand. These two objectives, however, have very different agendas (Valdés, 1997, p. 419).

CONTEXT

Nebraska is a state long characterized by the settling of immigrants—think of Willa Cather's classic novel *O Pioneers!* (1992/1913), which is also a movie and an opera, for the end of the 19th century and *Reviving Ophelia* author Mary Pipher's (2003) *The Middle of Everywhere* for the beginning of the 21st century. Yet Nebraska is also one noteworthy for its resistance to pluralism. Nebraska was the first state in the United States to pass an English-only law, way back in 1919. More recently, then-governor Dave Heineman outspokenly rejected any unaccompanied Central American minors connecting with extended family in Nebraska in 2015 (Catalano, 2017; Meckler et al., 2014). Even the state's ostensibly self-deprecating 2018 state tourism campaign—"Nebraska: Honestly, it's not for everyone"—can be understood as anti-pluralist if taken seriously. The role of schools in teaching or not teaching various languages has long been a means for Nebraska to multifariously welcome and not welcome the different peoples who have been attracted to this patch of America's heartland. In recent decades, as Nebraska has experienced demographic changes across both urban and rural areas, especially a growth in Latinx populations (see Morales et al., Chapter 2, this volume), there have been various efforts in support of preparing teachers to meet the needs of shifting populations of students (Reeves &

Hamann, 2008), as well as explorations of dynamic shifts in educational programs offered to support students' unique language acquisition needs.

One such program that has recently experienced growth across a variety of contexts in Nebraska, and the United States writ large, is dual language bilingual education (DLBE)—in particular, two-way bilingual education (TWBE), which uses immersion to co-teach students from different language backgrounds. By design, DLBE is intended to move away from the segregated nature of schooling often used for emergent bi/multilingual students. Instead of a focus on English language acquisition, these programs are informed by an additive approach that engages with and grows students' full linguistic repertoire. When done well, these programs also propose to critically integrate and engage students from different backgrounds for most or all of the school day in attempt to foster both cross-cultural competence (Bearse & de Jong, 2008) and critical consciousness (Cervantes-Soon et al., 2017). TWBE programs vary in model, outlining the time spent in instruction between the partner language and English in ranges from 90/10 to the more popular 50/50, with the aim of simultaneously supporting students' development of academic literacy in both languages as they employ them to study required academic content. While DLBE can match any two languages, we are particularly interested in Spanish/English DLBE programs that enroll Spanish as a heritage language learners (HLL) as a prioritized portion of the total enrollment.

Accompanying this growth in DLBE across the United States, an increasing body of research in the field is directed at better understanding the successes and shortcomings of program models (e.g., Cervantes-Soon, 2014; Thomas & Collier, 2002), teaching and leadership practices (e.g., DeMatthews & Izquierdo, 2017; Palmer & Martínez, 2013), and the overall goals of DLBE (e.g., Palmer et al., 2019). The two-way immersion (TWI) program model has been both lauded for its literacy and academic language benefit (de Jong, 2004; Thomas & Collier, 2012), as well as cautioned against for the ideological constraints that risk the gentrification of such programs (Hamann & Catalano, 2021; Palmer, 2010; Valdez et al., 2016). What is clear is that DLBE is neither a simple fix nor a guaranteed pathway toward equitable education for the populations of students it aims to serve. Meanwhile, Valdés's "Cautionary Note" (1997), shared as this chapter's epigraph, still looms large as it names the still-relevant critique that neoliberal forces center the interests of the dominant group and marginalize the needs of the minoritized in DLBE (e.g., Flores, 2016; Valdez et al., 2016). Her critique also underscores a hope articulated by a number of researchers that explores educators' critical pedagogical practices as a framework to counteract inequities in DLBE (Heiman & Yanes, 2018).

Drawing from lessons learned through not-yet-published research on a proposed-but-not-yet-initiated TWBE program in a midsized school district in Nebraska, this chapter reimagines the possibilities if an integrative framework of language policy for clearly defined DLBE in the state was articulated. Traditionally, the DLBE literature has described the three pillars of biliteracy, bilingualism, and bicultural competence as foundational program goals. But Cervantes-Soon et al. (2017) have called for a fourth pillar of DLBE—critical consciousness. This chapter argues this fourth pillar should be created and reinforced at a systems level (not just a program level) through the creation of policy that will create space for critical pedagogies that hold at the center the interests, goals, and realities of minoritized populations that DLBE should aim to serve.

This chapter describes a proposed TWBE Spanish-English program for a midsized school district in Nebraska, focusing on the Spanish-speaking and heritage Spanish–speaking population. While newcomer populations in Nebraska are not exclusively Latinx, nor are all Latinx residents of Nebraska "new," this proposal substantially but not exclusively endeavors to improve schooling for and with the NLD. Consistent with the requirements of my Institutional Review Board, some of the details have been changed to protect anonymity.

A BOARD OF EDUCATION MISSES THE POINT

On a sunny spring day in 2017 in the early evening, a group of parents, university professors, teachers, and interested community members who were all stakeholders in one of the more successful, rapidly growing, and better funded school districts in Nebraska spoke at the normally scheduled Board of Education (BOE) meeting. This was to follow up on their request that the local school district explore the addition of a two-way bilingual education (TWBE) program to the district's elementary school offerings. This was the second time this group had visited a BOE meeting to request that such a program be added to the educational offerings of the school district. At a meeting the year before, the group had also proposed that such a program be adopted, with a diverse group of parents, representing maintenance, heritage, and world language constituencies (Delavan et al., 2017) citing their hope of raising bilingual kids. Teachers who spoke described an interest in improving graduation rates for the Latinx population within the district. Teacher education faculty representatives from a local university also touted the research-based benefits of such a program.

The 2016 call had also addressed potential funding sources for the new program, explaining what existing funds the district could repurpose. They pointed to the possible use of federal Title III funds that were then directed by the district only to English language learning (ELL) programs. As advocates noted, such programs promote subtractive language models in the schooling of bi-/multilingual students not yet proficient in English. In such ELL programs, students' existing capabilities in languages other than English are ignored.

In sum, the community group that gathered in 2017 had previously laid out a well-rounded argument as to the need for, benefits of, and resources to be employed to start a TWBE pilot program. They had even identified an elementary school with a statistically higher enrollment of Spanish-speaking students. In their return to the BOE in the spring of 2017, the goal of the community group was to follow up on their initial request for TWBE to be offered beginning with one program in one elementary school, redoubling their efforts with additional, yet still diverse community constituencies advocating for this program as an important resource for the future of children in the community. Among the many voices posing varied reasons for wanting TWBE, those representing both maintenance and heritage language constituencies continued to be represented as a driving force of the community group. One of these parents made clear what she had lost in her own struggle to maintain and regain the language of her heritage.

> I can't tell you enough how much my father's culture, half of my culture means to me ... he was a migrant and traveled so much and I missed out on developing my Spanish fluency as a child. I can't tell you how much it would have meant to me to have been a part of a dual language program, and now that I'm an adult and in college I struggle to develop my fluency in Spanish and regain my heritage language and it's a whole lot harder when you're older, so much harder when you're older. I feel like there was a piece of my childhood and my culture that was lost because I couldn't speak as deeply or as engaged with my grandparents and my aunts and uncles on my father's side. It was such a loss. So, I have two little ones in the [school district] and they would most definitely benefit from a dual language program. (Representative of dual language community group speaking at Board of Education meeting, April 25, 2017)

For several of the parents and teachers representing this community group in front of the BOE, the benefit a TWBE program was supporting of language maintenance and revitalization for the Latinx population living and learning within the community. They were not asking for an enrichment program, but rather for access to equitable schooling that would allow for the use of their full linguistic repertoires as a resource and support their children's ability to connect with the identities of their current and heritage communities. The request they presented to the school district was to prevent further cultural and linguistic loss. Addressing this request would require district leadership to both understand and respond to the growing population of Latinx students and their unique needs both contemporarily and historically, to acknowledge and include the linguistic capital of this community as already present within the district, and finally to recognize that in offering a TWBE program they would be building opportunity to privilege the abilities and resources of a minoritized but growing population within the district.

In the months that followed the April 2017 meeting, the BOE revisited the topic of TWBE during strategic planning discussions for the 5-year strategic plan that was to be adopted by the school district. Quickly taken up alongside conversations of TWBE was the promotion of World Language (WL) content classes for *all* elementary students to have access to the study of languages other than English, and thus have the opportunity to benefit from bilingualism. In these discussions, Spanish was not understood as a language of the community, but rather as one of many foreign languages that would allow students access to global opportunity. What emerged from this misunderstanding of TWBE and its pairing with WL courses was a dominant discourse championing the social forces of gentrification within TWBE, centering the interests of the dominant group and quieting the needs and wishes of the minoritized (Flores, 2016; Valdez et al., 2016) who had advocated for the needs of their children and community.

During more than 6 months of strategic planning in 2017–2018, TWBE and WL elementary course offerings were considered as possible aims for programs to add to the district's offerings. While TWBE would offer the potential for students to gain literacy in Spanish and English through content study, WL is distinct for its teaching of languages as a content area of its own, independent from all other content and curricula accessed by students across the school day. Most prevalent in the BOE discourse was the ideological underpinning that languages other than English are not local resources, but rather their "value" comes from how they offer a competitive advantage on the global scale. This discourse of globalization was often present alongside the conflation of TWBE and WL offerings as aiming to achieve the same end goal, disregarding the unique hegemonic forces and issues of equity surrounding both program models.

As the quote from a board member below alludes to, a few members of the BOE had recently visited schools in China in order to contextualize educational offerings globally. While it was clear that a key takeaway from their experience was the importance of bi- or multilingualism, that clarity was coupled with an end goal that promoted bilingualism for global access, rather as a local or heritage concern.

> I do feel that the world language goal is incredibly important and that is my top and only priority on this page. I would also include the dual language program . . . maybe there are some creative ways that would need to be sized, but I would love to have us look into it and figure out some kind of a way to make that happen. Maybe each of you are sick of hearing us talk about what we saw in China, but the idea that has the, you know, this competitive advantage of being bilingual or multilingual as the world continues to shrink. It was just amazing and I want our kids to have that. So I would just have the one bold language goal on this page. (BOE member during BOE meeting, October 24, 2017)

This side-by-side consideration of WL and TWBE being added as offerings in K–5 education often resulted in the TWBE program competing for priority in the strategic plan. WL was positioned as a program that could be offered to all elementary students, and in a variety of languages, not just Spanish. Elsewhere in the state, such elementary WL programs usually meant kids from English-speaking households learned how to count, say colors, and greet each other in another language, but there was little building of true linguistic competence.

While WL was to be introduced across the whole district, the TWBE program was proposed for just a single school pilot program that aimed at benefiting specific constituencies of students rather than broadly impacting all students across the district at once. As a board member's quote (below) indicates, leaders' support for TWBE was tepid and reflected their limited understanding of the concept and limited prioritization of the Latinx parents in particular who had advocated for it.

> I am, I'm not against a dual language program. I don't see that as being something that is at this point a priority in the next five years. I think we need to get all kids going towards it and then we find a way to intensify it. (BOE member during BOE meeting, October 24, 2017)

Rather than considering current students' languages other than English as a resource to expand on, blanket language content policy was preferred as a one-size-fits-all solution. Missing from the BOE commentary on adding language study to the strategic plan was acknowledgment from the community group that the TWBE model offered the possibility of both revitalizing and building critical cultural and linguistic capital from within the community and its current, often transnational, resources.

There were some members of the BOE whose conflation of WL and TWBE programs further involved English language learner (ELL) programs and the populations served by this offering. Rather than understanding the proposed Spanish-English TWBE as serving both Spanish-speaking constituencies and English-speaking constituencies, TWBE was identified as further complication for ELL constituencies who lacked both Spanish and English.

> If we put it in a neighborhood school, as was proposed to us, I want to know where the students who don't speak Spanish or English go? And I'm thinking that the wonderful ELL teacher who says oh this is really good, my student now has to learn two new languages because they came here with a third language. (BOE member during BOE meeting, October 24, 2017)

Together with the conflation of TWBE for WL, the premise that some ELL constituencies (a constituency identified in deficit terms by the way) would be extra disadvantaged (a claim not supported by research) cemented the idea that language study as proposed was in fact not for all students. This further precludes the potential success of the community group in achieving its goal of connecting TWBE in the district with community language, identity, and even the potential for language pride. Using terminology made famous by Richard Ruiz (1984), superseding this appeal were both "language-as-problem" orientations toward students already served within ELL programs and neoliberal discourse that oriented "language-as-resource," but only for students who had already acquired English language proficiency.

Finally, one member of the BOE questioned the inclusion of language as a goal within the strategic plan at all. While the original goal of DLBE was largely ignored within the discourse, the group requesting that TWBE be added to the district was politicized for an attempt to influence the strategic plan.

> I wonder if we went to language because we were lobbied by a group that has something they're very passionate about. A good idea, it's a great idea, but is that really the way of a global ready citizen? (BOE member during BOE meeting, October 24, 2017)

The framing of the community group's request as "lobbying" further demonstrates the power of English language hegemony in language policy and planning in schools. All decisions about what languages to teach are political, but only the prospect of creating TWBE was characterized as such here. Even though this idea was presented by an organized group from the community following the process set by the BOE for communicating and sharing ideas and concerns, they were framed (and eventually disregarded) as lobbyists when requesting a program to meet the specific needs of a contemporarily and historically marginalized group of students. Rather than seeking to understand the varied interests of the constituencies represented by the community group, the BOE worked simply to understand the request for a TWBE program from their preexisting orientations of language learning and language education as additional content to be added to the district's educational offerings with disregard for the varied constituencies they serve and the languages they bring with them into the classroom. Lost in translation were the more complex needs and possibilities to be met by a TWBE and the benefits such a program could offer to all.

Ultimately, creating some version of two-way instruction was added to the district's 5-year strategic plan, with a feasibility study as a loosely characterized first step. However, it is now 5 years later as of this writing and no such study or plans for a program have been publicly shared by the district. What seems to have been a simple community-driven request—the addition of TWBE to a school district that thinks of itself as both strong and progressive—remains stalled even though the state has several DLBE programs, two of which have been successfully sustained for more than a decade and three more that are newer.

All of the chapters in this volume describe a problem and then challenge the author to propose ways to resolve that problem. I am claiming that it is problematic that we keep denying any value to preserving and enhancing Spanish for constituents who have Spanish as a heritage language. Furthermore, I am claiming that the existing structure that ostensibly allows for constituent advocacy to the school board is inadequate for Latinx parent and student constituencies to be heard. While it is easy (and accurate!) to describe these problems as hegemonic, I am proposing that TWBE could get a better reception if the state department of education laid out a framework regarding both how and why it could be pursued.

A STATE MISPLACES DLBE

It is no secret that competing interests exist within DLBE. The tension in top-down language education policy versus grassroots additive language practices has raised the need to warn against hard-to-shake embedded systems of inequity (Valdés, 1997). Scholars have noted the crucial role that language ideology plays in creating policies enacted every day in additive bilingual programs

(Freeman, 2004; Palmer, 2011; Pérez, 2004) and language policy seems implicated here in what was *not* created. Additionally, the neoliberal commodification of the non-English partner language within DLBE has proven problematic (Cervantes-Soon, 2014; Cervantes-Soon et al., 2017; De Jong & Howard, 2009; Delavan et al., 2017; Varghese & Park, 2010), resulting in additional possibilities for inequity. But DLBE being de facto blocked is not a better outcome than DLBE being gentrified.

Although there is evidence that teachers are central to language policy implementation through their interpretation of top-down language policy and, thus, their local construction of language policy at the classroom level (Hornberger & Johnson, 2007; Menken & García, 2010; Ricento & Hornberger, 1996), it must be underscored that local level policy is mediated by district, state, and federal language policies (Hamann & Lane, 2004). While teachers have agency within their classroom spaces, these same spaces are regulated by and consequently in tension with the structure built by top-down educational policies. For framings of agency in tension with structure, see Bourdieu (1991) and Foucault (1995).

The teachers who petitioned the BOE in favor of TWBE were not deferred to as experts, even as they (and the university professors) shared why TWBE would be a good idea. So let's situate the community organization's request for TWBE and the BOE's conflation of TWBE with WL in the larger context of the state of Nebraska's educational interaction with DLBE. A near contemporaneous 2019 review of the Nebraska Department of Education's (NDE) website looking for resources for DLBE found references to dual language immersion in both the WL and ELL state program sites. These positioned DLBE as both a WL and an ELL program and thus positioned students served by the program as either WL learners or English language learners (ELLs). There was no explanation or mediation offered for the different pedagogies or expected outcomes by students served by WL and ELL programs. The prospect of heritage learners of Spanish, who were not deficient in English (to use momentarily the intrinsic deficit framing of the labels EL and ELL) and who were neither WL nor ELL constituencies, appears to not have been considered. (A 2022 perusal of the NDE website showed that the pages reviewed in 2019 were unchanged and remained as the department's outward articulations of goals and strategy.)

Newer exploration of the state's site showed increasing misrepresentation of the populations and outcomes imagined for DLBE. Under the umbrella of ELL programs, the only offering was a link to an off-site tool kit for early childhood educators working with young children and families that speak multiple languages (https://www.education.ne.gov/natlorigin/dual-language-learners-toolkit/). This implied that only early childhood educators benefit from resources to work with multilingual students and families and setting up the question: What is/are the expected language(s) of education beyond early childhood? There was little else offered by way of information around DLBE on the ELL education site.

As of April 2, 2022, World Language Education included more detailed information about DLBE on three separate pages. These highlighted program benefits, instructional features, programs in the state, and a brief description of immersion programs. The benefits highlighted from the state's WL perspective included:

- Increase language skill and proficiency in two languages, no matter the student's first language.
- Build cognitive flexibility, increased attention and memory, and superior problem-solving skills.
- Increase performance on standardized tests in English.
- Generate more positive attitudes towards other cultures.
- Have higher attendance rates and fewer dropouts. (https://www.education.ne.gov/worldlanguage/educator-resources/dual-language/)

While this list includes benefits offered to multiple constituencies to be served within DLBE programs, the lack of detail masks which benefits might be of greater interest or outcome to one imagined constituency versus another. This leaves room for DLBE to be manipulated toward neoliberal interests. Finally, under the umbrella of World Language Education, the state has one additional page that details program models of "Elementary World Language," listing first "Dual Language Immersion Programs" followed by "Foreign Language in Elementary School." Although this site offers an improved contrast in these two program models, the discourse used to explain DLBE positions the different constituencies served in troubling ways.

> English language learners who are using their native language as the second language benefit in gaining academic ground otherwise lost to language barriers while building English literacy. Students who are native English speakers benefit from an enriched, high performing education. (https://www.education.ne.gov/worldlanguage/educator-resources/for-elementary-middle-and-high-school-programs/program-models-for-elementary-world-language/)

Thus, the state positions students that are native speakers of the partner language within DLBE from a "language-as-problem" (Ruiz, 1984) perspective while simultaneously offering native speakers of English an "enriched" education neoliberally commodified as "high performing." There is a noteworthy contrast in language orientation toward both groups. For native speakers of the partner language, language is a *problem* to be overcome for the purpose of increasing English literacy, whereas for native speakers of English TWBE offers language as a *resource* (Ruiz, 1984) to enhance their school performance. It is no wonder that the local BOE highlighted in the earlier case struggled in their positioning of TWBE as an offering to be added to the district's programming. Their conflation of TWBE as a WL program, as well as the contrasting language orientations offered to the different constituencies to be served, was mirrored in the state department of education's own framework. In other words, the imagining of what was possible and desirable at the BOE and state levels were similar.

STUDYING UP TO REIMAGINE DUAL LANGUAGE BILINGUAL EDUCATION IN THE NLD

Consistent with the goals of this edited volume, I now aim to reimagine the path forward to resist the furthering of inequities in schooling within the NLD. The task of how to endorse and disseminate information around DLBE is as complex as the converging of interests of the varied constituencies such schooling aims to accommodate. However, given the documented inequities faced by the minoritized population of students that DLBE aims to repair, state departments of education, such as the Nebraska Department of Education, need mechanisms to uphold fidelity to the equitable design of such models, to center the interests of the minoritized populations, and to communicate these ideas to school districts designing and implementing DLBE. While both parents and university professors were joining with the community group to advocate for TWBE as a model for schooling that could improve outcomes for the Latinx population of students served by this school district, their combined voices alone for a few minutes at a BOE meeting were not enough. The significant embedding of neoliberal language ideologies and the lack of a top-down framework to support an in-depth understanding of DLBE and the language constituency at the center of its design impeded the clear reception of their request.

DLBE and the TWBE models can falter by catering to the native English-speaking (read largely White) student population rather than to the Latinx population that brings Spanish (whether well developed or not) as a heritage language. Acknowledging that risk and monitoring to prevent its realization, however, are possible and certainly better than having no DLBE program at all. So, if school boards are prospective obstacles to the creation of language, culture, and identity-affirming DLBE programs (that also bring the academic advantages previously mentioned), then we need to "study up" (Hamann, 2003; Nader, 1972), to think through what kind of program evidence and from whom would be persuasive to a BOE. I propose that getting Nebraska's state department of education to describe criteria for a good TWBE program (or other DLBE models) might be a way to be persuasive to a body willing to ignore/reject the heterogeneous collection of stakeholders who pushed for a TWBE program in 2016 and 2017. Unlike a school board (which is composed of earnest and often elite local politicos whose expertise is usually not education), the state department of education is a body of professional educators who are charged with being up-to-date on the research and the programs that yield various desirable results.

Petitioning the Nebraska Department of Education to describe DLBE models positions that body more systematically and overtly to support and help guide what are currently varied and largely autonomous programs rising in various locales across the state. The same evidence reviewed earlier about both the virtues of DLBE and its various prospective pitfalls can be summoned to help the state department of education articulate its standards and build support capacity. Children benefit from communities in which the languages they speak are both supported and valued (Reese & Goldenberg, 2006) by placing English-dominant children in classrooms where a community language other than English is privileged for part or the majority of the day; the message we should be leaning on is that it is their responsibility to learn and use the languages of their community in addition to English, that they are important in schooling and community, and that they are to be shared in social and professional communities with the same privilege currently enjoyed by the status of English. To shift the position of students within these programs we need to study up and double-down on the call to expand "our understanding of who we call a student" (Hamann, 2003, p. 443). Boards of education ostensibly are willing to "listen to the experts" (even as they overlook the expertise of current teachers and nearby education scholars speaking as concerned citizens). That means we need to think about how to package that expertise in ways that will be compelling, holistic, and unlikely to be substantially distorted.

As a product for the Great Plains Equity Assistance Center, Hamann and colleagues (2022) recently published a *Planning Guide for Starting Dual Language Programs*. Their guide, echoing teacher Dan Moran's experience starting a dual language program in Fremont, Nebraska, after being part of one in Omaha, presumes that the initiative for a DLBE program will come from the grassroots. Clearly in the not-yet-realized case shared here, grassroots perspectives matter (failure to listen to parents' goals for their kids to "not lose a language" would be problematic), but also they were clearly not enough to successfully move the local BOE to action. By proposing that added capacity and articulation at the state level could reinvigorate and support the stalled effort that I have been studying, I am imagining a kind of pincer, that is both top-down and grassroots, with the top-down part attentive to how BOE members hear and heed (and how they do not). "Research says" was not enough; parents' articulations of "our children deserve" were not enough. But perhaps adding, "and pursuant to state parameters and guidance, we could . . ." would suffice to get the board to move from misunderstanding and mischaracterizing to actually hear and see what viable, responsive, and affirming programs can look like and why they would be desirable to multiple constituencies in the district. Utah has had substantial success starting DLBE programs (Delavan et al., 2017). If Nebraska followed Utah's lead, perhaps local Nebraska districts like the one I studied wouldn't almost begin a new program. Perhaps, instead, they would actually pull it off.

REFERENCES

Bearse, C., & de Jong, E. J. (2008). Cultural and linguistic investment: Adolescents in a secondary two-way immersion program. *Equity and Excellence in Education, 41*(3), 325–340.

Bourdieu, P. (1991). *Language and symbolic power*. Harvard University Press.

Catalano, T. (2017). When children are water: Representation of Central American migrant children in public discourse and implications for educators. *Journal of Latinos and Education, 16*(2), 124–142.
Cather, W. (1992). *O pioneers!* (Reissue ed.). Vintage. (Original work published 1913)
Cervantes-Soon, C. G. (2014). A critical look at dual language immersion in the new Latin@ diaspora. *Bilingual Research Journal, 37*(1), 64–82.
Cervantes-Soon, C. G., Dorner, L., Palmer, D., Heiman, D., Schwerdtfeger, R., & Choi, J. (2017). Combating inequalities in two-way language immersion programs: Toward critical consciousness in bilingual education spaces. *Review of Research in Education, 41*(1), 403–427.
De Jong, E. J. (2004). After exit: Academic achievement patterns of former English language learners. *Education Policy Analysis Archives, 12*, 50. https://doi.org/10.14507/epaa.v12n50.2004
De Jong, E. J., & Howard, E. (2009). Integration in two-way immersion education: Equalising linguistic benefits for all students. *International Journal of Bilingual Education and Bilingualism, 12*(1), 81–99.
Delavan, M. G., Valdez, V. E., & Freire, J. A. (2017). Language as whose resource? When global economics usurp the local equity potentials of dual language education. *International Multilingual Research Journal, 11*(2), 86–100.
DeMatthews, D. E., & Izquierdo, E. (2017). Authentic and social justice leadership: A case study of an exemplary principal along the US-Mexico border. *Journal of School Leadership, 27*(3), 333–360.
Flores, N. (2016). A tale of two visions: Hegemonic whiteness and bilingual education. *Educational Policy, 30*(1), 13–38.
Foucault, M. (1995). *Discipline and punish: The birth of the prison*. Vintage Books.
Freeman, R. (2004). *Building on community bilingualism*. Caslon Publishing.
Hamann, E. T. (2003). Imagining the future of the anthropology of education if we take Laura Nader seriously. *Anthropology & Education Quarterly, 34*(4), 438–449.
Hamann, E. T., & Catalano, T. (2021). Picturing dual language and gentrification: An analysis of visual media and their connection to language policy. *Language Policy, 20*(3): 413–434.
Hamann, E. T., Catalano, T., & Moran, D. (2022). *Planning guide for starting dual language programs*. Midwest and Plains Equity Assistance Center.
Hamann, E. T., & Lane, B. (2004). The roles of state departments of education as policy intermediaries: Two cases. *Educational Policy, 18*(3): 426–455.
Heiman, D., & Yanes, M. (2018). Centering the fourth pillar in times of TWBE gentrification: "Spanish, love, content, not in that order." *International Multilingual Research Journal, 12*(3), 173–187.
Hornberger, N. H., & Johnson, D. C. (2007). Slicing the onion ethnographically: Layers and spaces in multilingual language education policy and practice. *TESOL Quarterly, 41*(3), 509–532.
Meckler, L., Reinhard, B., & Nicholas, P. (2014). *Flood of child migrants spurs local backlash*. Wall Street Journal. http://online.wsj.com/articles/flood-of-child-migrants-spurs-local-backlash-1405294984
Menken, K., & García, O. (2010). Introduction. In K. Menken & O. García (Eds.), *Negotiating language policies in schools: Educators as policymakers* (pp. 1–12). Routledge.
Nader, L. (1972). Up the anthropologist: Perspectives gained from studying up. In D. Hymes (Ed.), *Reinventing anthropology* (pp. 284–311). Pantheon Books.

Palmer, D. (2010). Race, power, and equity in a multiethnic urban elementary school with a dual-language "strand" program. *Anthropology & Education Quarterly, 41*(1), 94–114.

Palmer, D. (2011). The discourse of transition: Teachers' language ideologies with in transitional bilingual education programs. *International Multilingual Research Journal, 3*(2), 72–79.

Palmer, D. K., Cervantes-Soon, C., Dorner, L., & Heiman, D. (2019). Bilingualism, biliteracy, biculturalism, and critical consciousness for all: Proposing a fourth fundamental goal for two-way dual language education. *Theory Into Practice, 58*(2), 121–133.

Palmer, D. K., & Martínez, R. A. (2013). Teacher agency in bilingual spaces: A fresh look at preparing teachers to educate Latina/o bilingual children. *Review of Research in Education, 37*(1), 269–297.

Pérez, B. (2004). *Becoming biliterate: A study of two-way bilingual immersion education.* Lawrence Erlbaum Associates.

Pipher, M. B. (2003). *The middle of everywhere: Helping refugees enter the American community.* Houghton Mifflin Harcourt.

Reese, L., & Goldenberg, C. (2006). Community contexts for literacy development of Latina/o children: Contrasting case studies. *Anthropology & Education Quarterly, 37*(1), 42–61.

Reeves, J., & Hamann, E. (2008). Preparing Nebraska teachers to see demographic change as an opportunity: Reflections on immigrant integration and the role of government, communities, and institutions. *Journal of Latino/Latin American Studies, 3*(1), 56–75.

Ricento, T. K., & Hornberger, N. H. (1996). Unpeeling the onion: Language planning and policy and the ELT professional. *TESOL Quarterly, 30*(3), 401–427.

Ruiz, R. (1984). Orientations in language planning. *NABE Journal, 8*(2), 15–34.

Thomas, W. P., & Collier, V. P. (2002). *A national study of school effectiveness for language minority students' long-term academic achievement.* Center for Research on Education, Diversity & Excellence.

Thomas, W. P., & Collier, V. P. (2012). *Dual language education for a transformed world.* Dual Language Education of New Mexico.

Valdés, G. (1997). Dual-language immersion programs: A cautionary note concerning the education of language-minority students. *Harvard Educational Review, 67*(3), 391–429.

Valdez, V. E., Freire, J. A., & Delavan, M. (2016). The gentrification of dual language education. *Urban Review 48*, 601–627.

Varghese, M. M., & Park, C. (2010). Going global: Can dual-language programs save bilingual education? *Journal of Latinos and Education, 9*(1), 72–80.

CHAPTER 13

The Bureaucratic Paradox
Newcomer Unaccompanied Children, Educational Access, and Strategies for Increasing Flourishing Through an Ecosystem of Care

Sophia Rodriguez, Lisa Lopez-Escobar, and Katya Murillo-Valencia

INTRODUCTION

In 2021, over 100,000 children registered with the Office of Refugee Resettlement (ORR) and were officially labeled unaccompanied minors. Of these youth, over 70% were between ages of 15 and 17 (ORR, 2022). This is just one segment of the migrant population to the United States, and our focus in this chapter is migrant youth, particularly those with unaccompanied status, who face barriers to accessing the social and educational resources and capital necessary to navigate many social and educational systems. We argue this population is made visible through institutional practices and labels while also being neglected and excluded largely due to the policies and institutions that claim to be helping them. Through our inquiry of terms and conceptual literature alongside our anecdotal data from an ongoing study, we aim to reveal how a neglect/surveillance paradox functions to potentially perpetuate inequality for newcomer immigrant youth and call for how we conceptualize supports.

The United States defines an unaccompanied minor as an immigrant who is under the age of 18 and not in the care of a parent or legal guardian at the time of entry, who is left unaccompanied after entry, and who does not have a family member or legal guardian willing or able to care for them in the arrival country. Unaccompanied minors, or "newcomer youth," are part of a large global migrant group that are settling in the United States due to high rates of violent crime, gang violence and recruitment, and severe economic insecurity in their home countries (Zak, 2020). Upon arrival in the United States, unaccompanied minors face strict and often inhumane policies, mistreatment, deplorable conditions, and procedures designed to keep as many of them in custody as possible. Currently, 8,500 migrant teens and children who crossed the border without their parents are being housed in Department of Health and Human Services shelters, with 87% of those in custody between the ages of 13 and 17 (Levinson, 2020; Miroff, 2021).

For unaccompanied immigrant youth who eventually settle in the United States, barriers to integration persist, including inadequate support for navigating complex immigration and K–12 education systems, as well as a legal system in which unaccompanied minors have no right to legal counsel, even when facing deportation. For the schools and districts that serve these students, a lack of federal financial assistance and a reliance on ad hoc local support systems only deepen existing obstacles. Yet, unaccompanied youth maintain educational rights despite challenges during and after the detention process (Wiseman et al., 2020). We approach this chapter through our positionalities as researchers and educators and our connections with immigrant communities. Having taught and/or worked with immigrant communities, especially newly arrived students, we know the multiple systems that this population enters into upon arrival to the United States. Knowing how complex bureaucratic processes and education and social systems can be, we ground this chapter in our lived experiences and also in those of the newcomers with whom we have worked (Rodriguez, 2019, 2021).

In this effort, we have several guiding questions and aims in this chapter that we hope will be useful to policy and practice. First, we aim to understand the various terms and names used to apply to this youth population. In many cases, we hear "newcomer" used at the local or school level, and or more legal terms at policy levels such as unauthorized or unaccompanied. Thus, the first part of this chapter seeks to understand the terminology for and about newcomer unaccompanied migrant youth. Second, we share preliminary findings from an ongoing longitudinal study of two school districts in Maryland—where we are situated—and where two of the largest school districts also receive the large numbers of unaccompanied children—approximately 3,000 in 2021. Conducting this study prompted reflection about terminology use, the labeling of young people, and access to resources. It also raised conceptual questions about how policy and practice ought to support newcomer youth. Third, and from our preliminary findings of challenges and barriers for newcomers, we offer a conceptual framework for policymakers and practitioners to improve the belonging and access for newcomer unaccompanied youth. We expect that framework to assist the imagineering of more inclusive, successful educational spaces.

Labels and Discursive Practice

We examined how the term or label "newcomer" was used or not used in the policy and scholarly literature and documents. This was prompted by the first author's (Rodriguez) previous research and encounter with the conflation of terms related to migrant youth and how such labels impact access to resources (Rodriguez, 2019). In addition, labeling is not something that occurs in a vacuum (Oboler,

1995); rather there are social and political consequences and effects that manifest as part of naming and labeling as a discursive practice (Hacking, 1999).

As part of this process, we generated a list of terms (Table 13.1) to investigate based on previous research, empirical findings, and our familiarity with terms used by practitioners in the field of migration. We were curious to learn whether these terms were used interchangeably in policies, since our findings from work with practitioners suggested variation in term use and oftentimes the conflation of terms like newcomer with unaccompanied. Initially, we simply started looking for definitions of the terms on the Internet and found that the best way to approach this was to start by looking for legal definitions of the terms, if they existed. Next, we looked for legal definitions in international-, federal-, and state-level contexts, often referring to United Nations conventions and websites as well as U.S. law and codes. With the terms "asylum seeker" and "refugee," for example, we found that there are both international and federal definitions of the terms that provide protection for people who fall under those categories. We included sources for both international and national definitions to note the consensus on the terms at the international level, but we found it particularly important to note the federal definitions as they provide clear services or protections to these populations in the United States.

Although many of the terms did have some degree of legal framing at the international, state, or local level, there were other terms—namely, "newcomer" and "undocumented," often understood as umbrella terms—that did not. For these terms, we looked for definitions used on nonprofit and education-related websites to gauge how practitioners understand them. For the table, we prioritized federal and international legal definitions when possible.

From this initial review of terminology, we found that while many of the terms used in research and in law provide certain protections and services, the terms practitioners use do not. Because these umbrella terms are conflated and there are no specific protections for the practitioners' terms, it becomes difficult for practitioners to provide the support that is necessary for students who fall under one or many of these terms. A teacher (and others) must work with a refugee in a certain way; there are no corresponding expectations for their work with newcomers even though the two terms can be referencing the same person. The legal limitations and disconnect between theory, law, and practice create what we refer to as a bureaucratic paradox (described later).

Newcomer Immigrants and Educational Barriers and Opportunities

We uncovered several themes relevant to understanding newcomers' experiences and immigrant youth specifically. They related to curriculum, language meaning, and adaptation to new contexts of reception that impact newcomers' experiences and pre- and post-migration effects (Bajaj & Bartlett, 2017; Heidbrink, 2020; Hernandez et al., 2019; Suárez-Orozco et al., 2010) and the types of schools newcomers attend—that is, traditional public or the international network of schools

Table 13.1. Newcomer Terms

Term	Level	Definition	Source/Citation
Asylum seeker	International	Any person whose claim for sanctuary has yet to be processed. Not every person who seeks asylum will attain refugee status.	United Nations High Commissioner for Refugees. (n.d.). *Asylum-seekers*. UNHCR. https://www.unhcr.org/en-us/asylum-seekers.html
	Federal	Any person who arrives in the United States through a port of entry, or who is already physically present in the United States, who meets the requirements determined by the Secretary of Homeland Security or the Attorney General under this section if the Secretary of Homeland Security or the Attorney General and applies for asylum.	Immigration and Nationality Act, 8 U.S. Code § 1158 (1952).
Displaced person	International	A person who has been deported from, or has been obliged to leave, their country of nationality or of former habitual residence. That is, persons who were compelled to undertake forced labor or who were deported for racial, religious, or political reasons.	62(I). Refugees and Displaced Persons
Disrupted schooling	Local/District	Learners who have had limited or no previous schooling or significant schooling gaps due to interrupted or disrupted education.	Montgomery County Public Schools. Multidisciplinary Education, Training, and Support (METS) Program—Montgomery County Public Schools, Rockville, MD. (n.d.). https://www.montgomeryschoolsmd.org/curriculum/esol/instruction/mets

Term	Level	Definition	Source
Newcomer	Federal	A person who was not born in the United States and has recently arrived to the country; the term is often used to refer to a broad category of immigrants such as asylum-seeking children, immigrant children and youth, English language learners, unaccompanied youth, etc.	U.S. Department of Education, Office of English Language Acquisition. (2016). *Newcomer tool kit*. https://www2.ed.gov/about/offices/list/oela/newcomers-toolkit/ncomertoolkit.pdf
Refugee	International/Federal	Any person who is outside of their national country, or for someone who has no national country, the country of most habitual residence, who is unable or unwilling to return to that country for fear of persecution based on race, religion, nationality, membership in a particular social group, or political opinion.	Convention Relating to the Status of Refugees, July 25, 1951. Immigration and Nationality Act, 8 U.S. Code (USC) § 101(a)(42) (1952).
Unaccompanied	Federal	A child who (a) has no lawful immigration status in the United States, (b) is under 18 years of age, and (c) has no parent or legal guardian in the United States, or no parent or legal guardian in the United States available to provide care and physical custody.	6 USC § 279(g)(2) (2011).
Unauthorized	Federal	A foreign-born person who is not currently a legal resident of the United States. An unauthorized person may have entered the United States without inspection or was admitted into the country temporarily and overstayed their visa.	U.S. Government. (n.d.). *Estimates of the unauthorized immigrant population residing in the United States*. Homeland Security. https://www.dhs.gov/immigration-statistics/population-estimates/unauthorized-resident#:~:text=The%20unauthorized%20resident%20immigrant%20population,they%20were%20required%20to%20leave

(continued)

Table 13.1. Newcomer Terms (continued)

Term	Level	Definition	Source/Citation
Undocumented	International	Often previously used interchangeably with irregular, an undocumented person is a migrant who has not met the requirements to enter or stay in their country of destination.	United Nations Population Fund. (2014). *Programme of Action of the International Conference on Population Development.* https://www.unfpa.org/sites/default/files/pub-pdf/programme_of_action_Web%20ENGLISH.pdf
	Federal*	A person who resides in the United States without legal status, including but not limited to people who entered the country without inspection, entered with legal status and overstayed their visa, individuals who have or have had Deferred Action for Childhood Arrivals (DACA), are currently in the process of legalizing their status, and other vulnerable immigrants.	Immigrants Rising. (n.d.). *Defining undocumented.* https://immigrantsrising.org/resource/defining-undocumented/

*While we choose to locate this particular definition under federal, there is no U.S. law that defines or uses the language of "undocumented migrant/person"; rather, it is a term that is widely defined and often used as an umbrella term for broad categories of migrants.

(Jaffe-Walter et al., 2019; Villavicencio et al., 2021). Previous research about newcomers focuses on questions related to the services they receive upon arrival to the United States, referred to as post-release services, and how they adapt to school, new language and cultures, as well as the variety of contexts they encounter. Attending to the educational success of immigrant students may be perceived as primarily the responsibility of teachers or social workers who are more likely than other personnel to have direct contact with these students (Jaffe-Walter, 2018; Rodriguez et al., 2022), yet we know how problematic it is to rely on one individual actor rather than a system of support for immigrant students, which provides the foundation for our conceptualization of newcomer immigrant belonging (described later). Simultaneously, newcomers are subject to ad hoc support systems, if any, while also being subject to a variety of bureaucratic systems to navigate. We label this *bureaucratic paradox* and call for an intervention into supporting newcomers.

Newcomers, Policies, and Practice

Scholars have argued that many of the policies in place for newcomers lead to more harm than good for newcomers (Grace & Roth, 2020), and clash with the realities of the everyday lives of migrant communities and families (Heidbrink, 2017). Regarding the management of and legal processes of unaccompanied immigrant children (or undocumented migrant or refugee children more broadly), some scholars have addressed the issue using rights-based approaches (Monico et al., 2019).

Ataiants et al. (2018) argue that "multiple components of the human rights framework are relevant to protect the dignity, health and wellbeing of children arriving to the US" (pp. 1003–1004). Scholarship on the rights of unaccompanied minors often takes one of two angles. Some scholars, using both international and domestic perspectives, discuss the right to migration (Byrne, 2018), whereas others address the right to education (Booi et al., 2016; Sanchez, 2020). Scholarship points to international conventions, such as the Convention of the Rights of the Child, and domestic laws such as *Plyler v. Doe*, the Flores Settlement Agreement, and the Trafficking Victims Protection Act (TVPRA) to discuss rights unaccompanied minors have to basic protections, such as standards of care and education (Booi et al., 2016; Byrne, 2018; Sanchez, 2020).

The United Nations Convention on the Rights of the Child, like U.S. law, defines a child as a person who is below the age of 18, unless they attain majority status through their country's legal system (United Nations, 1989). The convention delineates the rights and protections of children, as well as the responsibilities of the states, under the following four principles: nondiscrimination, best interests of the child, the right to survival and development, and the views of the child (UNICEF, 2019). Within these principles, specifically the right to development, the convention declares education as a right. Under U.S. law, *Plyler v. Doe* (1982) denied state and local officials the right to refuse service to undocumented children. Despite rejecting the concept of education as a fundamental right, the Supreme Court believed that "denying K–12 education to undocumented children amounted to creating a lifetime of hardship for this population and a permanent underclass of individuals" (Gonzales et al., 2015, p. 319). Meanwhile, TVPRA—which partially codified the 1997 Flores Settlement Agreement—set a minimum standard of care, such as providing children with (a) proper housing; (b) access to medical care, including physical, dental, and mental health services; (c) access to legal assistance; and (d) educational services, for unaccompanied children detained in federal facilities (Ataiants et al., 2018; ORR, 2021; Wiseman et al., 2020).

Despite these existing policies' intentions, the reality of how these policies and protections impact newcomers is very different. As far as unaccompanied immigrant children in detention, Wiseman et al. (2020) address the gap between rights-related policies at the international, federal, and state levels and actual educational opportunities of unaccompanied minors in U.S. federal custody. According to their findings, "variation among shelters and questions about which federal or state policies apply to specific situations means that equitable, quality education is often unavailable to unaccompanied im/migrant children" (p. 10).

For newcomers beyond detention, scholars argue that there is a tension between their rights as children through the policies mentioned above and their legal status as immigrants (Grace & Roth, 2020; Roth & Grace, 2018; Roth et al., 2019). Grace and Roth (2020) criticize federal institutions for curtailing their responsibilities by assuming that because newcomers' legal categorization as children grants them certain rights, they will have access to them. Specifically referring to post-release services, ORR in practice only offers referrals, and it does not follow up to ensure children are accessing and using the services, leaving children and their families to navigate these systems alone (Grace & Roth, 2020). Further, scholars argue that this disregard for immigrant children's safety does not meet the standards of TVPRA (Roth & Grace, 2018). Above all, for undocumented newcomers, their legal status remains a barrier. Pierce (2015) found that even after unaccompanied minors' cases have been resolved in court, they are given informal relief and only rarely formal legal status. This means while newcomers navigate federal institutions and policies, they may still be subject to deportation at any point (Roth & Grace, 2018). The lack of accountability of federal institutions can result in more harm than good for newcomers as this process becomes more of a burden than a system of support (Grace & Roth, 2020). This tension addressed by scholars supports Heidbrink's (2017) claim that the realities of newcomers' lives as immigrant children with limited legality and complex family structures clash with these policies and institutions.

Education Systems and Practices

Scholars have examined how these harmful policies and institutions have, in practice, failed newcomers and undocumented students more broadly. López (2021) finds that, among other violations of rights and policies, a major concern in public schools is educators' and education leaders' inadequate understanding of *Plyler* and other laws. Where some school districts may purposefully be causing harm by, for example, straight out rejecting *Plyler* and petitioning for the removal of unaccompanied children, other education leaders' lack of knowledge of these policies unintentionally results in restrictive practices (López, 2021; Rodriguez & Crawford, 2022; Rodriguez & McCorkle, 2020). Even further, while these policies are in place and where school districts may be trying to support newcomers, federal support is gravely lacking (Pierce, 2015). Although some case managers try to fill the gaps that larger institutions miss, case managers often provide this support at their own expense, meaning their additional support is limited and newcomers who do not get this support are faced with the realities of bureaucratic neglect (Grace & Roth, 2020).

Exemplifying this paradox is a recent study by Rodriguez and McCorkle (2020), where the authors surveyed 5,190 educators (e.g., teachers) about their awareness of policies impacting immigrant students. The authors found that teachers largely held false narratives about immigration policies or an overall lack of awareness, which led to neglect of resources. This combination of being part of a system (e.g., a school) where actors lack awareness but are also part of larger bureaucracies that can broker resources is critical to address. Yet, helping immigrant students access resources is often ad hoc or left up to particular key support personnel, such as teachers and school social workers (Rodriguez et al., 2022). While the strategic actions of teachers and other personnel helps newcomers navigate the bureaucratic systems, at times it is also an example of how they are labeled, subjecting them to a set of institutions and policies, while also leaving their educational opportunities and access to chance. These failures have prompted scholars to call for enhancing communication and cooperation between the multiple institutions involved in supporting newcomers, such as ORR advising districts about releases so districts are better prepared (Greenberg et al., 2021; Pierce, 2015).

School Environment

In addition to federal laws and policies, and their awareness or lack of by school-based personnel, additional components related to systems of neglect are evident. At the school level, much of the previous research on newcomer students has focused on language and curriculum (Bajaj & Bartlett, 2017; Bartlett, 2007; García & Bartlett, 2007; García et al., 2011; Pacheco & Brown, 2022; Valdés,1998), and the criminalization and adultification of immigrant youth due to assimilationist principles (Diaz-Strong, 2021; Hamann & Harklau, 2010; Rodriguez, 2019, 2020). The literature calls for U.S. schools to radically rethink the fundamental assumptions of the national schooling system that marginalizes immigrants (in addition to minoritized groups broadly) and replace it with what we term an ecosystem of care (Rodriguez et al., 2024), which we return to later.

Language and Curriculum

Newcomer students who are recently arrived migrants to the United States are often categorized as English language learners (ELLs). Today, ELLs are one of the fastest-growing populations in schools across the United States, according to the National Education Association (2020). Despite this increase, schools have not been able to adapt instruction to meet the needs of ELLs. The National Center for Education Statistics (2022) reported that only 63% of ELL students graduate compared to 82% of students nationwide. Therefore, it is no surprise that much of the scholarship on newcomer students is devoted to understanding school language policy and curriculum (Bajaj & Bartlett, 2017; García et al., 2011; Valdés, 1998).

Two challenges commonly cited in the literature regarding schooling of newcomer students are difficulty addressing individual needs due to newcomer students' diverse backgrounds and having to learn academic content while simultaneously navigating a new culture and society (Diaz-Strong, 2021; Pacheco & Brown, 2022; Valdés, 1998). In their recent comparative case study of two 9th-grade biology classrooms in the southeast United States, Pacheco and Brown (2022) illustrate how diversity in language and cultural backgrounds of newcomers makes it difficult for the predominantly white teaching force to incorporate students' funds of knowledge in the classroom: "A biology teacher would need to know not only how to construct explanations with certain language functions, like justifying or defining, but also how to support EBs [emergent bilinguals] in asking questions from partners and using other relevant communication norms" (p. 5). Pacheco and Brown assert the importance of ELLs needing to learn language and comprehend content.

Additionally, many scholars argue that the current widespread model for educating English as a second language (ESL) students is an ineffective tool (Bajaj & Bartlett, 2017; Bartlett, 2007; García & Bartlett, 2007; García et al., 2011; Valdés, 1998). Valenzuela (1999) uses the term "subtractive schooling" to describe the ESL model that "reproduces [immigrant] youth as monolingual, English-speaking, ethnic minority, neither identified with [their home country] nor equipped to function competently in American mainstream" (p. 3). Such an ESL model leads ELLs to perform poorly on exams, lag behind their peers in academic achievement, and graduate or drop out without the needed English level to thrive in their new home. As a result, schools are undereducating a large part of the population, leaving them without the tools to express their full potential as contributing members of U.S. society. Accordingly, Bajaj and Bartlett (2017) explain that

> . . . most US high school curricula are normed to white, middle-class, native English-speaking, college bound, and non-working students with increasing standardization forced by high stakes testing. Moreover, social studies curricula in the U.S. focus on political socialization, presuming that all students are current and/or future

citizens of the U.S. Such curricular are problematic when thinking about the exclusion of newcomer immigrant youth who may not have immigration status or who may be troubled by the meaning and status of U.S. citizenship, or who may hope to return to their countries of origin. (p. 26)

This further demonstrates how migrant youth are alienated in schools. While this literature draws attention to newcomers' needs, we caution the focus on English-only perspectives and language segregation practices. In hindsight, this scholarship also links back to how the bureaucratic hyper-surveillance persists by creating categories and conflating newcomers' experiences, often racialized, with language deficits.

Criminalization of Youth Through Assimilationist Approaches

Education policies that target newcomer youth, such as ESL, have often led to marginalization and experiences of unbelonging. This is because schools may use outdated assimilationist approaches that apply to English-only programs and create isolation coupled with an unwelcoming climate just for the hope of a better life (Rodriguez, 2020). Assimilationist theories view immigrants as gradually losing the sociocultural norms of their origin country to assume the norms and values of the host country. As more international and internal migration occurs, states not previously known for housing large Latinx and immigrant populations are using improvised educational responses (Hamann & Harklau, 2010). These local communities often develop racialized views of Latinx and immigrants based on mass media coverage (Hamann, 2003; Hamann & Harklau, 2010). Established views on linguistic, cultural diversity, and education policies lead to the use of assimilationist approaches rationalizing colorblind methods that view newcomer students' underachievement as cultural deficits rather than problems of structural racism and racialization (Rodriguez, 2019, 2020). Thus, the criminalization youth face through the immigration system extends into the school classroom where ESL programs segregate youth. Limited mental health services leaves trauma from migration unaddressed, and teachers lack the training and professional development to educate newcomers (Greenberg et al., 2021; Hamann & Harklau, 2010; López, 2021; Pacheco & Brown, 2022).

BEST INTERESTS OF THE CHILD?

In addition to clarifying terminology, we hope our argument so far illuminates the hyper-surveillance and bureaucratic paradox immigrant communities enter into, as well as the lack of attention to their needs across multiple educational and social systems. While research shows the misalignment between migrant youths' experiences and the services that are available to them and eventually provided to them, we know less about the ways that institutions create bureaucracy and, in turn, forms of surveillance while also sustaining bureaucratic neglect of this populations.

Some scholars have drawn attention to the "best interests of the child" paradigm in child welfare policy toward immigrant students (e.g., Heidbrink, 2014). This approach is laden with subjective processes and deficit-based "deservingness" assumptions (Patel, 2015) about types of migrant groups. (The needier, the most desperate, the saddest, and so forth become the most deserving.) It is critical to explore these paradigms because they often determine which resources and types of educational and social pathways migrant youth can obtain. By showing these terms and relationships between labels in policy and practice, and the realities migrant youth encounter in the United States, we aim to demystify the processes, structures, and actors that newcomers are entangled with as they navigate educational and social systems.

To discuss our focus on bureaucracy and to put forward this notion of a paradox that we observe in policy, research, and practice, we acknowledge how contexts of reception—as the major framework for understanding immigrant integration (Portes & Rumbaut, 2001)—often downplays the important ways migrants are living in/under racialized immigration surveillance apparatus (Rodriguez, 2022; Rodriguez & Acree, 2020). We utilize previous research as a starting point of conceptualizing bureaucracy, but we aim to move past its organizational colorblindness and race neutrality.

The general assumption with minoritized groups is that their political incorporation (through engagement in electoral politics) precedes the establishment of positive relationships with bureaucrats who help with their transition. In this view, minoritized groups receive political rights and benefits prior to being granted social rights in lower-order bureaucratic institutions. Bureaucratic institutions, therefore, tend to follow political responses to minoritized groups rather than dictating them. Marrow (2011) explains that principal-agent theories (theories of bureaucratic incorporation) critique this top-down perspective, claiming that there is a conflict between elected officials—principals—and bureaucratic agents. Thus, according to this framework, while principals will struggle to get the bureaucrats "in line," the latter will often engage in actions that undermine those directives. Thus, the relationship between the two is described as more reciprocal, with bureaucrats exerting their own degree of control and autonomy over their own actions and also influencing decisions made by principals. In this sense, what might look like political action, is in fact a result of autonomous bureaucratic decisions in the context of goal consensus. It is clear from our examination of terms/labels and policies and actors in agencies alongside our current empirical study (Rodriguez, 2021) that decisions and processes appear in the best interests of migrant youth but are also made in abstract ways. We complicate Marrow's work by noting that the web of actors that engage with migrant youth and determine their access to resources reveals layers of potential inequalities.

Marrow's case of immigrant integration demonstrates the validity of competing theories that go even beyond the principal-agent reciprocal relationship to suggest that not only does political incorporation fail to precede bureaucratic incorporation, but that it also follows it. Analysis of immigrant integration in new destination cities in California indicates that local law enforcement officers responded more positively to newcomer communities than did elected officials. Similarly, research in communities in Washington, DC, reveals more positive responses to newcomer immigrants among local school administrators than politicians. These school administrators and school staff instituted policies supportive of immigrant youth, attempting to engage in resource redistribution to meet these students' needs. The first author's own unpublished research in eastern North Carolina underscores the significance of bureaucratic incorporation, albeit in conjunction with, or interacting with, political processes. Research there highlighted that local bureaucrats responded more inclusively to Latinx newcomers than elected officials.

In our empirical study, we have already observed that one district's relationship with local county officials improve services, or the potential for them, for newcomer immigrant youth. In the case of North Carolina, Latinx newcomers enjoyed little representation in local politics and were generally excluded from participation in political life until the attainment of naturalization (which typically takes a long time if it happens at all). Additionally, local and state politicians lacked substantive knowledge about the needs of newcomer communities. In contrast, bureaucrats working in elementary school systems in eastern North Carolina not only recognized the needs of their newcomer immigrant youth, but also took concrete steps to address those needs, including hiring bilingual ESL program coordinators and assistants and instituting policies designed to increase parental involvement for immigrant families. Relatedly, similar research that took place in Georgia indicated that schools "were among the first institutions . . . to develop programs and policies to incorporate immigrants" (Marrow, 2009, p. 762) in contrast to state policies, which remained restrictive and punitive.

The North Carolina case study illustrates the interactional nature of the relationship between bureaucratic interests and political processes. The elementary schools' positive response to newcomers is justified by their professional interests, defined as "an internal variable intrinsic to local bureaucracies . . . distinct from professional norms" (Marrow, 2009, p. 762) shaping how bureaucracies respond to demographic changes. The growth of the Latinx population in areas such as eastern North Carolina proved beneficial to school bureaucrats because it justified an increase in schools' fiscal resources and funding for both native and newcomer students. A more important factor in the positive response, however, has been bureaucrats' strong client-serving ethic stemming from the notion of education as a public good and "shared norms about promoting equity and opportunity" (p. 763). Inclusive federally mandated government policies (political processes) also contributed to the positive response to newcomers. Such policies reflected the administration's push for inclusivity for newcomer students and the view that they constitute "clients to be served . . . regardless of their potential undocumented status" (p. 762). Thus, both inclusive federal government policies and the strong local bureaucratic culture of public schools shaped school actors' positive interactions with newcomers.

This example is useful for understanding the importance of bureaucracies and actors within it. Our hope is to build upon this research and to point out the colorblind and often intentionally confusing aspects of bureaucracy that mask and perpetuate inequalities. In our empirical project, we aim to unravel funding and relationships among bureaucratic actors. Additionally, we problematize such relationships for the best interest, deficit-based perspectives outlined. Additionally, scholars have noted how violence, symbolic and real, is created and sustained through bureaucratic process (Menjívar, 2014; Roth & Grace, 2018), such as immigration authorities' ongoing monitoring of those released at the border and the unrelenting confusion of immigration courts (Terrio, 2019). Thus, we call for understanding bureaucratic neglect and surveillance.

METHODS AND A CALL FOR AN ECOSYSTEM OF CARE

This chapter's attention to the harm of the bureaucratic paradox that governs the lives of newcomer immigrant youth stems from an ongoing mixed-methods comparative case study of how two school districts in a mid-Atlantic state manage the welcome of Central American newcomers. The aim of the ongoing study is to (a) examine the various organizational actors in school districts and local social service organizations, and (b) to identify structures and networks of support to reduce inequality for immigrant youth. We focus on Latino/x newcomers because, like many states, the Hispanic population in Maryland is substantial. According to the 2022 American Community Survey data referenced in Chapter 1 (U.S. Census Bureau, n.d.), Maryland has the seventh-largest under-18 Latinx population in the NLD, trailing only Massachusetts, Nevada, North Carolina, Pennsylvania, Virginia, and Washington. Increasingly, unaccompanied youth are a topic of discussion and have persistently arrived over the past decade in the thousands. To date, we have interviewed district and school officials and engaged in participant observations at community- and district-level events. While this chapter engages with the discursive labeling of newcomer migrants and an inquiry into conceptualizing the bureaucratic paradoxes that newcomers face, we rely on our data that prompted these interests to illustrate these challenges and tensions.

Thus far, we have learned about three challenges that districts face (Rodriguez, 2021). Research in school districts indicates that the sheer number of newly arrived unaccompanied students presents challenges to districts in part because the government does not provide financial assistance to local communities that serve these students. In the summer of 2021, a community-based organization staff member who works with the school district reported, "They [unaccompanied children] are coming to us in record numbers, and we don't know what to do." Moreover, these students are often ineligible for health insurance or social services due to their immigration status (i.e., citizen, undocumented, unaccompanied minor). In addition to the lack of federal funding and ad hoc local support systems, districts must manage major challenges, such as (a) enrollment and registration processes, including complicated registration systems and language barriers; (b) a lack of personnel to manage the enrollment process and a lack of background knowledge about working with newcomer immigrants; and (c) fear of immigration enforcement in local communities that necessitates trauma-informed approaches to serving these students.

The systems that families and youth must navigate, and the lack of personnel to support them, leads to an overall lack of district capacity to enroll the newcomer students—let alone to support them once enrolled (for expanded discussion about these challenges, see Rodriguez, 2021). Related to the complexity, bureaucratic processes and systems are obtuse for many families. For example, to enroll in a public school in the United States, families must first provide multiple documents. For unaccompanied newcomers, providing documentation such as proof of residence in the school district, a birth certificate, and vaccination records can be a considerable obstacle. Some districts in the United States have made the decision at the state level to not require documentation, with one district official explaining:

> We have a big issue with immigration taking away all of their documents, and not providing them with the proper paperwork, especially in detention. It depends on the family. But most of the time, the unaccompanied youth [minors under age 18 who migrate without a parent] have nothing. ZERO. Another explained: "A lot of times, parents when kids are released from detention to a sponsor [a family member or distant relative] they don't even have anything showing that they're the parent or relative. We have to dig through the immigration-related paperwork packets that they do have, and we kind of connect the information and we use that. When people migrate, they don't usually carry paperwork with them, yet we ask for it.

This practice of "connecting the dots" is necessitated by the complicated nature of the immigration system and the seemingly arbitrary requirements for enrolling in school, the second bureaucratic system after immigration customs and enforcement. The reality is that newcomers face unimaginable conditions and experiences before, during, and after migration; their life trajectories are restricted or expanded by the nature of complex bureaucratic surveillance through immigration enforcement and yet a lack of services and support in school systems.

After reviewing the previous scholarship and discursive labeling, and reflecting upon our anecdotal data, we acknowledge the bureaucratic paradox that newcomers grapple with upon arriving to the United States. To advance the conceptual understanding of bureaucratic paradox, we hope that districts will consider an ecosystem of care (Rodriguez et al., 2024) when envisioning how to best support newcomers. Indeed, what prompted the first author's study was an interest by school districts to serve this population given the migrant crisis, which is both new and old. Instead of focusing on the always-in-crisis mode, since newcomers, especially unaccompanied youth, have consistently been arriving for at least the last five years to bureaucratic systems and neglect, we call for a vision that includes multiple types of social-emotional support and actors coordinating with one another (Figure 13.1).

Figure 13.1. An Ecosystem of Care: Supporting Newcomer Immigrant Youth

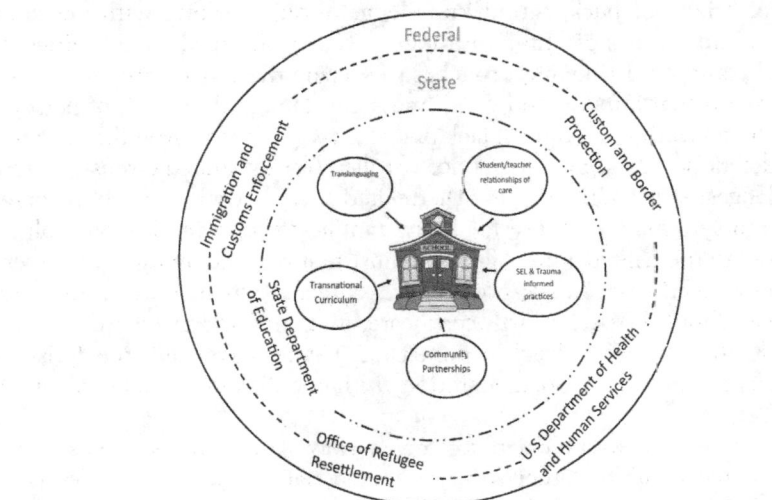

Ecosystem of Care

In our effort to reconceptualize how newcomers are supported by schools and communities, we envision several terms/key points in Figure 13.1 that relate to research-based approaches to working with newcomer immigrant populations. Key concepts in our conceptual model include translanguaging (García & Kleyn, 2016), teacher–student relationship-based authentic caring (Valenzuela, 1999), community-based partnerships and relationships (Rodriguez, 2020; Suárez-Orozco et al., 2009, 2010), and critically sustaining pedagogy and transitional curriculum.

Translanguaging is a practice that places the students' native language, culture, and prior knowledge in high status and presents a form of additive schooling where students can learn English without sacrificing their native language and culture (Bajaj & Bartlett, 2017). Translanguaging should occur in and out of the classroom in group projects, morning announcements, bulletin boards in the hallways, and graduation portfolios. It is a signal to teachers, parents, and students that all are welcomed in the school regardless of linguistic ability. Schools must also strive to employ high-quality teachers who reflect the community they serve. Teachers who speak the same language as their students have similar backgrounds, and sometimes similar immigration statuses can use these similarities to foster relationships with their students and between the school and community. It is important for students to see themselves reflected in their teachers so that they can begin to imagine themselves as professionals and watch as their teachers navigate U.S. and home culture (García & Bartlett, 2007). Whether or not teachers share similar backgrounds with their students, they should approach their work with an asset-based mentality and authentic caring where students' needs are at the center and the teacher role is to facilitate learning.

In addition, recognizing the trauma that comes with being an unaccompanied minor, refugee, asylee, and/or student with interrupted formal education, a trauma-informed approach to teaching is essential to building successful relationships with students. Schools should focus on professional development that will add to teachers' and any school-based personnel such as school social workers knowledge of students' cultures and communities but also the way trauma affects learning and the brain (Bajaj & Suresh, 2018; Rodriguez et al., 2022). Schools must strengthen social-emotional services with daily/weekly adviser check-ins and wellness centers, and by partnering with organizations or individuals who can address students' needs with cultural and linguistic competency. Community partnerships can help schools provide holistic wrap-around services (Martin & Suárez-Orozco, 2018). Through community partnerships, schools can provide legal service information sessions, internship opportunities, mental health services, and recreational activities. Schools are also able to engage families through these same services along with food drives and even community gardens (Bajaj & Suresh, 2018). With this community model, the school becomes a welcoming environment for all and the bedrock of the community.

Lastly, classroom curriculum cannot ignore the realities immigrant students are witnessing firsthand. Rather, classroom teaching and learning must connect to real-life examples of activism and civic engagement so that students develop a critical consciousness of the social inequalities in the United States and globally and know how to respond to it through political actions in their own lives. This can be done through culturally sustaining pedagogy (Paris, 2012) and a transnational curriculum that does not privilege Western narrative but that honors the knowledge and desires immigrant students have. Bajaj and Bartlett (2017) state that "culturally and socio-politically responsive approaches to schooling for immigrants and refugees must recognize that students' identities and their sense of belonging must extend beyond or across national boundaries" (p. 27). With these local school practices, we can begin building a community of care for immigrant students, although that alone may not be enough.

Discussion and Conclusion

The failure of schools to help newcomers thrive is especially abhorrent. Not only does this violate the spirit of *Plyler v. Doe* and result in the undereducation of a large part of the population, leaving them without the tools to express their full potential as contributing members of U.S. society, but because schools are crucial to the success of these children through their positioning as one of the only institutions newcomer youths engage with daily, schools have the capability to provide critical support and connections to resources and community (Greenberg et al., 2021; Rodriguez, 2019). From ORR facilities and post-release providers inflicting harm and trauma to immigrant youth and families, to classroom teachers and school counselors, what newcomer students require is an ecosystem of care that expands on and is rooted in newcomer experiences.

At the school level, this can be done through holistic student-centered wrap-around services. Whether supporting the use of translanguaging (Bajaj & Bartlett, 2017; García et al., 2011), social emotional and trauma-informed practices (Bajaj & Suresh, 2018), community partnerships (Martin & Suárez-Orozco, 2018; Rodriguez, 2019), or culturally sustaining and critical pedagogy (Bajaj & Bartlett, 2017; Valdés, 1998), these policies and practices all advocate for placing the humanity, agency, and knowledge of newcomer youth at the forefront. Adapting these policies and practices would reject assimilationist principles that alienate youth to schools, but a true ecosystem of care would require more cooperation and coordination between all institutions.

REFERENCES

Ataiants, J., Cohen, C., Riley, A. H., Tellez Lieberman, J., Reidy, M. C., & Chilton, M. (2018). Unaccompanied children at the United States border, a human rights crisis that can be addressed with policy change. *Journal of Immigrant and Minority Health, 20*(4), 1000–1010. https://doi.org/10.1007/s10903-017-0577-5

Bajaj, M., & Bartlett, L. (2017). Critical transnational curriculum for immigrant and refugee students. *Curriculum Inquiry, 47*(1), 25–35.

Bajaj, M., & Suresh, S. (2018). The "warm embrace" of a newcomer school for immigrant & refugee youth. *Theory Into Practice, 57*(2), 91–98.

Bartlett, L. (2007). To seem and to feel: Situated identities and literacy practices. *Teachers College Record, 109*(1), 51–69.

Booi, Z., Callahan, C., Fugere, G., Harris M., Hughes A., Kramarczuk, A., Kurtz, C., Reyes, R., & Swaminathan, S. (2016). *Ensuring every undocumented student succeeds: A report on access to public education for undocumented children.* Georgetown Law Human Rights Institute. https://www.law.georgetown.edu/human-rights-institute/wp-content/uploads/sites/7/2017/07/2016-HRI-Report-English.pdf

Byrne, O. (2018). Promoting child rights-based approach to immigration in the United States. *Georgetown Immigration Law Journal, 32*(1), 59–98.

Diaz-Strong, D. X. (2021). "When did I stop being a child?" The subjective feeling of adulthood of Mexican and Central American unaccompanied 1.25 generation immigrants. *Emerging Adulthood, 10*(5), 1286–1298. https://doi.org/10.1177/2167696821992141

García, O., & Bartlett, L. (2007). A speech community model of bilingual education: Educating Latino newcomers in the USA. *International Journal of Bilingual Education and Bilingualism, 10*(1), 1–25. https://doi.org/10.2167/beb364.0

García, O., Flores, N., & Chu, H. (2011). Extending bilingualism in US secondary education: New variations. *International Multilingual Research Journal, 5*(1), 1–18. https://doi.org/10.1080/19313152.2011.539486

García, O., & Kleyn, T. (2016). *Translanguaging theory in education.* Routledge.

Gonzales, R. G., Heredia, L. L., & Negrón-Gonzales, G. (2015). Untangling *Plyler*'s legacy: Undocumented students, schools, and citizenship. *Harvard Education Review, 85*(3), 318–341. https://doi.org/10.17763/0017-8055.85.3.318

Grace, B. L., & Roth, B. J. (2020). Bureaucratic neglect: The paradoxical mistreatment of unaccompanied migrant children in the US immigration system. *Journal of Ethnic and Migration Studies, 47*(14), 3455–3472. https://doi.org/10.1080/1369183X.2020.1788378.

Greenberg, M., Grow, K., Heredia, S., Monin, K., & Workie, E. (2021). *Strengthening services for unaccompanied children in U.S. communities.* Migration Policy Institute. https://www.migrationpolicy.org/research/services-unaccompanied-children-us-communities

Hacking, I. (1999) *The social construction of what?* Harvard University Press.

Hamann, E. T. (2003). *The educational welcome of Latinos in the New South.* Praeger.

Hamann E. T., & Harklau, L. (2010). Education in the new Latino diaspora. In E. G. Murillo, Jr. (Ed.), *Handbook of Latinos and education: Theory, research, and practice* (pp. 157–169). Routledge.

Heidbrink, L. (2014). *Migrant youth, transnational families, and the state: Care and contested interests.* University of Pennsylvania Press.

Heidbrink, L. (2017). Assessing parental fitness and care for unaccompanied children. *Russell Sage Foundation Journal of the Social Sciences, 3*(4), 37–52. https://doi.org/10.7758/RSF.2017.3.4.03

Heidbrink, L. (2020). *Migranthood: Youth in a new era of deportation.* Stanford University Press.

Hernandez, E., Suárez-Orozco, C., Cerda, J., Osei-Twumasi, O., Corral, M., García, Y., Katsiaficas, D., & Ruedas-Gracia, N. (2019). Immigrant-origin students in community college: How do they use their time on campus? *Teachers College Record, 127*(7), 1–48. https://doi.org/10.1177/016146811912100702

Jaffe-Walter, R. (2018). Leading in the context of immigration: Cultivative collective responsibility for recently arrived immigrant students. *Theory Into Practice, 57*(2), 147–153.

Jaffe-Walter, R., Miranda, C. P., & Lee, S. J. (2019). From protest to protection: Navigating politics with immigrant students in uncertain times. *Harvard Educational Review, 89*(2), 251–276. https://doi.org/10.17763/1943-5045-89.2.251

Levinson, A. (2020, August 27). *Unaccompanied immigrant children: A growing phenomenon with few easy solutions.* Migration Policy Institute. https://www.migrationpolicy.org/article/unaccompanied-immigrant-children-growing-phenomenon-few-easy-solutions

López, R. M. (2021). *The (mis)treatment and (non)education of unaccompanied immigrant children in the United States.* National Education Policy Center. http://nepc.colorado.edu/publication/immigrant-children

Marrow, H. B. (2009). Immigrant bureaucratic incorporation: The dual roles of professional missions and government policies. *American Sociological Review, 74*(5), 756–766. https://doi.org/10.1177/000312240907400504

Marrow, H. B. (2011). *New destination dreaming: Immigration, race, and legal status in the rural American south.* Stanford University Press.

Martin, M., & Suárez-Orozco, C. (2018). What it takes: Promising practices for immigrant origin adolescent newcomers. *Theory Into Practice, 57*(2), 82–90. https://doi.org/10.1080/00405841.2018.1425816

Menjívar, C. (2014). Immigration law beyond borders: Externalizing and internalizing border controls in an era of securitization. *Annual Review of Law and Social Science, 10,* 353–369. https://doi.org/10.1146/annurev-lawsocsci-110413-030842

Miroff, N. (2021, March 10). *At border, record number of migrant youths wait in adult detention cells for longer than legally allowed*. Washington Post. https://www.washingtonpost.com/national/unaccompanied-minors-detention-cells/2021/03/10/a0d39390-81c6-11eb-bb5a-ad9a91faa4ef_story.html

Monico, C., Rotabi, K. S., & Lee, J. (2019). Forced child–family separations in the Southwestern U.S. border under the "zero-tolerance" policy: Preventing human rights violations and child abduction into adoption (Part 1). *Journal of Human Rights and Social Work, 4*(3), 164–179 https://doi.org/10.1007/s41134-019-0089-4

National Education Association (2020). *Toolkit: English language learners*. https://www.nea.org/resource-library/english-language-learners

Oboler, S. (1995). *Ethnic labels, Latino lives: Identity and the politics of (re)presentation in the United States*. University of Minnesota Press.

Office of Refugee Resettlement. (2021). *ORR unaccompanied children program policy guide*. Administration for Children and Families. https://www.acf.hhs.gov/orr/policy-guidance/children-entering-united-states-unaccompanied

Office of Refugee Resettlement. (2022). *Unaccompanied children: Facts and data*. Administration for Children and Families. https://www.acf.hhs.gov/orr/about/ucs/facts-and-data

Pacheco, M. B., & Brown, J. C. (2022). Newcomer emergent bilingual students' meaning-making in urban biology classrooms: A communities of practice perspective. *Urban Education, 59*(1), 447–478. https://doi.org/10.1177/00420859211073893

Paris, D. (2012). Culturally sustaining pedagogy: A needed change in stance, terminology, and practice. *Education Researcher 41*(3), 93–97.

Patel, L. (2015). Deservingness: Challenging coloniality in education and migration scholarship. *Association of Mexican American Educators Journal, 9*, 11–21.

Pierce, S. (2015). *Unaccompanied child migrants in U.S. communities, immigration court, and schools* [Issue Brief]. Migration Policy Institute. https://www.migrationpolicy.org/research/unaccompanied-child-migrants-us-communities-immigration-court-and-schools

Plyler v. Doe, 457 U.S. 202 (1982).

Portes, P. & Rumbaut, R. (2001). *Legacies: The story of the immigrant second generation*. University of California Press and Russell Sage Foundation.

Rodriguez, S. (2019). "We're building the community; it's a hub for democracy": Lessons learned from a library-based, school-district partnership and program to increase belonging for newcomer immigrant and refugee youth. *Children and Youth Services Review, 102*, 135–144. https://doi.org/10.1016/j.childyouth.2019.04.025

Rodriguez, S. (2020). Community-school partnerships as racial projects: Examining belonging for newcomer migrant youth in urban education. *Urban Education*.https://doi.org/10.1177/0042085920959126

Rodriguez, S. (2021). "They let you back in the country?": Racialized inequity and the miseducation of Latinx undocumented students in the new Latino south. *Urban Review, 53*, 565–590. https://doi.org/10.1007/s11256-020-00594-8

Rodriguez, S. (2022). "Immigration knocks on the door . . . We are stuck": A multi-level analysis of undocumented youths' experiences of racism, system failure, and resistance in policy and school contexts. *Teachers College Record, 124*(6), 3–37.

Rodriguez, S., & Acree, J. (2020). Biopolitical power and paradoxes in evaluation research with transnational migrant youth. *Evaluation, 26*(4), 456–473. https://doi.org/10.1177/1356389020914314

Rodriguez, S., & Crawford, E. (2022). School-based personnel advocacy for undocumented students through collective leadership in urban schools: A comparative case study. *Journal of Research on Leadership Education, 18*(3), 347–377. https://doi.org/10.1177/19427751221081887

Rodriguez, S., Lopez-Escobar, L., & Pippin-Kottkamp, S. (2024). Toward race-conscious care-based healing to support Latino immigrant youth. *Educational Policy.* https://doi.org/10.1177/08959048241265509

Rodriguez, S., & McCorkle, W. (2020). On the educational rights of undocumented students: A call to expand teachers' awareness of policies impacting undocumented students and strategic empathy. *Teachers College Record, 122*(12), 1–34.

Rodriguez, S., Roth, B., & Villarreal Sosa, L. (2022). "Immigration enforcement is a daily part of our students' lives": School social workers' perceptions of racialized nested contexts of reception for immigration students. *AERA Open.* https://doi.org/10.1177/23328584211073170

Roth, B. J., & Grace, B. (2018). Structural barriers to inclusion in a Latino immigrant new destination: Exploring the adaptive strategies of social service organizations in South Carolina. *Journal of International Migration and Integration, 19*, 1075–1093. https://doi.org/10.1007/s12134-018-0587-8

Roth, B. J., Grace, B. L., & Seay, K. D. (2019). Mechanisms of deterrence: Federal immigration policies and the erosion of immigrant children's rights. *American Journal of Public Health, 110*(1), 84–86. https://doi.org/10.2105/AJPH.2019.305388

Sanchez, A. (2020, May 6). This comment joins the developing debate and discusses the right to education in the United States and whether this right [Comment on the article "Zero tolerance, zero education: Reconsidering the right to education in the aftermath of the zero tolerance policy"]. *Houston Law Review.* https://houstonlawreview.org/article/12760-zero-tolerance-zero-education-reconsidering-the-right-to-education-in-the-aftermath-of-the-zero-tolerance-policy

Suárez-Orozco, C., Onaga, M., & Lardemelle, C. (2010). Promoting academic engagement among immigrant adolescents through school-family-community collaboration. *Professional School Counseling, 14*(1), 15–26. https://doi.org/10.1177/2156759X1001400103

Suárez-Orozco C., Pimentel, A., & Martin, M. (2009). The significance of relationships: Academic engagement and achievement among newcomer immigrant youth. *Teachers College Record, 111*(3), 712–749.

Terrio, S. J. (2019). *Illegal encounters: The effect of detention and deportation on young people.* New York University Press.

UNICEF. (2019, June 24). *Four principles of the Convention on the Rights of the Child: Four principles that together form a new attitude toward children.* https://www.unicef.org/armenia/en/stories/four-principles-convention-rights-child

United Nations. (1989). Convention on the rights of the child. *Treaty Series, 1577*, 3. https://treaties.un.org/doc/Treaties/1990/09/19900902%2003-14%20AM/Ch_IV_11p.pdf

U.S. Census Bureau. (n.d.). *American Community Survey 2022: Annual State Resident Population Estimates for 6 Race Groups by Age, Sex, and Hispanic Origin.* U.S. Department of Commerce. Retrieved Aug. 1, 2024, from https://www.census.gov/data/datasets/time-series/demo/popest/2020s-state-detail.html

Valdés, G. (1998). The world outside and inside schools: Language and immigrant children. *Educational Researcher, 27*(6), 4–18. https://doi.org/10.3102/0013189X027006004

Valenzuela, A. (1999). *Subtractive schooling: US Mexican youth and the politics of caring*. State University of New York Press.

Villavicencio, A., Jaffe-Walter, R., & Klevan, S. (2021). "You can't close your door here": Leveraging teacher collaboration to improve outcomes for immigrant English learners. *Teacher and Teacher Education, 97*, 1–11. https://doi.org/10.1016/j.tate.2020.103227

Wiseman, A. W., Damaschke-Deitrick, L., Park, M. F., & Bell, J. C. (2020). Caught between a rock and a hard place: The gap between rights-related policies and educational opportunities for unaccompanied im/migrant children in detention. *Journal of Latinos and Education*, 1–15. https://doi.org/10.1080/15348431.2020.1850458

Zak, D. (2020, November 2). *Fact sheet: Unaccompanied migrant children (UACs)*. National Immigration Forum. https://immigrationforum.org/article/fact-sheet-unaccompanied-migrant-children-uacs/

CHAPTER 14

The Praxis of More Welcoming, More Just, More Successful Schooling in the New Latino Diaspora

Edmund T. Hamann, Socorro G. Herrera, Stanton Wortham, and Enrique G. Murillo

A paradox of schooling and other educational processes is that they are potent vehicles for inclusion, capacity-building, and enfranchisement, but they are often instead vehicles of stratification, alienation, and disempowerment (Flores, 2021). As in locations where Latino populations have long been present, in the NLD too often those who could be included are excluded; those who could be bolstered are ignored or harassed; and those who are vital to the future building of safe, creative, purposeful, and responsive communities are instead undermined by educational systems that should know and do better.

We know the challenges are sometimes much bigger than just education system challenges. Consider the perspective of Meg Juarez, daughter of one of the victims of the White supremacist shooter who killed 23 Latino customers at an El Paso Walmart in 2019, who has harrowingly pointed out that 25 Republican governors have contemporarily (i.e., 2024) endorsed the xenophobic "invasion" language of Texas Governor Abbott (Mathias, 2024). Those include governors in the NLD from several states highlighted in the volume—Georgia, Idaho, Missouri, Nebraska, South Carolina, and Tennessee—as well as Alabama, Alaska, Arkansas, Indiana, Iowa, Louisiana, Mississippi, Montana, Nevada, New Hampshire, North Dakota, Ohio, Oklahoma, South Dakota, Utah, Virginia, West Virginia, and Wyoming. This xenophobia and racism from the top precipitates but also reflects ignorance, discomfort, and hate from other societal tiers and offers an uncomfortable background to what happens in educational spaces. However, it remains the case that the misinformation and vitriol that undergird these stances are also contestable in education spaces; indeed, in a world that harbors the NLD well, they must be.

One way to read the previous 13 chapters is to see them as additional accounts of where/how education systems fall short with Latino stakeholders in the 41 states where the presence of Latino families in large scale is "newer." Yet, as readers already know, that would be an incomplete reading of those chapters. It would skip how each outlines what better praxis/could should look like at a scale as modest as assuring competent staffing to lead a university's freshman seminar (Beck et al., Chapter 3); as broad as better deploying existing educator expertise (Yammine & Lowenhaupt, Chapter 9); as abstract as interrupting pernicious discourses (Herrera et al., Chapter 10); or as concrete as reimagining and expanding who we must listen to (Rodriguez et al., Chapter 13).

The goal here is to look across these 13 earlier chapters and to use them as examples for the articulation of an encompassing vision of more welcoming, just, and successful schooling. With praxis in the chapter title referencing where theory meets practice, each of those terms—welcoming, just, and successful—merit more scrutiny.

"Welcoming" is a good word and an optimistic one, and it is clearly the stance of the various chapter authors that educational structures and practices encountered by Latino stakeholders in the NLD (be they parents, students, teachers, or others) should be welcoming. However, there is one dimension of welcoming that merits interruption for more inclusive praxis and outcomes. "Welcome" can imply a welcomer, or host, but also one who is to be welcomed, or a guest. In this construct, more established populations (typically White) get to play the role of host and the "newer" Latino population gets trapped in a framing as visitor, newcomer, guest, or even guestworker. There are more pejorative possible roles than host and guest—think of Gray's phrasing (Chapter 6) of "xenophobic messages of unwelcome" for example—but this host/guest dichotomy nonetheless keeps imagining Latino children, youth, and adults as not fully *of* where they now live. Indeed, as Hamann and Harklau (2022) recently acknowledged in the second edition of the *Handbook of Latinos and Education* (Murillo, 2022), definitionally even the term diaspora references a homeland and identity from that homeland that is somewhere else. Full Latino inclusion will require "Latino" to be a descriptor of not only those to be welcomed, but increasingly those who are also understood as welcomers.

Looking at Hopkins and Weddle's contribution (Chapter 11), they describe compellingly a framework of welcome that involves community partnerships, welcoming processes, innovative staffing models, and instructional programs. The above paragraphs are not intended to push back on their second dimension—welcoming processes—as it remains the case that those arriving do need to be welcomed and to find welcome, but it is from their other three dimensions that it is possible to position Latino constituents to be welcomers, namely community partnerships, innovative staffing, and changed instructional programs. Gallegos Buitron and Anthony-Stevens (Chapter 7) invoke Yosso's (2005) notion of community cultural wealth to further explore "with whom?" dimensions of community partnership. As an unorthodox strategy for innovative staffing, Morales and colleagues (Chapter 2) point to youth participatory action research (YPAR) as a vehicle for connecting high school students from majority Latino high schools to teacher education pathways. Finally, Mitchell-McCollough (Chapter 12) imagines changed instructional programs that better welcome Latino stakeholders, although the empirical case she describes lays out frustrating paths not taken.

Examining "more just praxis" centers the consideration of what counts as fair and according to whom. As Sierk's (Chapter 8) invocation of Crenshaw's (1991) and Love's (2019) notions of intersectionality emphasizes, this cannot simply involve consideration of Latino versus not-Latino. Issues of gender, class, employment, language(s), indigeneity, sexual orientation, religion, and other dimensions of ascribed and asserted identity come into play, but the insistent voice across all of the chapters is that better/fairer is not only possible, but necessary.

Gray (Chapter 6) invokes Dewey (1916/2011) to remind us of the intention that education serves as a "midwife" of democracy and that, in turn, democracy is a key vehicle of enfranchisement. It follows that "more just praxis" in the NLD must enfranchise and foster belonging, while attending to particularities of context. This is true at multiple scales. At a small scale, we can remember the case of Mateo from Chapter 6, who was interpreting for his father during his father's immigration case, which meant Mateo needed to have his cell phone and to be able to use it while at school, contrary to school rules. More just praxis would not pit Mateo's language assistance to his family (assistance made possible in part through his schooling) as contrary to the wishes and expectations of school.

At a bigger scale, more just praxis can imagine higher/more respected status for ESL and bilingual teachers (see McConnochie, Chapter 5). It entails transformed practice—that is, a dual language program—that allows students to continue developing their multilingual skills rather than having a family/community language other than English be devalued and excluded (Mitchell-McCollough, Chapter 12). More just praxis need not be rocket science; it can have the quotidian face of adapted teacher professional development (Dorner & Crawford, Chapter 4), but it needs to hold those with power accountable for acting as agents of inclusion and justice.

More just praxis will be more successful practice. Here is where we start turning from processes to outcomes—higher graduation rates, increased school attendance, fewer mental health challenges, better academic achievement. These benefits will likely reach beyond students and even reimagine what should count as success. English language competence, for example, is incomplete as a desired school outcome, and if we are considering a student whose parents use Spanish as a first language and whose grandparents use Kaqchikel, for example, even bilingualism may be too limited as a definition of success. Educational systems need to help students become who they can be and who they deserve to be and elevate students' means and prospects to reach their full potentials. State education agencies and local school boards should get to weigh in on that, but so, too, should students and their families.

One of the intended strengths of this volume is to draw attention to the multiple and varied niches where making educational systems more responsive to Latino constituencies is possible. That involves diversifying who becomes an educator, changing what counts as educational competence and teacher excellence, attending to local contexts, and insisting on two outcomes: first, that the promise made in the U.S. Constitution's 14th Amendment and advanced by the *Brown v. Board* (1954) decision that public entities, including schools, should be vehicles for all "person[s]" to have "the equal protection of the laws" in terms of funding, treatment, and input into what gets understood as "success"; and second, following Gloria Ladson-Billings (2021) on culturally relevant pedagogy that students "are entitled to expect their learning to be meaningful" (p. 6).

Meaningful is necessarily at least partially in the eye of the beholder. That means meaningful learning for Latino learners in education systems needs to be relevant/satisfactory on their terms. We cannot reengineer education systems *for* the NLD, with an unnatural and unnecessary division between an *us* of the system and a *them*. Rather we need to do this *with* Latino learners, and we think the contributors to this volume have articulated a number of means for *how*.

REFERENCES

Crenshaw, K. (1991). Mapping the margins: Intersectionality, identity politics, and violence against women of color. *Stanford Law Review 43*(6), 1241–1299.

Dewey, J. D. (2011). *Democracy and education* (Simon & Brown ed.). Simon & Brown. (Original work published 1916)

Flores, A. (2021). *The succeeders: How immigrant youth are transforming what it means to belong in America*. University of California Press.

Hamann, E. T., & Harklau, L. (2022). Changing faces and persistent patterns for education in the new Latinx diaspora. In E. G. Murillo, Jr. (Ed.), *Handbook of Latinos and education: Theory, research, and practice* (2nd ed., pp. 81–92). Routledge.

Ladson-Billings, G. (2021). *Culturally relevant pedagogy: Asking a different question*. Teachers College Press.

Love, B. L. (2019). *We want to do more than survive: Abolitionist teaching and the pursuit of educational freedom*. Beacon Press.

Mathias, C. (2024). A white supremacist killed her dad in El Paso. Now, GOP politicians sound like the shooter. *Huffington Post* (Feb. 4). https://www.huffpost.com/entry/el-paso-shooting-anti-immigrant-rhetoric_n_65bbe7a2e4b0102bd2d84f24

Murillo, E. G., Jr. (Ed.). (2022). *Handbook of Latinos and education: Theory, research, and practice* (2nd ed.). Routledge.

Yosso, T. J. (2005). Whose culture has capital? A critical race theory discussion of community cultural wealth. *Race Ethnicity and Education, 8*(1), 69–91. https://doi.org/10.1080/1361332052000341006

Index

The letters *f* or *t* following a page number denote a figure or table, respectively.

Abu-El Haj, T., 40
ACCESS examination, 64–65
Acevedo, N., 99
Achinstein, B., 127
Acree, J., 180
Acuña, 132, 134
Agarwal, G., 113
Aiello, A. E., 138
Akiba, M., 113
Alcoff, L. M., 133
Allen, R. L., 146
Allexsaht-Snider, M., 22
Amanti, C., 75, 83, 90, 114, 128
American Community Survey, 5, 88
American Dream, 139, 141
Americanization, 133
Anderson, G. L., 41
Antiracist, 47
Anzaldúa, G., 137
Apple, M. W., 83
Arar, K., 40
Arzubiaga, A. E., 87
Asmelash, L., 89
Aspirational capital, 90, 93–94
Ataiants, J., 175, 176
Auerbach, S., 100
Ayala, J. M., 13
Azano, A. P., 88

Baetens, B. H., 137
Bajaj, M., 90, 153, 171, 177–178, 184–186
Bang, M., 91
Barajas-López, F., 91
Barko-Alva, K., 141
Bartlett, 177
Bartlett, L., 90, 153, 171, 177–178, 184–186
Bearse, C., 157

Beck, S., 4, 22, 25–27, 192
Bejarano, C., 95
Bell, J. C., 170, 176
Bell, J. M., 123
Benevolent racism, 2
Berry, T., 10
Berubé, B., 40
Bettez, S. C., 146
Bettini, E. A., 127
Bickham-Mendez, J., 141
Biddle, C., 88
Billingsley, B. S., 127
BIPOC (Black, indigenous, and people of color), 3, 8–17, 89
Bjorklund, P., 146, 147
Black, 3, 15, 21, 22, 29, 31, 44, 45, 48, 105–107
Black, P., 27Black Lives Matter, 22
Blanca Dabach, D., 146, 147
Blomstedt, M., 14
Bode, P., 10
Bodur, Y., 4, 25, 27, 192
Bogotch, I., 41
Bonilla-Silva, E., 123
Booi, Z., 175
Bourdieu, P., 163
Brant, K., 40
Brezicha, K., 146, 147
Bright, D. J., 120
Brimeyer, T., 22
Bristol, T., 127
Brooks, F. E., 21
Brooks, J. S., 41
Brooks, M. D., 100
Brown, J. C., 177–179
Brown, K., 11
Brown, T. M., 13
Brown v. Board of Education, 136

bureaucratic paradox
  child interests, 179–182
  criminalization of youth, 179
  ecosystem of care, 182–185, 184f
  education systems and practices, 176–177
  educational barriers, 171, 175
  labels and discursive practice, 170–171
  language and curriculum, 178–179
  newcomer immigrants, 171, 172–174t, 175
  opportunities, 171, 175
  ORR facilities, 185
  overview, 169–170
  policies and practice, 175–176
  school environment, 177
  unaccompanied immigrant youth, 170
Bush, G. W., 138
Byrne, O., 175

Cáceres, B., 137
Calderón, D., 108
Callahan, C., 175
Callahan, R. M., 40, 41
Call-Cummings, M., 89
Cammarota, J., 13–14
Caraballo, L., 14
Carter, N. P., 103
Carver-Thomas, D., 11
Cary, N., 23
Casanova, S., 109
Castañeda Shular, A., 134
Castrellón, L. E., 43
Catalano, T., 110, 156, 157, 166
Cather, W., 156
"Cautionary Note" (Valdés), 157
Cerda, J., 171
Cervantes-Soon, C. G., 40, 157, 163
Challenges to improvements, 1–6
Chavez, L., 133
Chesler, M., 113, 114
Chilton, M., 175, 176
Chishti, M., 43
Choi, J., 157, 163
Christensen, D., 12
The Chronicle of Higher Education, 23–24
Chu, H., 177, 178
The Circuit, 30
Civil Rights Movement, 134
Cockrell, K. S., 113
Cocreating, 15
Co-facilitators, 14, 1513
Cohen, C., 175, 176
Collier, V. P., 157

Colomer, S. E., 126
Commins, N. L., 124
Common Read, 20, 25, 32, 33
Contreras, F., 40, 137
Corral, M., 171
Cotter Public School District (CPSD), 118, 120
County Latino Coalition, 69
COVID-19 pandemic, 13, 32, 40, 41, 92, 147, 153
Crawford, E., 38–40, 120, 137, 177, 193
Crenshaw, K., 103, 193
Creswell, J., 25
Critical Latinx Indigeneity (CLI), 103, 106, 109, 111, 113
Crucet, C., 24, 27, 32, 33
Crucet, J. C., 4, 6, 20
Cuban, L., 72, 73
Cy in Chains (Dudley), 33
Cytron-Walker, A., 113, 114

Dabach, D. B., 39–41, 120, 123, 124, 147
Damaschke-Deitrick, L., 170, 176
Daniels, H., 26
Dantley, M., 41
Datasets, 9, 27, 30, 105
Davis, B., 25
Davis, J., 27
Dawson, A., 22
Day of Tears (Lester), 33
Dearien, C., 88
Deferred Action for Childhood Arrivals (DACA), 3
De Jong, E. J., 157, 163
Delavan, M., 157, 160, 163, 166
Delgado Bernal, D., 90
DeMatthews, D., 39–41, 157
DeNicolo, C., 90
Deschenes, S., 73
Dewey, J. D., 72, 193
Diaz-Strong, D. X., 177, 178
Dilworth, M. E., 11
Dobbin, F., 22
Dorner, L., 38, 40, 120, 157, 163, 193
Dual Language Bilingual Education Agenda, 161
Dual language bilingual education (DLBE), 157
  education board, 158–162
  ELL programs, 158
  in NLD, 165–166
  overview, 156–158
  state misplacement, 162–164
  TWBE program, 158, 159
"Dual Language Immersion Programs," 164

Index

Dudley, D., 33
Duran, E., 80
Dykema, J., 27
Dyrness, A., 90

Easton-Brooks, D., 11
educator expertise
   district context, 119–120
   interview participants, 121
   nuanced understandings, 124–127
   one-on-one interviews, 120
   overview, 118–119
   reengineering practices, 127–130
   viewing Latinx students, 121–124
Educators Rising Standards, 12, 13
Ee, J., 120, 146
Elementary and Secondary Education Act, 136
"Elementary World Language," 164
Ellis, B., 40
Ellis, L., 20, 23, 24, 33
Emergent multilinguals, 57
Emerson, R. M., 120
English as a second language (ESL), 56, 178
English language learner (ELL) programs, 157, 158, 161, 163, 178
English learners (ELs), 147
English learning (EL) program, 71
English to Speakers of Other Languages (ESOL), 119
Erickson, F., 10
Estep, K., 146
"The Excluded Student," 136
Expanding Definitions of Giftedness (Valdés), 6

Falbo, T., 1
Fals-Borda, O., 13
False hope (1960–1990), 136–137
Familial capital, 90, 94–95
Farm Worker Awareness Week, 94
Fasching-Varner, K. J., 105
Fernández-Rhodes, L., 138
Fine, M., 13, 14
First-Year Experience (FYE), 20–25, 27, 32–33
Flores, N., 1, 56, 57, 67, 157, 160, 177–178, 191
Flores Settlement Agreement, 175–176
Fones, A. K., 39
"Foreign Language in Elementary School.," 164
Ford, D. Y., 135
Foucault, M., 163
Foy, N., 88
Free Application for Federal Student Aid (FAFSA), 96

Freeman, J., 22, 146
Freeman, R., 163
Freire, J. A., 157, 160, 163, 166
Freire, P., 39, 113
Fretz, R. I., 120
From Risk to Opportunity: Fulfilling the Educational Needs of Hispanic Americans in the 21st Century, 138
Fugere, G., 175
Furman, G., 41, 42, 53
Future Teachers of Color (FTOC), 15

Gándara, P., 40, 120, 137, 146
García Bedolla, L., 146
García, O., 57, 84, 110, 112, 137, 163, 177–178, 184, 186
García, Y., 171
Gardiner, M. E., 88, 89
Gentemann, K. M., 77
Georgia Southern educators, 4
Getz, L. M., 135, 136
Ginorio, A., 10
Ginwright, S., 14
Gist, D., 127
Goldenberg, C., 166
Goldhaber, D., 9
Gonzales, R. G., 40, 123, 133, 135, 137, 176
Gonzalez, L. M., 141
González, M., 90
Gonzalez, N., 75, 83, 90, 114, 128
Gonzalez, R. G., 100
Gottfried, M. A., 146
Grace, B. L., 175–177, 182
Gray, T., 73, 193
Great Plains Equity Assistance Center, 166
Greenberg, M., 177, 179, 185
Greene, M., 33
Grow, K., 177, 179, 185
Guerrero, P. M., 22
Gurin, P., 108, 114
Gusman, J., 80
Gutiérrez, K. D., 73, 89–90, 99

Haan, M. N., 138
Habersham, R., 22
Hacking, I., 171
Hackle, A., 23
Hager, E., 38
Hairston, S., 39
Hamann, E. T., 1–5, 22, 23, 29, 40, 71, 104, 137, 155–157, 163, 165–166, 177, 179, 192
Han, S., 113

Handbook of Latinos and Education, 192
Hansen, M., 11
Harklau, L., 1, 5, 40, 104, 126, 177, 179, 192
Hartmann, D., 123
Hartman, S. L., 88
Hatch, T. J., 57, 59
Healthcare, 43
Heath, S. B., 111
Heidbrink, L., 171, 175, 176, 180
Heiman, D., 40, 157, 163
Heineman, D., 156
Henkenius, A. L., 25
Heredia, L. L., 176
Heredia, S., 177, 179, 185
Heritage language learners (HLL), 157
Hernandez, E., 137, 171
Herrera, S., 33, 133, 135
He, Y., 146
Higinbotham, S., 25
Historically Black colleges and universities (HBCU), 22
Hodgins, D. W., 41
Holmes, M., 33, 133, 135
Hondo, C., 88, 89
hooks, b., 10
Hopkins, M., 39, 40, 124, 146–147
Hornberger, N. H., 163
Howard, E., 163
Humanizing Education for Immigrant and Refugee Youth, 90
Huq, N., 141
Hurtig, J., 90
Huston, M., 10

Idaho, NLD
   aspirational capital, 90, 93–94
   community cultural wealth, 89–91
   diversity and rurality in education, 88–89
   educational resiliency, 97–99
   FAFSA, 96
   familial capital, 90, 94–95
   implications, 100
   K–12 schools in, 91
   La Familia, 91–93, 99–100
   leveraging institutional resources, 96–97
   methods of data collection, 92–93
   nondominant groups, 90
   overview, 87
   participant information, 92
   social capital, 95
Iftody, T., 25
Imagineering teacher education
   BIPOC teachers, 8
   diversifying teaching force, 10–11
   enrollments and teacher retention, 9
   grow-your-own (GYO) effort, 14
   Nebraska's teaching force, 12–13
   non-urban K–12 education, 112–115
   UNL'S teacher education program, 13–15
   YPAR projects, 15
Immigrant, 87–89, 91, 99, 176
Immigrant Children in Transcultural Spaces (Orellana), 6
Immigration and Customs Enforcement (ICE), 40, 60
Immigration Reform and Control Act, 137
Impacto sin Quemarse
   FYE speech, 20
   imagineering, 32–34
   immediate causes, 23–24
   long-term context, 21–23
   participant freshmen, 27
   planning and implementation, 24–25
   qualitative data, 29–32
   quantitative data, 27–28, 28t
   speculation, 33
   theory, pedagogy, and data collection, 25–27
Indigeneity/indigenous, 3, 103–104, 106, 108–109, 111–112, 115, 193
Ingersoll, R., 11
Ingram, H. M., 146
Institutional Review Board (IRB), 26
Ishimaru, A. M., 91
Izquierdo, E., 39–41, 157

Jackson, P. W., 75
Jaffe-Walter, R., 40, 41, 175
Jean-Marie, G., 41
Jefferies, J., 41
Jennings, J., 38
Johnson, D. C., 163
Johnson, F., 22
Johnson, J., 88
Johnson, M., 24
Journal of Latino Education (JLE), 4
Juarez, M., 191

K–12 school district structures
   community partnerships, 148–150
   innovative staffing, 152
   instructional programs, 152–154
   overview, 146–147
   research study, 147–148

teacher professional learning, 153–154
welcoming processes, 150, 151
Kalev, A., 22
Kasper, J., 40
Katsiaficas, D., 171
Kavimandan, S., 135
Kim, K. H., 135
Kim, Y., 27
Kiramba, L., 4, 156
Kirksey, J. J., 146
Kleifgen, J. A., 57
Klein, R., 88
Klevan, S., 175
Kleyn, T., 184
Koyama, J., 40
Kramarczuk, A., 175
Kubota, R., 111
Kumar, A., 40
Kurtz, C., 175

Lac, V. T., 127
Ladson-Billings, G., 10, 73, 124, 194
Lady Liberty's Shadows: The Politics of Race and Immigration in New Jersey (Rodriguez), 59
La Familia
  implications, 100
  stories and experiences, 99–100
Lakoff, G., 27
The Land (Taylor), 33
Lane, B., 163
Lardemelle, C., 171, 184
Larson, J., 73
Latine/o/x identity
  claiming of language, 134–136
  dimming of the dream, 139–142
  dismissive/malicious notions, 133
  false hope (1960–1990), 136–137
  first do no harm, 142
  forced displacement, 134–136
  irreplaceable loss, 141
  marginalization and exclusion, 138–139
  overview, 132–133
  predominant deficit view, 135
  reaching from the margins, 140–141
  standardized national examinations, 135
  systemic characterizations, 134
Latino Education and Advocacy Days (LEAD), 4
"Latino" *vs.* "Hispanic," 4
Latinx students, reengineering practices
  conceptualize leadership, 129–130
  engage teachers, 129
  identify specific supports, 128

Lau v. Nichols, 135
Lee, C., 40
Leeman, J., 111
Lee, S. J., 41, 175
Legwork, 14
Leonardo, Z., 107
Lester, J., 33
Levin, B., 146
Levinson, A., 170
Lewis, J., 33
"Limited English proficient," 64
Linguistic capital, 90
Liou, D. D., 96
Little, B., 89
Lone Star Republic, 132
Long-standing, 5, 8, 17, 71, 133–134, 136, 146
López, F., 39
López, G. R., 43
López, R. M., 176, 177
Lopez-Escobar, L., 177, 183
Love, B. J., 73, 83, 103–104, 111
Love, B. L., 193
Lowenhaupt, R., 39–40, 118, 120, 124, 192
Lozenski, B. D., 14
Lyiscott, J., 14, 114
Lynn, C., 21

Macedo, D., 111
Make Your Home Among Strangers (Crucet), 4, 20
Malsbary, C. B., 124
Mangual Figueroa, A., 120, 124
March (Lewis), 33
Marrow, H., 22, 180, 181
Martin, K., 133
Martin, M., 184
Martínez, G., 90, 153
Martinez, R., 4, 13, 156
Martínez, R. A., 157
Martinez, S., 135
Martin, M., 185, 186
Mathias, C., 191
Maxwell-Jolly, J., 40
May, H., 11
McCarty, T. L., 111
McConnochie, M., 193
McCorkle, W., 41, 177
McLaughlin, M., 14
McLaughlin, M. W., 83
Meacham, S., 25
Meckler, L., 156
Mehta, 135–136

Meier, K., 10, 127
Menjívar, C., 182
Menken, K., 64, 163
Merchant, N. H., 39
Metacognitive activities, 114
Miller, E., 138
Miramontes, O., 124
Miranda, C. P., 41, 175
Miroff, N., 170
Mitchell-McCollough, J., 193
Moberg, D. P., 27
Moll, L., 75, 83, 90, 114, 128
Monin, K., 177, 179, 185
Monreal, T., 2
Moraga, C., 137
Morales, A., 10
Morales, P. Z., 4, 12, 110, 124, 156
Morales, S., 90
Moran, D., 166
Moreno, M., 90
Morrell, E., 14
Mosley, M., 108
Motsinger, C., 23
Murillo, E. G., Jr., 2, 4, 23, 29, 71, 192
Murry, K. G., 133, 135

Nadeau, A., 124
Nader, L., 165
Nagda, B. A., 108, 113–114
National Center for Education Statistics, 178
National Education Association, 178
Navigational capital, 90
Nebraska Department of Education (NDE), 163
Nebraska's Latinx public school enrollment, 9
Neff, D., 75, 83, 90, 114, 128
Neo-nativism, 6
New Jersey Administrative Code (NJAC), 63
New Jersey's Bilingual Education Code, 63
New Latino Diaspora (NLD), 11, 38, 57, 59, 71, 147
  DLBE in, 165–166
  education in, 2
  emergent multilinguals, 59–60
  geography of, 2
  in Idaho, 87–100
  Latino students in, 5
  reengineer equity, 57
  reengineering PD, 51
  stakeholders in, 192
  substantial concern, 5
  successful schooling, 191–194
Newton, L., 146

Nicholas, P., 156
Nieto, S., 10, 115
Nieves-Martinez, A., 96
No Child Left Behind (NCLB), 63, 138
Noguera, P., 14
Noguerón, S. C., 87
Non-urban K–12 education
  data collection and analysis, 105
  findings, 105–106
  imagineering, 112–115
  intersectionality, 103
  overview, 103–104
  rationale and definitions, 106–112
  sites and participants, 104–105
Normore, A. H., 41

Oakes, J., 146
Oboler, S., 170
Office of Refugee Resettlement (ORR), 169
Ogawa, R., 127
Oluo, I., 113
Onaga, M., 171, 184
Ong, A., 57
Ontiveros, R. J., 134
O Pioneers! (Cather), 156
Orellana, M. F., 6
Orfield, G., 40
Osberg, J., 14
Osei-Twumasi, O., 171
Owens, A., 135
Ozuna, C. S., 146

Pac, T., 135
Pacheco, M. B., 177–179
Palmer, D., 40, 157, 163
Palmer, D. K., 157
Paraeducator, 74–76, 84
PARCC examination, 64–65
Paris, D., 124, 185
Park, C., 163
Park, M. F., 170, 176
Parmar, P., 88
Pascarella, E. T., 15
Patel, L., 180
Pérez, B., 163
Pérez-Iribe, M. F., 110
Peterson, B. S., 25
Phillipson, R., 135
Pierce, S., 176–177
Pierson, C. T., 15
Pimentel, A., 184
Pippin-Kottkamp, S., 177, 183

Index

Planning Guide for Starting Dual Language Programs, 166
Plano Clark, V., 25
Plyler v. Doe, 175, 185
Pollock, M., 123
Pompa, D., 147
Porter, L., 147
Portes, P., 180
Poza, L., 100
Praying for Sheetrock (Greene), 33

Q'anjob'al, 108, 111
Quinn, R., 146
Quintero, D., 11

Raciolinguistic ideologies, 56–57
Radford, J., 40
Reengineering inclusive schooling
   care among students, 75–76
   codifying better, 83–84
   constructing citizenship, 72–81
   cultivating inclusive spaces, 79–81
   demonstrated care, 78–79
   enacting better, 84–85
   mismatch of school policies, 73–75
   noticing what can and ought to be better, 82–83
   overview, 71–72
   paraeducator, 76–78
   students' dual realities, 73–75
Reengineering professional development
   case studies, 51–52
   challenges, 38–39
   discussion and participants' positionalities, 44–45
   inclusive leadership, 41–42
   intersections among immigration status, 52
   law enforcement/police, 45–51
   Missouri's NLD, 42
   NLD recommendations, 51
   perspective taking, 47–48
   professional development, 41–42
   real and immigrants, 49–51
   schooling practices, 39–41
   time and space, 52–53
   training for families, 48
   undocumented immigrants, 45–51
   workshop design, 43–44
Reese, L., 166
Reeves, J., 155, 156
Reframing emergent multilinguals
   citizenship, 60–68

   cultural citizenship, 57
   ESL/bilingual teachers, 56
   imagineering NLD discourses, 68–69
   New Latino Diaspora, 59–60
   raciolinguistic ideologies, 56, 57
   right to instructional space, 60–68
   Smithtown community and school, 58–59
Reidy, M. C., 175–176
Reinhard, B., 156
Resistance capital, 90
Revisiting Education in the New Latino Diaspora, 2
Reviving Ophelia (Pipher), 156
Reyes, P., 41
Reyes, R., 175
Ricento, T. K., 163
Riley, A. H., 175–176
Rivarola, A. R. R., 43
Rivera, M., 13
Robinson, K., 41
Rodriguez, J., 142
Rodriguez, L. F., 13
Rodriguez, S., 41, 59, 170, 175, 177, 179–180, 182–186
Rogers, R., 108
Rogoff, B., 89, 90, 99
Romaní, L., 90
Romo, H., 1
Rosa, J., 56, 57, 67
Rosaldo, R., 57, 73, 81
Rosenblatt's reader-response theory, 25
Roth, B., 175–177, 182, 185
Rotheram-Fuller, E., 96
Ruedas-Gracia, N., 171
Ruiz, R., 161, 164
Rumbaut, R., 180
Rumburger, R., 40
Rury, J. L., 40
Rymes, B., 73

Sáenz, B. A., 6
Salant, P., 88
Sandoval, J. S. O., 38
San Miguel, G., 132–133, 135
Santa Ana, O., 133
Sapien, Y., 88–89
Saravia, L. A., 110
Sattin-Bajaj, C., 146
Scanlan, M., 39
Schneider, A. L., 146
Schneider, B., 135
Schueths, A. M., 22

Schwerdtfeger, R., 157, 163
Seay, K. D., 176
Serna v. Portales, 135
Shaw, L. L., 120
Shefelbine, J., 80
Shields, C., 128
Shin, H., 111
Shohamy, E., 58, 64, 70
Shohat, E., 112
Showalter, D., 88
Sierk, J., 110, 114, 193
Simmons, J. C., 113
Smith, T., 25
Social capital, 90, 95
Solorzano, D. G., 99
Sommers, J., 134
Sowell, E. R., 25
So You Want to Talk About Race: (Oluo), 113
Spillane, J. P., 129
Spradley, J. P., 105
Stacy, J., 23, 29
Stein, G. L., 141
Stevenson, A., 4, 22, 26, 192
Stevenson, J., 27
Stewart, J., 10, 127
Stirgus, E., 27
Strobel, K., 14
Student essays
  economics, 30–31
  political engagement, 31–32
  previous preconceptions, 29–30
  young adult novels, 30
Students with limited or interrupted formal education (SLIFE), 147
Stuesse, A., 22
Suárez-Orozco, C., 10, 171, 184–186
Suárez-Orozco, M., 10
Successful schooling, 191–194
Sullivan, A. L., 87
Sumara, D., 25
Supporting Effective Educator Development (SEED) program, 16
Suresh, S., 185, 186
Swaminathan, S., 175
Sweet, T., 124

Taxel, J., 25
Taylor, M., 33
Tellez Lieberman, J., 175–176
Terenzini, P. T., 15
Terrio, S. J., 182
Tharoor, S., 142

Theobald, R., 9
Theoharis, G., 41
Thomas, W. P., 157
Thompson, K., 147
Thompson, P. M., 25
Tillman, L. C., 41
Tirado, J., 2
Todres, J., 25
Toga, A. W., 25
Toolset, 108
Torree, M., 13
Town, C., 25
Trafficking Victims Protection Act (TVPRA), 175
Treaty of Guadalupe Hidalgo, 132–134
Trump, D., 22, 25, 43, 104, 142, 146
TWBE pilot program, 158
Two-way bilingual education (TWBE), 157–165
Two-way bilingual education (TWBE) program, 157, 158
Two-way immersion (TWI) program model, 157
Tyack, D., 72, 73

Umansky, I. M., 40, 147
"The Unfinished Education," 136
United Nations Convention on the Rights of the Child, 175
University of Nebraska-Lincoln's (UNL) teacher education program, 13–15
Urrieta, L., Jr., 108
U.S. border as Migrant Protection Program, 147

Valdés, G., 6, 76, 100, 128, 157, 162, 177–178, 186
Valdez, V. E., 157, 160, 163, 166
Valencia, R., 40, 132–133, 135
Valenzuela, A., 178, 184
Valverde, M., 95
Van Houtum, H., 110
Varghese, M. M., 163
Vavrus, M., 103
Viesca, K., 73
Villarreal Sosa, L., 175, 177, 185
Villavicencio, A., 175
Villenas, S., 2, 90
Vines, A. I., 138
Viramontes, H., 6

Walker-DeVose, D. C., 22, 25
Walsh, D., 90, 153

Ward, J. B., 138
Warner Elementary School, 56, 61
Washington River High School (WRHS), 71–72
Weber, J., 22
Weddle, H., 146–147, 192
Welcome, S. E.
  Toga, A. W., 25
Welner, K., 146
White, 3, 8, 10–11, 15, 20–21, 23, 27, 29–31, 33, 38–40, 43–46, 48, 52, 56, 71, 84, 88, 98, 104, 106, 112–113, 118–119, 133–134, 136, 138, 141, 146, 165, 178, 191–192
Whitehead, T. L., 77
Whyte, W. F., 14
Williams, J. P., 29
Williams, T. O., 127
Wiseman, A. W., 170, 176
Wolniak, G. C., 15

Workie, E., 177, 179, 185
World-Class Instructional Design and Assessment (WIDA), 99
World Language Education, 163, 164
World Language (WL), 159
Wortham, S., 2, 71

Yammine, J., 192
Ybarra-Frausto, T., 134
Yonezawa, S., 146
Yosso, T. J., 89, 90, 94–95, 192
Youth participatory action research (YPAR), 10, 13–16, 192

Zabelina, D., 135
Zak, D., 169
Zentella, A. C., 67
Zúñiga, X., 113–114
Zwiers, J., 134

About the Editors and Contributors

Vanessa Anthony-Stevens is an associate professor in the Department of Curriculum & Instruction in the College of Education, Health, and Human Sciences at the University of Idaho. Vanessa's research highlights the gifts of Indigenous community-centered education and the tenacity of critical participatory research to advance local educational equity. She is most interested in participating in settler-scholar response-ability to change in colonial institutions such as schools and universities, and delights in bending anthropological tools to build anti-oppressive learning communities. Vanessa's work has been featured in the *Journal of Teacher Education*; *Diaspora, Indigenous, and Minority Education*; the *Journal of American Indian Education*; and *Anthropology & Education Quarterly*.

Katherine Barko-Alva is associate professor and program director of ESL/bilingual education at the William & Mary School of Education. Currently, she serves as codirector for WMSURE (W&M Scholars Undergraduate Research Experience). In addition, she serves on the executive board for the Virginia Dual Language Educators Network (VADLEN). She has been awarded the Virginia Latino Advisory Board Latinx Leadership Award in Education and the Janet Brown Strafer Award at William & Mary School of Education, recognizing her efforts promoting equitable and inclusive learning spaces. Her research explores the role of language, equity, and agency in Dual Language/ESL contexts and family engagement in multilingual contexts.

Scott Beck is a professor of teaching linguistically and culturally diverse students at Georgia Southern University. His research focuses upon the New Latinx Diaspora in the Rural South and the use of literature for young people as a means to address controversial issues such as immigration, Islam, and LGBTQ+ equity.

Yasar Bodur is a professor of elementary education. His research interests include multicultural education, diversity issues in teacher education programs, field-based teacher education, classroom management, and reflective practice.

Emily Crawford is an associate professor in the Department of Educational Leadership and Policy Analysis (ELPA) at the University of Missouri-Columbia.

Her research explores issues related to leadership and immigration in PK–12 public schools across geographic contexts. Specifically, she examines the intersections among immigration and education policy, leadership, and ethics. Her projects seek to understands the ways PK–12 educators—particularly school leaders—perceive and provide educational and schooling access for immigrant students and families of mixed legal status. She received her PhD in educational theory and policy from Penn State University.

Lisa M. Dorner is a professor in the Department of Educational Leadership and Policy Analysis and director of the Cambio Center at the University of Missouri-Columbia. Striving to work alongside communities to disrupt inequities, her research focuses on the politics and discourses of bilingual education, educational policy enactment, and immigrant childhoods, especially children's and families' integration in "new" spaces. Read more at lisamdorner.com.

Eulalia Gallegos Buitron's homes are rural Idaho and Tacámbaro y Nocupétaro, Michoacán, Mexico. Through an interdisciplinary research approach, Gallegos Buitron considers how class, race, language, colonization, and geography intersect to understand the experiences and histories of Mexican migrants and Chicanx people in Idaho. Gallegos Buitron's academic trajectory and public service career have focused on asset-based approaches to understanding the experiences of nondominant people and transforming public institutions to serve nondominant communities.

Tricia Hagen Gray is an assistant professor of practice at the University of Nebraska–Lincoln. Her experience as a high school Spanish teacher in contested spaces—including an urban context, a public school located on Native American tribal lands, and an exurban community experiencing demographic change—inform her work. Her research questions explore the construction of citizen identities among young people in school and aim to promote more equitable and justice-oriented schooling. Information Age Publishers recently published her book, *Learning to Hide: The English Learning Classroom as Sanctuary and Trap* (2024).

Edmund T. Hamann is a professor in the Department of Teaching, Learning, and Teacher Education at the University of Nebraska. An anthropologist of education, he has long studied the local development of education policy in response to demographic change, particularly to the transnational migration of students and families between the United States and Latin America. He began his career leading a bilingual family literacy program that concurrently asked how Mexican newcomer parents were making sense of their children's U.S. schools and how those schools were regarding these parents and their children.

Socorro G. Herrera is a professor in the Department of Curriculum and Instruction, College of Education at Kansas State University, and the executive director of the Center for Intercultural and Multilingual Advocacy (CIMA). As an international keynote speaker, district consultant, and trainer of trainers, she has collaborated with families, teachers, and administrators in charting new paths for the success of culturally and linguistically diverse students. Dr. Herrera has authored six textbooks and numerous articles for publication in journals such as *Bilingual Research Journal*, *Journal of Research in Education*, *Journal of Latinos and Education*, and *International Journal of Multicultural Education*.

Megan Hopkins is professor and chair in the Department of Education Studies at the University of California, San Diego. Her research focuses on policy and leadership with a specific emphasis on the education of multilingual learners in the K–12 education system.

Lydiah Kiramba is an associate professor of applied linguistics at the University of Nebraska–Lincoln. Born in Kenya, she later was a teacher and then teacher educator there before coming to the United States to earn an MA and PhD from the University of Illinois Urbana-Champaign. She is an expert in second/additional language acquisition and has studied the U.S. school experiences of African immigrant youth.

Lisa Lopez-Escobar is a doctoral candidate specializing in urban education in the Teaching and Learning, Policy, and Leadership Department at the University of Maryland, College Park. She has experience in mixed-methods, community-engaged research, including qualitative research methods such as in-depth interviews, focus groups, and qualitative survey design. Her content expertise spans immigration, education, and the role of schools in creating spaces of belonging for youth. Her journey began in after-school spaces, working with Latinx immigrant and newcomer youth, which sparked her interest in education policy and advocacy.

Rebecca Lowenhaupt is a professor in Boston College's Department of Educational Leadership and Higher Education where she teaches aspiring school principals and superintendents. Her mixed-methods research investigates educational policy and school leadership with a focus on immigrant-serving schools and districts.

Ricardo Martinez is an assistant professor of mathematics education in the Department of Curriculum and Instruction at Pennsylvania State University's College of Education. Before earning a doctorate in mathematics education and a master of education in curriculum and instructional technology, both) from Iowa State University, Ricardo was a high school mathematics teacher in McFarland, California, and Colo, Iowa. His lifework is rooted in critical youth studies and spiritual activism, where the goal is to create spaces for young people to liberate themselves both in the classroom and within the community through collective action.

Meredith McConnochie is an associate professor of education at the University of Saint Joseph in West Hartford, CT. She earned a BS in psychology with a minor in Hispanic studies from Carnegie Mellon University and an MA in bilingual-bicultural education from Teachers College, Columbia University. She received a PhD in education from Rutgers University with a concentration in language education. Early in her career, she was a preschool, kindergarten, and 1st-grade teacher in various multilingual communities.

Amanda R. Morales is an associate professor of education at the University of Nebraska–Lincoln. Her research addresses issues of equity and access for minoritized students across the PK–20 education continuum. Her current work focuses on teacher diversification pathways; critical mentoring for teachers of Color (TOCs); teacher preparation for working with (im)migrant, multilingual, and minoritized students; and the experiences of preservice and inservice TOCs in predominately White institutions. She teaches both graduate and undergraduate courses on multicultural education, intercultural communication, and critical, de-colonial/anticolonial theories in education.

Enrique G. Murillo, Jr. is a professor in the Department of Teacher Education and Foundations at California State University, San Bernardino, where he is director of doctoral studies. He is the founding editor of the *Journal of Latinos and Education* and has been the lead editor for both volumes of the *Handbook on Latino Education*. He is also founder of LEAD (Latino Education and Advocacy Days).

Katya Murillo is a PhD candidate in the international education policy program in the College of Education at the University of Maryland, College Park. Her academic interests include education in conflict and crisis settings as well as migration and education. Her research focuses on schooling for unaccompanied (im)migrant children in U.S. shelters/facilities.

Lisa Porter is an associate professor of sociology at James Madison University where she teaches courses on the sociology of education and nonprofit organization. Her research interests include educational inequalities and community engagement specifically examining the marginalization of immigrant families within K–12 schooling. Prior to teaching at the university level, she spent several years teaching in migrant education programs in K–12 schools and ESOL programs in adult education. She has led various cultural sensitivity trainings and enjoys the opportunity to learn from and collaborate with community members on projects that seek social justice and educational reform.

Sophia Rodriguez is an associate professor of educational policy studies and sociology at New York University's Steinhardt School of Culture, Education, and Human Development. Her work examines the experiences of immigrant youth with varying legal statuses and how schools and community-based organizations cultivate belonging for them. Her work has been generously supported by the William T. Grant and Spencer Foundations and appears in *Educational Researcher*, *Teachers College Record*, and *Urban Education*, as well as the *Washington Post*.

Jessica Sierk is an associate professor of education at St. Lawrence University in Canton, New York. Her research has been featured in journals like *Critical Inquiry in Language Studies* and *Discourse: Studies in the Cultural Politics of Education*, as well as in books like *The Price of Nice: How Good Intentions Maintain Educational Inequity* (edited by Angelina Castagno, published by University of Minnesota Press) and *Pedagogical Translanguaging: Theoretical, Methodological, and Empirical Perspectives* (edited by Päivi Juvonen and Marie Källkvist, published by Multilingual Matters).

Alma Stevenson is a professor of literacy at Georgia Southern University. Her research explores the power of home languages and cultures to support educational equity and positive identity formation. She uses sociocultural and critical approaches to literacy and literature to construct culturally responsive and sustaining curricula that advocate for social justice.

Hayley Weddle is an assistant professor of education policy at the University of Pittsburgh. Her research examines how leaders across K–12 and higher education implement policies in ways that enable or constrain equity.

Stanton Wortham is Charles F. Donovan, S.J., Dean of the Lynch School of Education and Human Development, Boston College. At the University of Pennsylvania before Boston College and at Bates College before Penn, early in his career he noted that Latino high school boys and Latina high school girls in Maine often had distinct education trajectories from each other, with girls experiencing more academic success and boys turning more to trades and vocational activity.

Julie Kim Yammine completed her doctorate at Boston College in the Lynch School of Education and Human Development. She is currently a middle school science teacher in the Boston Public Schools.